HARDY AND THE SISTER ARTS

By the same author

THE POEMS OF HENRY CONSTABLE (*editor*)
THE SPENSERIAN POETS

HARDY AND THE SISTER ARTS

Joan Grundy

First published 1979 by
THE MACMILLAN PRESS LTD
London and Basingstoke
Associated companies in Delhi
Dublin Hong Kong Johannesburg Lagos
Melbourne New York Singapore Tokyo

Typeset in Great Britain by Santype Ltd., Salisbury

Printed in Great Britain by offset lithography by
Billing & Sons Ltd, Guildford, London and Worcester

British Library Cataloguing in Publication Data

Grundy, Joan
  Hardy and the sister arts
  1. Hardy, Thomas, b.1840 – Criticism
  and interpretation
  823'.8   PR4754

  ISBN 0-333-24106-1

*To Helen Pilkington
and the memory of Richard*

Contents

Preface

My published work having been hitherto mainly in the Elizabethan field, I feel in publishing a book on Hardy something of a gate-crasher, and a gate-crasher upon an already crowded party. But the fields of literature are subject to no Enclosure Act, and the works of Hardy have been a long-time love of mine. The book began as an exploration: it was written not, at first, because I had something I was burning to say, but rather because there was something I wished to find out. Briefly, I wanted to know what made Hardy so good; even what made Hardy Hardy. I was convinced that the answer lay not, as so many critics were telling me at the time, in either his philosophy, his moral standpoint, or his sociology, but rather in his art, which was still relatively ignored, belittled, or denied to exist. Seeking a more detailed know-ledge of the nature of this art, of its roots and affinities, I sought also to understand it in relation to Hardy the writer's most striking single quality, that habit of compassion which in More's *Utopia* is said to be 'the most human affection of our nature'. Since that time (about nine years ago) the winds of change have blown increasingly in this direction, and works such as J. Hillis Miller's *Thomas Hardy, Distance and Desire* (1970), Penelope Vigar's *The Novels of Thomas Hardy: Illusion and Reality* (1974), and Paul Zietlow's *Moments of Vision, The Poetry of Thomas Hardy* (1974) have confirmed some of my own early findings. My entire enterprise (explained more fully in the Introduction) has been most encouragingly (if unwittingly) endorsed by P. N. Furbank, in his Introduction to the

New Wessex edition of *Tess of the d'Urbervilles*, where he presents
a view of Hardy's achievement very close in its essential features
to my own. More recently, and since my second chapter was
written, two admirable treatments of the subject of Hardy's pictorial
art have appeared, by F. B. Pinion in his *Thomas Hardy: Art
and Thought* (1977) and by Norman Page in his *Thomas Hardy*
(1977), both treatments differing considerably in scope and intention
from mine, as also from each other.

All these, being more substantial than mere straws in the wind,
suggest that there is a growing recognition both of the importance
of Hardy's artistry, and of how much there is still to be known
about it. Writers on Hardy, like diggers for treasure in the Thames
mud, may be numerous, but the treasure is not yet exhausted. I
hope that I have been able to recover a little more of it.

I should like to record my gratitude to the friends, colleagues,
and students who have encouraged me by the interest they have
shown in this work, in particular to Professor Barbara Hardy and
Dr Katharine J. Worth, who each read some of it in manuscript;
to Royal Holloway College, who granted me the two terms of
sabbatical leave without which its completion would have been
delayed much longer; and to my niece Mrs Helen Pilkington,
who devotedly and uncomplainingly prepared the typescript.

Reference Abbreviations

References to the novels are to the New Wessex edition (hardback) (London, 1975). Page references for prose and verse are given only where quotations are not readily identifiable through their context. References to *The Dynasts* specify part, act and scene: thus 2.1.i signifies Part Second, Act I, scene one.

DR	*Desperate Remedies*
UGWT	*Under the Greenwood Tree*
PBE	*A Pair of Blue Eyes*
FFMC	*Far from the Madding Crowd*
HE	*The Hand of Ethelberta*
RN	*The Return of the Native*
TM	*The Trumpet-Major*
L	*A Laodicean*
TT	*Two on a Tower*
MC	*The Mayor of Casterbridge*
W	*The Woodlanders*
TD	*Tess of the d'Urbervilles*
JO	*Jude the Obscure*
WB	*The Well-beloved*
CP	*The Complete Poems of Thomas Hardy*, ed. James Gibson, New Wessex edition (London, 1976)
SS	*The Short Stories of Thomas Hardy* (London, 1928)
Dyn.	*The Dynasts*, in *The Poetical Works of Thomas Hardy*, vol. II: '*The Dynasts*' and '*The Famous Tragedy of the Queen*

of Cornwall' (London, 1930)

Life   F. E. Hardy, *The Life of Thomas Hardy* (London and New York, 1965)

1 Introduction: The Sentient Seer

In *The Life of Thomas Hardy*, chapter 25, Hardy, speaking through his wife Florence Emily, the nominal author of the work, answers the critics who at the publication of *Wessex Poems* in 1898 were sceptical of his 'modulation' from prose to poetry. There was, he suggests, 'in the art-history of the century . . . an example staring them in the face of a similar modulation from one style into another by a great artist', namely Verdi. And he (or his wife) continues,

> But probably few literary critics discern the solidarity of all the arts. Curiously enough Hardy himself dwelt upon it in a poem that seems to have been little understood, though the subject is of such interest. It is called 'Rome: The Vatican: Sala delle Muse'; in which a sort of composite Muse addresses him.

The poem, first published in *Poems of the Past and the Present* (1901) and dated 1887, runs as follows:

> I sat in the Muses' Hall at the mid of the day,
> And it seemed to grow still, and the people to pass away,
> And the chiselled shapes to combine in a haze of sun,
> Till beside a Carrara column there gleamed forth One.
>
> She looked not this nor that of those beings divine,
> But each and the whole – an essence of all the Nine;

With tentative foot she neared to my halting-place,
A pensive smile on her sweet, small, marvellous face.

'Regarded so long, we render thee sad?' said she.
'Not you,' sighed I, 'but my own inconstancy!
I worship each and each; in the morning one,
And then, alas! another at sink of sun.

'To-day my soul clasps Form; but where is my troth
Of yesternight with Tune: can one cleave to both?'
– 'Be not perturbed,' said she. 'Though apart in fame,
As I and my sisters are one, those, too, are the same.'

– 'But my love goes further – to Story, and Dance, and Hymn,
The lover of all in a sun-sweep is fool to whim –
Is swayed like a river-weed as the ripples run!'
– 'Nay, wooer, thou sway'st not. These are but phases of one;

'And that one is I; and I am projected from thee,
One that out of thy brain and heart thou causest to be –
Extern to thee nothing. Grieve not, nor thyself becall,
Woo where thou wilt; and rejoice thou canst love at all!'

The composite lady's appearance and affirmations are hardly enough
to establish all that she and the *Life* claim for her, even with
the help of Marcus Aurelius ('Be not perturbed; for all things
are of the nature of the Universal' – quoted also by Paula Power
in *A Laodicean*); nevertheless, the poem is interesting for what it
tells us about Hardy. His Muses are not quite the usual ones;
we recognise Clio and Terpsichore and Polyhymnia, but 'Form',
the first named, has no exact counterpart among the Nine. Hardy
seems to be combining a statement about the qualities that appeal
to him in literature with an avowal of his devotion to the sister
arts generally. His soul clasps Form today because he is admiring
a work of sculpture (the 'chiselled shapes'); at other times he
finds 'the quality which makes the Apollo and the Aphrodite a
charm in marble' in painting, or in narrative. The phrase occurs
in his essay on 'The Profitable Reading of Fiction', where a little
earlier he had written,

Probably few of the general body denominated the reading public consider, in their hurried perusal of novel after novel, that, to a masterpiece in story there appertains a beauty of shape, no less than to a masterpiece in pictorial or plastic art, capable of giving to the trained mind an equal pleasure.[1]

The thoughtlessness of the reading public as described here resembles that of the critics censured in the *Life*: both groups in their experience of art are in Hardy's view missing a great deal by their rigidly compartmentalised approach.

The poem seems to be more, however, than simply an avowal of the principle of synaesthesia, or *Ut pictura poesis*. Not only, according to this 'essence of the Nine', are all the arts fused, or capable of fusion, in any particular work of art, whatever its medium ('I and my sisters are one'), but the constituent elements of those arts, represented here by Form, Tune, Story, Dance and Hymn, are one and the same, being all of them projections from the poet's own brain and heart – 'Extern to thee nothing'. The subjectivism of the latter part of this argument is confirmed elsewhere in Hardy's critical writings, as when, for instance, he writes of the incidents of Barnes's lyrics that 'they are tinged throughout with that golden glow – "the light that never was" – which art can project upon the commonest things'.[2] But the lines may also be taken as a restatement of Hardy's oft-repeated, indeed his central, artistic principle, that art is a matter of the artist's personal impressions, an expression of 'what appeals to [his] own individual eye and heart in particular', and the work of art itself, though it involves a 'going to Nature', 'no mere photograph, but purely the product of the writer's own mind' (*Life*, 184, 153). The unifying factor, making Form, Tune and the rest one and the same, is therefore no doubt emotion. Hardy can worship all the Muses because they are all vehicles of emotion; and this is true whether the allusion is to the practice of the art or simply to its enjoyment. 'The Poet takes note of nothing that he cannot feel emotively', Hardy wrote in 1908 (*Life*, 342). And it is worth observing that when he refurbished his unsigned review of Barnes's *Poems of Rural Life* (October, 1879), for an obituary essay in the *Athenaeum* (October, 1886), he altered his statement concerning 'the light that never was' from 'which art can project' to 'which the emotional art of the lyrist can project', which, although by contracting the general term 'art' to 'the art of the lyrist' it seems more limiting, gains in significance from the use of the word 'emotional' in relation to the artist's 'projections'.[3]

The composite Muse may also represent ideal beauty. In this respect the poem recalls Hardy's treatment of the theme of the pursuit of the Well-Beloved, both in the novel and in the lyric of that name. The 'Shape' who appears to the speaker in the lyric seems a counterpart in the sphere of human experience to what the Muse is in the realm of art, and Hardy worshipping the Muse in all her various guises is like Jocelyn Pierston loving 'the masquerading creature wherever he found her', whether in the three Avices, Marcia, 'Lucy, Jane, Flora, Evangeline, or what-not'. Hardy does not mention beauty in the poem, except possibly by implication in 'her sweet, small, marvellous face', but it seems unthinkable that the idea was not present in his mind. Beauty always mattered a great deal to him: this is obvious alike from his artistic practice; from his regard for woman's beauty, which makes him morbidly, even cruelly, sensitive to its withering; and from his various reflections on the subject, such as that art lies in making Nature's defects 'the basis of a hitherto unperceived beauty', or that 'To find beauty in ugliness is the province of the poet' (*Life*, 114, 213).

The poem, then, whatever its intrinsic merits, has some value as a commentary on Hardy's own art, and offers me a convenient starting-point for the argument I wish to pursue. This study began as an attempt to answer certain questions that puzzled me. Liking Hardy all my life, I found that I did not much care for the critical study of him, either my own or that of others. His merits and defects seemed alike obvious, writ large and frequently repeated. Did the difficulty of probing his work arise, then, from the fact that there was nothing there to probe? Was he indeed merely the superlatively gifted and literate popular writer some have held him to be, and should I in my regard for him simply rejoice to concur with the common reader, acknowledging that romance, sensationalism, and an emotional wallow in attractive surroundings were irresistible to us both? It seemed the sensible course; and yet an obstinate impression remained with me that where all seemed surface there was in fact depth; that Hardy's apparent simplicity concealed a real complexity. It was to test this impression that I embarked on this study; to test its validity by attempting to discover the nature of that complexity, supposing it to exist. And the conclusion I have come to is that Hardy's work has indeed at once the simplicity and complexity of life itself, of the actual process of living; and that it has it in part at least because Hardy's method of creation involves the fusion of several different arts to create an illusion of living. His adoption of this method is partly deliberate, partly instinctive, or, to use Hardy's preferred word, intuitive. Beyond the art-concealing art on which he prided himself there was a further art, concealed even from him.

Throughout all his work, whether prose, verse, or drama, Hardy has one theme, and one theme only, namely what Angel Clare calls 'this hobble of being alive'. This theme he seeks to render with complete fidelity, not the photographic fidelity of a Zola but an imaginative fidelity that selects and intensifies in order to achieve a heightened verisimilitude. Being alive involves being 'an existence, an experience, a passion, a structure of sensations' (*TD*, 119). This is the central, inescapable involvement which each individual faces alone and in isolation, 'each dwelling all to himself in the hermitage of his own mind' (*TM*, 120). But it also involves being in a place, an environment ('this planet', Europe, Wessex), and surrounded by a set of circumstances which 'hit upon the little cell called your life' (*JO*, 42), thus modifying and partly determining the nature of the 'existence, experience', etc., although without reducing its uniqueness and isolation as *felt*. This environment is itself composed very largely of other, similar 'existences': each separate existence has its part in the whole, helping to form the environment of its fellows. In doing so, each becomes an object of contemplation for the rest: the being who is for himself 'an existence, an experience, a passion, a structure of sensations' is for others a thought or an image. The most eloquent exposition of this idea in Hardy's prose comes from Cytherea Graye in chapter 13 of *Desperate Remedies*, but it is also, as will be recognised, fundamental to many of his poems and an essential part of his vision. Between the two modes of being, the 'existence' one is to oneself and the 'thought' one is to others, there is an unbridgeable gap: as Cytherea says of the world outside,

they will not feel that what to them is but a poor thought, easily held in those two words of pity, "Poor girl!" was a whole life to me; as full of hours, minutes, and peculiar minutes, of hopes and dreads, smiles, whisperings, tears, as theirs: that it was my world, what is to them their world, and they in that life of mine, however much I cared for them, only as the thought I seem to them to be. Nobody can enter into another's nature truly, that's what is so grievous.

There is, of course, 'a certain small minority who have sensitive souls' (*Life*, 185) who will appreciate this state of affairs and through fellow-feeling go some way towards remedying, or at any rate ameliorating, it. And lovers may occasionally achieve 'that complete mutual understanding' known to Jude and Sue, 'in which every glance and movement was as effectual as speech for conveying intelligence between them', making them 'almost the two parts of a single whole' (*JO*, 304). Nevertheless, the uniqueness of the isolated existence remains: 'You are you and I am I'; thought may bring insight and compassion, but it can never actually become flesh. The 'hobble' of being alive relates to other causes besides this, of course: notably to the Unfulfilled Intention and the cruelty and injustice of Circumstance, or of one creature to another. But the loneliness so fundamental to the experience of Hardy's heroes has its roots here. For Hardy, no less than for Cowper or Virginia Woolf, 'We perish, each alone', as even those 'two parts of a single whole', Jude and Sue, discover in the end.

A further, painful complication arises from the fact that the individual 'existence, experience', etc., is also an image, not simply in the minds of those contemplating it, but also, in some sense, actually in itself, through the transitoriness of life. 'But O, the intolerable antilogy / Of making figments feel!' This cry of the Pities in *The Dynasts* echoes throughout Hardy's work. The intolerableness for the sentient being comes through his sentience. His awareness of himself as a figment, a mere image-existence, is relatively limited (he is 'self-unconscious', 'self-unseeing'), although it comes upon him increasingly with age as he looks back on his past selves, as Hardy does in the poem 'Wessex Heights', for example. But essentially the imagistic nature of existence, its fragility and ephemerality, is felt by him through his perception of it in others. Thus this second mode of being – as a thought in the mind of others – itself becomes assimilated to the 'structure of sensations' (predominantly painful ones): each of us, by being a mere figment, becomes potentially a source of painful experience to our fellows, by the painful knowledge we offer. In our apprehension of life, seeing the feeling are intimately related. Comprehending our fellow-creatures inevitably only as thoughts or images, we can never truly *feel* their existences. We can, however, both feel and perceive the poignancy of them.

Hardy himself is haunted by his sense of the countless individual existences that are, have been, or will be, most of them so infinitely incomprehensible as realities, though knowable as facts. Even the 'old and dry mud-splashes from long-forgotten rains' that disfigure the spring-cart in which Æneas Manston is driven after his capture at the end of *Desperate Remedies* give him, one surmises, an almost metaphysical shudder. Like Keats's Grecian urn, they 'tease him out of thought, as doth Eternity': that is why he mentions them. Similarly with the 'infinite cows and calves of bygone years, now passed to an oblivion almost inconceivable in its profundity' which in *Tess of the d'Urbervilles* have rubbed the posts of Dairyman Crick's sheds to a glossy smoothness with their flanks; with the 'spinning leaves' of the poem 'The Later Autumn', which

> join the remains shrunk and brown
> Of last years display
> That lie wasting away,
> On whose corpses they earlier as scorners gazed down
> From their aery green height

or with the 'Proud Songsters' piping 'As if all Time were theirs':

> These are brand-new birds of twelve-months' growing,
> Which a year ago, or less than twain,
> No finches were, nor nightingales,
> Nor thrushes,
> But only particles of grain,
> And earth, and air, and rain.

All these are now, or soon will be, nothing; yet they have been, or at present are, something. And because they are, or have been, they *matter* to Hardy: we might almost say that for Hardy, as for God, the hairs of a man's head are numbered. His consciousness of the amount of feeling, thinking, experiencing, that is going on in the world is abnormally acute. Thus, on one of his periodic visits to London, in March 1888, he notes in his diary,

> Footsteps, cabs, etc., are continually passing our lodgings. And every echo, pit-pat, and rumble that makes up the general noise has behind it a motive, a prepossession, a hope, a fear, a fixed

thought forward; perhaps more – a joy, a sorrow, a love, a revenge. (*Life*, 206)

Probably Hardy's best-known pronouncement on his own art
is the entry made in his notebook on 3 January 1886: 'My art
is to intensify the expression of things, as is done by Crivelli,
Bellini, etc., so that the heart and inner meaning is made vividly
visible' (*Life*, 177). It is not, I think, often noticed that this is
to be linked with an entry for the previous day:

> Cold weather brings out upon the faces of people the written
> marks of their habits, vices, passions, and memories, as warmth
> brings out on paper a writing in sympathetic ink. The drunkard
> looks still more a drunkard when the splotches have their margins
> made distinct by frost, the hectic blush becomes a stain now,
> the cadaverous complexion reveals the bone under, the quality
> of handsomeness is reduced to its lowest terms.

The juxtaposition is instructive; it enlarges the phrase, 'the expression
of things', confirming us in our impression that Hardy is speaking
of an art which represents the internal in and through the external.
The association of warmth ('intensifying') with cold brings us momentarily close to Yeats's view of art, to his 'It must be packed
in ice', and his poem 'cold and passionate as the dawn'. We
may also be reminded of Hopkins: 'Self flashes off frame and
face'. It does this at all times for Hopkins, whereas for Hardy
it requires special, heightened conditions; when these are not present,
what we see is not the self, or at any rate not the self at its
most complete and absolute, but at best a pale superficial 'reading'
of the external clues.

It is this approach to the internal through the external which
gives the quality of substantiality to Hardy's art. Impressions may,
as he insists so often, be all that we are capable of receiving
in life and all that he as an artist is able to express, but the
impressions themselves have all the appearance of being solid and
substantial. As Lionel Johnson says, 'he gives us the comfortable
sense of dealing with realities'.[4] He is able to do this because
his own grasp of what he calls 'the substance of life' is so thorough.
He knows things by their shape and touch, sight, sound, and
smell: his senses are keen. Even Time is apprehended in this material
way: 'To-day has length, breadth, thickness, colour, smell, voice.

As soon as it becomes *yesterday* it is a thin layer among many layers, without substance, colour, or articulate sound' (*Life*, 285).

The qualities that define 'to-day' derive essentially from its events, from the happenings and experiences it contains. These are important to Hardy, for they help to define human beings also. We are known to others through our actions and speeches, through 'shape and voice and glance' (*CP*, 144), but life itself is known to us through experience and event, and we are in part, for ourselves if not for others, the sum-total of our experiences. (Only in part, of course; our innate impulses and desires help to make up the balance.) The celebrated poem 'Afterwards' provides an illustration: here Hardy wonders whether, when his 'tremulous stay' is over, he will be defined aright through the things he has seen and heard and cared for: 'He was a man who used to notice such things.'

This last point is particularly relevant to Hardy's treatment of the personages in his novels. These have unmistakably the breath of life in them: they are shrewdly observed and embody subtle psychological insights. And this is true not only of his most celebrated character-creations, the heroes and heroines of his major novels, but also of the relatively less well-known ones, people such as Elfride, Henry Knight and Parson Swancourt, or Anne Garland and her mother. All of these have a well-authenticated and convincing individual life. Yet of all of them, major and minor figures alike, it could be said that the psychological strength of the portrayal comes more through intuition, whether in the form of a sudden flash of insight or of a flow of sympathy 'gentle but continual', than it does through analysis. Hardy does not really go in for character-*study*: he does not, that is, reveal the thought-processes of his characters in any detail. Or, if he does so, we may feel conscious of a gap, if not actually a discrepancy, between the character as described and the character as shown. 'His countenance was overlaid with legible meanings' Hardy tells us in his set-piece introducing Clym Yeobright. These 'legible meanings' he proceeds to read for us. In doing so, however, he tells us far more than we ever see in action: the legible meanings remain on the countenance only. In his behaviour towards Eustacia and his mother he is simply the perennial male, and his 'face' in this respect is that of the past as much as of the future. ('In Clym Yeobright's face could be dimly seen the typical countenance of the future', Book Third begins.) Clym 'lives' by reason of his emotional experience

and his actions, but his inner world of thoughts remains dark
to us. With other, more fully dramatised and perhaps more genuinely
dynamic characters, such as Tess or Henchard, we are given a
little more information concerning the thought-processes, the actual
inner development, of the character, although still not a great
deal. The mental characteristics and mental paths that lead Tess
to such a reflection as the following, for example, are never clearly
shown us, as they would have been had she been a character
in a George Eliot novel:

> The trees have inquisitive eyes, haven't they? – that is, seem
> as if they had. And the river says, – 'Why do ye trouble me
> with your looks?' And you seem to see numbers of to-morrows
> just all in a line, the first of them the biggest and clearest,
> the others getting smaller and smaller as they stand farther away;
> but they all seem very fierce and cruel and as if they said,
> 'I'm coming! Beware of me! Beware of me!'

Even having passed the Sixth Standard in the National School
seems inadequate to account for this speech. Hardy, however, finds
it sufficient to explain it in terms of Tess's experience. 'Experience',
he reminds Angel Clare and us, 'is as to intensity, and not as
to duration. Tess's passing corporeal blight had been her mental
harvest.'

Here it may be helpful to recall the statement concerning Tess
part of which has already been quoted (p. 5): 'She was not an
existence, an experience, a passion, a structure of sensations, to
anybody but herself.' Not, we may add, until *Tess of the d'Urbervilles*
was written, for this is what she was to Hardy himself, and what
he intends her to be for the reader. Hardy's characters, even considered in their inwardness, are not primarily psychological or moral
entities; they are *experiencing* creatures, and their inner life is a
fusion, a meeting-place or battle-ground, of internal impulses and
external pressures. The emphasis in his portrayal of them is on
life, on living, the 'feel of old terrestrial stress'. We are taken
into their situations, rather than into their minds: we know how
life *felt* to them, what they experience, rather than what they
themselves are psychologically and morally.

Thus, while psychological and moral problems certainly have
their place in Hardy's novels, they are not the central point of
concern which some recent critics (Morrel, Southerington, for exam-

ple) have considered them to be. In the *Life* Hardy asserts his lack of interest in the novel as a picture of manners, and grumbles about the tedious obligation 'to get novel padding' by attendance at such places as police-courts and music-halls. He says nothing about the novel as a picture of morals, but perhaps, if the truth were known, he found this aspect only slightly less irksome than the former. What he really wanted was to write poetry, and, when, thwarted, economically at any rate, in this ambition, he turned to novel-writing instead, his aim became to keep his narratives 'as near to poetry in their subject as the conditions would allow' (*Life*, 291). And the subject of poetry is not morals: it is emotion, as Hardy insists repeatedly – in, for instance, his definition of poetry as 'emotion put into measure' (*Life*, 300). Life itself too was for him primarily an emotion: three times at least the *Life* tells us of his 'constitutional tendency to care for life only as an emotion and not as a scientific game' (p. 87). So that, when T. S. Eliot, in *After Strange Gods*, describes Hardy as 'an author who is interested not at all in men's minds, but only in their emotions; and perhaps only in men as vehicles for emotions'[5], I think he is basically right, barring some slight exaggeration in that 'not at all'. Where he is wrong is in the hostile inferences he draws: Hardy's is not necessarily a less profound or less serious art because it finds its centre here. Choosing emotion as his subject does not inevitably commit an author to emotional indulgence. No doubt Hardy *is* emotionally indulgent at times, as in the episode of the deaths of the three children in *Jude the Obscure*, but essentially he confronts emotion as a problem, and a painful one. 'The emotions have no place in a world of defect', he notes (9 May, 1881), 'and it is a cruel injustice that they should have developed in it' (*Life*, 149). '. . . a cruel injustice': cruelty is an area in which Hardy was always prepared to pass a moral judgement and to make a moral recommendation, of the exercise of altruism, of loving-kindness. But the cruelty he indicts is of impersonal as well as personal forces, so that even here man is an object as much for pity as blame. Hardy is one of those to whom 'the miseries of the world / Are misery, and will not let them rest'. His novels, no less than his other works, are an expression of that restlessness.

What I am seeking to define is the nature of the experience Hardy offers to us, his readers. I have been suggesting that, as far as the personages of his novels are concerned, this has relatively little to do with 'character' in the sense of moral and psychological

characteristics, and much more to do with experience and emotion
and their interaction, which together almost constitute 'character'
for Hardy. He is aware, of course, of individual differences between
people: he protests, for instance, in his essay 'The Dorsetshire
Labourer', against the notion of 'Hodge', the typical farm labourer;
on actual acquaintance with this class, he suggests, Hodge disinte-
grates 'into a number of dissimilar fellow-creatures, men of many
minds, infinite in difference'.[6] And he himself has a shrewd countryman's eye for telling traits and eccentricities of conduct. But his
keen sense of individuality relates primarily to feeling and experiencing: these are the individual's own; no one can deprive him of
or rescue him from them; and there is scope in them for infinite
variation and difference, as between one individual and another.
Hardy's perception of individuality in this sense extends beyond
man to all sentient things, to animals, plants, even at times to
the inanimate world (Jude, for instance, is moved by the cruelties
inflicted on the ancient buildings of Christminster 'as he would
have been moved by maimed sentient beings'). And so the cry
of the Pities goes up: 'But O, the intolerable antilogy / Of making
figments feel!' If the feeling is one of pleasure, yet still the fact
that it cannot last makes it ultimately pain; so 'pain is never
done'. Herein lies the 'hobble' of being alive.

Unwaveringly throughout his long life, it was his perception of
this state of affairs, together with his personal pain at it, that
Hardy wished to express through his writing. This is 'that pattern
among general things which his idiosyncrasy moves him to observe',
'what appeals to [his] own individual eye and heart in particular'
(*Life*, 153, 184). In his verse he found unchartered freedom for
such expression, so that the *Collected Poems* may strike a reader
as less a collection of separate poems than a continuous lifelong
meditation on a theme. In his novels, on the other hand, he
had to accommodate himself to the exigencies of the form. His
occasional failures to do so show themselves in the often-enumerated
'faults' – mechanical plotting, rudimentary characterisation, stilted
and unnatural dialogue. Such failures to adapt himself to the novel
form, however, matter less in the long run than the ability he
discovered in himself to adapt the novel form to his own needs,
so that if, as he maintained, his creations were not 'novels proper',
they were, the best of them at any rate, great works of some
kind. He loved story-telling, of course: *event* forms a prominent
colour or thread in that pattern in the carpet he follows, and

he is both fascinated and appalled by the odd, complicated or dreadful things that can happen to people. His interest, however, does not end with the event; it extends, as I have suggested, to the effect of event upon his personages, to their *feelings* about it; event thus becomes part of that 'expression of things' – the 'something glaring, garish, rattling' that 'hit[s] upon the little cell called your life' – by which 'the heart and inner meaning' (the 'little cell' itself) is made 'vividly visible'. Thus, if he writes 'sensation novels', as has sometimes been said, it is because he sees his characters as 'structures of sensations'. Superficially, Hardy's novels deal far more with externalities, both of action and setting, than do those of most novelists of his calibre. But it is through them that he takes us into the heart of his characters' experiences, bringing home to us what it feels like to be living this particular life, to *be* this 'existence'. His success in doing so is attested by that 'curious effect' noted by Lionel Johnson, which many readers surely would confirm:

> A curious effect is produced by the patient elaboration of story and of style, in these novels: it brings a strange conviction home to the reader, a comfortable assurance. Line upon line, as characters unfold, and passions wake, and motives meet or cross, the reader's mind falls into step with the writer's: to vary the figure, I might say that the reader answers the writer's call, as one instrument another, by sympathy.[7]

And he adds a little later the statement already quoted: 'he gives us the comfortable sense of dealing with realities'. Perhaps with this should be coupled Albert J. Guerard's equally endorsable observation, 'A basic fact about Hardy's novels is that they are very hard to put down', and his reference to 'some primary energy' to explain this.[8]

The sympathy between writer and reader to which Johnson alludes is created, it seems to me, largely by Hardy's practice of putting the reader in the same position as himself *vis-à-vis* his characters: that is, in the position of sympathetic observer. His habit of presenting his action through the eyes of a hypothetical observer, with whom we are implicitly invited to identify ourselves, is too familiar to require much demonstration here. We meet it frequently in *The Return of the Native*, for example, as at the beginning of Book I, chapter 3 – 'Had a looker-on been posted in the immediate vicinity

of the barrow, he would have learned that these persons were
boys and men of the neighbouring hamlets' – or in the description
of Clym's face as it appeared to 'the observer's eye'. Within the
novels themselves, the characters watch each other, and are watched
in their turn by the rest of Nature, even by inanimate objects
(the lamps of Christminster, for example, which 'winked their yellow
eyes dubiously' at Jude as he first arrived in the town). The
characters acquire their experience of life largely through watching,
seeing, and interpreting what they see. Watching, it seems, is an
essential part of being: 'I watch and am watched; therefore I
am.' How obsessively Hardy felt this ability of *looking* to affect
the nature of the object looked at comes out in an entry in his
notebook on 28 April 1893: 'The worst of taking a furnished
house is that the articles in the rooms are saturated with the
thoughts and glances of others' (*Life*, 254). And, of course, to
exist for others as a thought or image – the only existence they
can normally have for others – human beings must be seen. Jude
is 'obscure' because he does not 'exist' for others, is never 'seen'
by them. In his first experience of Christminster he becomes a
'self-spectre', the sensation being that of 'one who walked but
could not make himself seen or heard'. And this experience is
repeated throughout his career: the 'real' Jude is never seen, so
that he can declare at the end, in the words of Antigone, 'I
am neither a dweller among men nor ghosts.' Similarly, Sue's
cry 'Don't turn away from me! I can't *bear* the loneliness of
being out of your looks!' epitomises the sufferings of them both.

   To watch the characters watching is therefore for us a means
of entering into their experience. It is more than simply watching
them. Merely to watch them would be for them to remain simply
images or thoughts for us; to watch them watching is to realise
them as 'existences'. 'Inside this exterior, over which the eye might
have roved as over a thing scarcely percipient, almost inorganic,
there was the record of a pulsing life', writes Hardy, of Tess
on her walk to Flintcomb-Ash. To bring this 'pulsing life' home
to us, making us too prove it upon the pulses, he show us not
only Tess herself, but also what she sees, which includes the scenery
around her as well as the things that happen to her. (Hence,
in part, the importance of landscape in Hardy's work. It is part
of our experience, and therefore part of us: 'Whatever Miss T.
eats turns into Miss T.') He also shows us her reactions to what
she sees – that is, her emotional responses. In doing this, he is

going beyond the ordinary observer, and becoming the *sympathetic* observer that it is possible for him, as an artist, to be, writing, we might say, with the 'sympathetic ink' he mentions in the passage quoted above on p. 8. For, through the 'emotional perceptiveness' that has developed among 'thinking and educated humanity' (*JO*, 351), we may become 'feeling observers' (*TM*, 41), feeling not only for ourselves but also for the object observed, and so going beyond the object to the reality. This may come about through 'the insight which is bred of deep sympathy', such as enabled Melbury to discern 'the interior of Grace's life only too truly, hidden as were its incidents from every outer eye' (*W*, 237). Or, slightly more deliberately, the 'true quality' of what would otherwise remain 'a shape in the gloom', 'a conjectural creature', such as Grace was to the people of Sherton Abbas, may 'be approximated by putting together a movement now and a glance then, in that patient attention which nothing but watchful loving-kindness ever troubles itself to give' (*W*, 69). Hardy employs both forms of insight, the spontaneous and the deliberate, the former particularly perhaps in his portrayal of Tess. But always he creates in a spirit of watchful loving-kindness, and as an artist is the 'sentient seer' ('The Graveyard of Dead Creeds'), feeling with the 'figments' he both sees and creates.

'My art is to intensify the expression of things . . . .' Here 'expression' carries two meanings. The primary meaning is that of aspect, facial expression: Hardy is saying that he heightens the appearance of his subjects, emphasising one feature, suppressing or distorting another, so as to bring out the truth beneath the appearance. But 'expression' may also refer to literary expression: if he intensifies the expression things wear, he must do it by a form of writing that is itself in some respects intensified. And it is here that the composite Muse comes to his aid. The pictorial arts, drama, music, dance, song and story all assist him in his re-creation of a vision of life that at its best is 'more truthful than the truth'; that indeed goes beyond vision (something seen) to become also experience (something both seen and felt). From a concentration of Art (meaning here aesthetic modes, rather than craft or skill as such), a concentrated effect of Life is obtained.

Hardy's employment of the arts in this way develops naturally out of his activities as a 'sentient seer'. His emphasis on the visual leads him inevitably to the visual arts. Conscious always of the image and the scene, he sees life as every kind of show: as picture, play, pantomime, magic-lantern slide (and, by anticipation, motion-picture), conjuring-show ('I have no philosophy,' he wrote in 1920, '– merely what I have often explained to be only a confused heap of impressions, like those of a bewildered child at a conjuring show' (*Life*, 410). No figure is involved: since human-kind and the rest of the creatures are mere 'figments' for Hardy, they are already artistic creations. As Sir Thomas Browne says in a sentence Hardy recorded in his notebook, 'Nature is the Art of God.' Even in a God-less world this may still be so, and the patterns blindly woven by the Immanent Will be acknowledged as 'artistries'. The complexity of these patterns itself suggests the dance, and it is in part his perception of the complicated interrelationships between individual lives, the way they meet and touch and part and regroup themselves to form fresh patterns, that leads Hardy to give an underlying dance-structure to his novels. As he observed of *Jude the Obscure*, 'the involutions of four lives must necessarily be a sort of quadrille' (*Life*, 273). But dance is also a sensuous thing and its instrument is the body. In this respect it goes closely with music: both music and dance express emotion, and thus become for Hardy one of the primary means by which he conveys to us not only the fact that these 'figments' feel, but also what they feel.

There is a fundamental reason for Hardy's use of music and dance, and particularly music, in this way. It starts with the pulse, the heart-beat. The 'feeling' of his figments starts here too, of course, as he shows by his use on numerous occasions of such words as 'pulse', 'beat', 'throb', 'palpitate'. Thus, in *Tess of the d'Urbervilles*, besides the phrase 'the record of a pulsing life', already quoted, we read of 'the great passionate pulse of existence'; 'the beats of emotion and impulse'; or of young girls 'under whose bodices the life throbbed quick and warm'. In the poem 'I Look Into My Glass', Hardy himself grieves that Time

shakes this fragile frame at eve
With throbbings of noontide.

In 'The Darkling Thrush' the whole earth is involved, as we read of 'the ancient pulse of germ and birth'. Hardy's awareness of the close link between the beat of the human heart, the pulse of life, on the one hand, and the beat and pulse of music on the other, which is the basis for his use of this sister art in his work, may at this stage be established by quoting two further examples: first, his allusion to the 'joyous throb of a waltz' at the end of *Jude the Obscure*, heightening by contrast the sense of the cold, still form of Jude; and from *A Laodicean* the statement, 'The room was beating like a heart, and the pulse was regulated by the trembling strings of the most popular quadrille band in Wessex.'

Art, like life, is for Hardy a matter of seeing and feeling. The identity he asserts between the various arts relates to this: it is through their expression of these fundamental aspects of experience that the arts become 'one and the whole'. Hardy, in his experience of the arts, without confusing their identity, found in them ultimately the same things. And he used them in his own art, again without confusing their identity, to express the same things, 'overing and overing' them, as Hopkins would say, but at the same time greatly strengthening and enriching that expression, in ways which this book goes on to explore.

2 Pictorial Arts

I

The fact of Hardy's literary pictorialism requires no demonstrating. It is self-evident, has been often noted, and has sometimes been deplored. To deplore it, however, as for instance Lloyd Fernando does in his article 'Thomas Hardy's Rhetoric of Painting',[1] is at bottom to wish Hardy other than he is. It is to deny him the right, for instance, to make of the novel 'an impression, not an argument' (Fernando complains of the difficulty his pictorial manner creates for 'the interpreter of Hardy's themes'). It is also to reject the impression itself, to which a sense of the inescapably visual nature of experience and of the identity of the visual and the pictorial is central. The eye of the ordinary beholder, although, as Wordsworth says, it 'cannot choose but see', does not necessarily see pictures, or at any rate not consciously. Hardy's eye does. If he gives us in his work not simply pictures but, as Fernando says, pictures of pictures, this is because life shapes itself in that way to him. Writing to A. C. Benson of 'Poems of 1912–13', which he described as 'very intimate, of course', Hardy confided, 'but the verses came; it was quite natural; one looked back through the years and saw some pictures; a loss like that makes one's old brain vocal!'[2] It was always 'quite natural' to him to see pictures, both directly and, to use his own expression, through 'mindsight'. In reproducing these pictures, he is both painter and observer. If our discovery of this fact produces in us at first a sense of alienation, and of disappointment that what we took to be a re-creation of actuality is rather a re-creation of a *picture* of actuality (the picture the writer has seen), this is as it should be. It is only towards the end of his life that Michael Henchard discovers the world to be 'a mere painted scene'; the 'subtle-souled' Elizabeth-Jane, like her creator, knew it all the time.

Hardy in his novels is a painter using words as his medium instead of paint. He makes no attempt to disguise or camouflage this fact; on the contrary, he draws attention to it by his use of the technical language of the painter: 'foreground', 'middle distance', 'perspective', 'plane', 'line', 'curve', 'tone', 'chromatic effect'. The effect of the introduction of such technicalities is to distance the action or scene for us (particularly when distance is actually referred to), so that the style itself might be said in this respect to provide a frame for the picture, an over-all frame additional to the particular ones supplied by such things as windows (in pictures of Fancy, Grace, Viviette, for example) or doors ('this picture of to-day in its frame of four hundred years ago', the shearing-barn at Weatherbury).

Even when technical language is avoided, the technique of the painter is often still being employed, as we may see by comparing two passages:

The open hills were airy and clear, and the remote atmosphere appeared, as it often appears on a fine winter day, in distinct planes of illumination independently toned, the rays which lit the nearer tracts of landscape streaming visibly across those further off; a stratum of ensaffroned light was imposed on a stratum of deep blue, and behind these lay still remoter scenes wrapped in frigid grey. (*RN*, 132)

With their minds on these things they passed so far round the hill that the whole west sky was revealed. Between the broken clouds they could see far into the recesses of heaven as they mused and walked, the eye journeying on under a species of golden arcades, and past fiery obstructions, fancied cairns, logan-stones, stalactites and stalagmite of topaz. Deeper than this their gaze passed thin flakes of incandescence, till it plunged into a bottomless medium of soft green fire. (*W*, 226)

In the first of these examples the technical language – 'planes', 'toned', 'stratum' – makes it clear that this is a painter's point of

view, even a painter's analysis: we are reminded equally of Turner
and of some of Ruskin's analyses of Turner. In the second passage
it is Giles's and Grace's experience that is being rendered: the
sky *appears* to them in the form of 'golden arcades', 'fancied cairns',
and so on. Nevertheless, the movement of the eye, their eyes and
through them the eye of the reader, is being controlled and directed
as in a painting, though without the use of technical language.
The eye is led, just as much as in the former passage, from the
foreground of 'broken cloud' along a perspective line of 'golden
arcades' to a middle distance of 'fiery obstructions', etc., and so
on to an imagined vanishing-point in a 'bottomless medium of
soft green fire'. On a rather different level, effects of comedy
or caricature are achieved by the use of the distinctly 'painterly'
device of overlapping, again without resort to technical language.
Thus Miller Loveday, reading his son Bob's letter, finds that he
is being assisted by various neighbours 'whose persons appeared
in the doorway, partly covering each other like a hand of cards,
yet each showing a large enough piece of himself for identification'
(*TM*, 128). In *Under the Greenwood Tree*, the choir's visit to Parson
Maybold's to protest about the introduction of the church-organ
is presented in the same way. Earlier in this novel there is the
description of Dick's first call on Fancy, when 'the door opened,
and three-quarters of the blooming young schoolmistress's face and
figure stood revealed before him; a slice on her left-hand side
being cut off by the edge of the door'. The stance is familiar
and easily visualised, but only a writer thinking in painterly terms
would have described it in this way.

Hardy's composition of the scenes in his novels into pictures
by means of light and shade and colour is sufficiently obvious
and ubiquitous to require no stressing here. It is probably the
chief means by which descriptions are transmuted into pictures.
Effects of *chiaroscuro* abound: sun, moon, and fire-light, lamps, candles
and lanterns, even the light from glow-worms and buttercups, all
are called into play, shining upon the just and the unjust to unite
them in a single picture. The degree to which the characters themselves are conscious of or affected by these particular effects varies
considerably, but whatever the nature of their involvement, it is
towards the reader's eye that the picture is primarily directed.
Thus it is in these passages that the purely pictorial nature of
the writing is likely to be felt most strongly. In the passage from

The Return of the Native quoted above, for example, the reaction of Thomasin and Mrs Yeobright to the peculiar light-effect is not recorded: we see them walking on the heath in this peculiar light, and that is all. At this point, they are truly 'figures in a landscape', and no more. This is not to say that Hardy tells us *nothing* about their experience: he tells, or rather shows, us that one afternoon in their lives was passed in this particular 'atmosphere'; he adds one further detail to his account of their rural experience, an authentic one for those who know the countryside, and one serving therefore to actualise their lives for us. But it is an actualisation achieved through the eye alone, the eye of the reader (and of the author). Again, in the description of the rick-yard fire in *Far from the Madding Crowd*, we read that Gabriel's 'weary face now began to be painted over with a rich orange glow'. 'Weary' tells us something about the state of Gabriel's feelings as well as his appearance, but the rest of the description is given from an observer's point of view, and, as there is at this point no 'living soul' about and Gabriel cannot see himself, is clearly directed towards the reader-as-spectator. Even when a detail is given from the point of view of one of the characters, this may still be so. When Knight, Elfride and Stephen meet in the Luxellian vault, the scene is mentioned as one 'which was remembered by all three as an indelible mark in their history'. The carefully composed and striking picture that follows this statement, however, seems again directed outward to the spectator. Only he, after all, can see all three figures; Elfride, for instance, cannot see herself receiving 'most of the light' from the entrance, though she can see Stephen standing in the candle-light. To Stephen himself, we are told, 'the spot of outer sky visible above the steps was as a steely blue patch, and nothing more'. This certainly gives Stephen's view-point, but it also completes the picture for us *as* a picture, comparably with the 'yellow spot on the wall' in Vermeer's *View of Delft* so celebrated in Proust's *Du Côté de Chez Swann*.

Although the visual element is still strong, this pictorial method of presentation is less marked, certainly less obtrusive, in Hardy's poems. Hardy is here less concerned with the reader–spectator, more given up to and absorbed in self-expression: 'So I unto myself alone shall sing'. The observer's eye at work, although still a painter's eye, is content to appear as simply a natural, or perhaps a poet's eye. In the opening of 'The Wind's Prophecy',

I travel on by barren farms,
And gulls glint out like silver flecks
Against a cloud that speaks of wrecks,
And bellies down with black alarms

the painter's sensibility has contributed to the description, forming
the details into a rapid Ruisdael-like landscape, bringing earth
and sky into relationship, establishing the mood by means of the
contrast between the black, threatening cloud and the glint of
sunshine on the gulls' wings, yet the description itself does not
advertise the fact. In 'By the Runic Stone', the pictorialism of
the opening stanza may be more deliberate and self-evident:

By the Runic Stone
They sat, where the grass sloped down,
And chattered, he white-hatted, she in brown,
Pink-faced, breeze-blown.

Here the elements of colour seem to serve to create a momentary
Impressionist picture (Monet? Seurat?), the white of the hat standing
out by contrast with the larger area of brown. Yet, if the picture
is there, it is not insisted on. In 'Midnight on the Great Western',
on the other hand, the pictorial skills familiar to us from the
novels are undisguisedly at work, creating a picture of 'the journeying
boy' for us, with 'the roof-lamp's oily flame' playing down on
his 'listless form and face', its light picked up again by the key
round his neck,

That twinkled gleams of the lamp's sad beams
Like a living thing.

And towards the end of his life, writing in a quietly contemplative
fashion, Hardy produced a number of poems which are predominantly
or wholly word-paintings. They occur mostly in the volume *Human
Shows, Far Phantasies*, and include 'A Bird-Scene at a Rural Dwelling',
'Last Week in October', 'An East-End Curate', 'Coming Up Oxford
Street: Evening', 'A Spellbound Palace', 'A Sheep Fair', 'No Buyers,
A Street Scene', and others.[3] Most of these poems are composed
into pictures by means analogous to those employed in the novels,
but, again, generally less obtrusively. In 'A Sheep Fair', rain unites
all the disparate elements into a vivid *genre* picture: as 'the auctioneer

wrings out his beard', he is at one with his victims, the ewes, whose wool 'is like a sponge / With the daylong rain'. Similarly, in 'No Buyers' the pony is explicitly related to the man:

A yard from the back of the man is the whiteybrown pony's
    nose:
He mirrors his master in every item of pace and pose.

And in 'A Light Snow-Fall after Frost', it is again the painter's eye that in the third stanza links the man's beard and coat with the colour of the holm-trees:

A second man comes by;
His ruddy beard brings fire to the pallid scene:
    His coat is faded green;
    Hence seems it that his mien
    Wears something of the dye
Of the berried holm-trees that he passes nigh.

There is undoubtedly a painter *manqué* in Hardy. He looks at the world around him with the eye of a painter, and describes what he sees with an eloquence and an enthusiasm uncannily close to those of Van Gogh in his letters; only, whereas Van Gogh has painted or is about to paint the scenes re-created in words for the benefit of his correspondents, Hardy goes no further than to shape his observations into a *word*-picture. But to acknowledge this is not to concede that these pictures have a merely decorative or 'rhetorical' function. Most of the time in reading his work, especially the novels, we know, though with varying degrees of awareness, that we are looking at pictures. But the effect, after that first sense of alienation I referred to earlier has worn off, is to heighten rather than to diminish our sense of reality. The pictures are so vivid that they have life, as actual pictures (which are static only in the sense that they cannot get up and walk away) have it. Their effect is simultaneously to idealise and to reify. The pictures have such finish and perfection *as* pictures that we seem to see the scenes and objects depicted with an almost hallucinatory clarity. To take a simple example, the description of Keeper Day's house in Yalbury Wood:

A curl of wood-smoke came from the chimney and drooped

over the roof like a blue feather in a lady's hat; and the sun shone obliquely upon the patch of grass in front, which reflected its brightness through the open doorway and up the staircase opposite, lighting up each riser with a shiny green radiance and leaving the top of each step in shade.

Here the detail about the sunlight and the 'green radiance' reflected from the grass upon the stair-rods informs us at once that we are looking at a picture; it stirs memories, vague but strong, of actual pictures we have seen, especially perhaps of Dutch and Flemish interiors. The moment seems as much arrested and fixed as are the figures of Keats's Grecian Urn, or the 'lady and a lap-dog' who in 1774 stood on the lawn of Oxwell Hall 'in a strenuously walking position', according to a plate in the County History (*TM*, 71). The scene acquires a quality of timelessness through its picture-character, yet at the same time the content of that picture gives it a convincing temporality. The open door invites us in, as do similar doors in Dutch paintings, and the reflected sunlight suggests the warmth and brightness of the home, so that we fully accept Hardy's statement that 'it was a satisfaction to walk into the keeper's house, even as a stranger, on a fine spring morning like the present'. We see the bloom on the picture, yet we feel its actuality too. The description is in keeping with Hardy's various pronouncements concerning the nature of art, both art in general and his own art in particular: that it is able to make the defects of Nature 'the basis of a hitherto unperceived beauty, by irradiating them with "the light that never was" on their surface, but is seen to be latent in them by the spiritual eye' (*Life*, 114); that its aim is to be 'more truthful than the truth' (compare Van Gogh's expressed desire to paint 'yes, lies if you like – but truer than the literal truth');[4] above all, that his own art 'is to intensify the expression of things, as is done by Crivelli, Bellini, etc., so that the heart and inner meaning is made vividly visible' (*Life*, 177).

The artists named in this comparison were well chosen. The work of Crivelli (1435? – 92) still has a Gothic flavour about it: his expressiveness is achieved above all through line. Hardy refers to him three times in the novels, each time in terms that show that it was this aspect of his art that he appreciated. 'A narrow bony hand' (*DR*, 172), the 'skinny legs' of storks (*L*, 292) suggest comparisons with him, and of Angel Clare on his return from

Brazil Hardy writes,

> You could see the skeleton behind the man, and almost the
> ghost behind the skeleton. He matched Crivelli's dead *Christus*. . . .
> The angular hollows and lines of his aged ancestors had succeeded
> to their reign in his face twenty years before their time.

Revelation of 'heart and inner meaning' in fleshly form could
scarcely go further, and it is, of course, Hardy's ultimate vision
of this existence in which 'We come to live and are called to
die': in Clare's *Christus*-like appearance the stark facts of Clare's
and every man's being and destiny, his past and his future, stand
revealed. In *The Dynasts* the same X-ray-like vision was to give
Hardy his 'transparencies'. Bellini (1430?–1516), by contrast, is
never mentioned again by Hardy,[5] yet the parallel is equally apt.
Hardy's sense of affinity with this most lyrical and tender of painters
must surely have been great, and it could have been from Bellini
primarily that he learned how to unify and intensify the emotion
of a scene through the transfigurative power of light. An example
of what I have in mind occurs in *Tess of the d'Urbervilles*. Here,
unlikely as it may sound, Hardy's treatment of Tess's arrest at
Stonehenge seems to have been influenced by Bellini's *Agony in
the Garden* (in the National Gallery, London). There are differences,
of course: it is Tess who sleeps, while Angel and her captors
watch, and there is a silveriness in Hardy's picture not found
in Bellini's. But it is the same moment, the mysterious time just
before dawn, that is depicted; there is the same breadth and spaciousness in the landscape, with the central figures in the foreground,
Tess lying on the Stone of Sacrifice, Christ kneeling among the
rocks of the Garden. Hardy writes,

> All waited in the growing light, their faces and hands as if they
> were silvered, the remainder of their figures dark, the stones glisten-
> ing green-gray, the Plain still a mass of shade. Soon the light
> was strong, and a ray shone upon her unconscious form, peering
> under her eyelids and waking her.

Earlier he had noted how 'the band of silver paleness along the
east horizon made even the distant parts of the Great Plain appear
dark and near', and had shown Tess's captors moving towards
her from this verge. In Bellini's picture the far-distant horizon

is pink with the first flush of dawn, the pale (golden rather than silver) light of which is already touching the feet of Christ and the sleeping disciples; the plain, across which the Roman soldiers are winding to his arrest, is, like Hardy's, still a 'mass of shade'. Although Bellini's scene is painted predominantly in tones of rose and gold, Hardy's in silver and grey, the play of light in each case serves both to heighten the drama of the situation and to subdue it, introducing a quiet tone of pathos and reconciliation. How similar Hardy's method is in this respect to Bellini's may be seen by comparing his description with the *Agony in the Garden* of Bellini's brother-in-law Mantegna, which itself suggested part of Bellini's design. Here, although the increased stoniness of the setting and the magnitude of the stones afford a closer parallel with Stonehenge, the absence of these tonal gradations – the scene is depicted in full daylight – makes any significant connexion with Hardy's scene unlikely.

II

Within the medium of words to which he is limited, Hardy becomes a 'chameleon painter'. The whole realm of painting lies at his command: he can adopt the style of any individual artist or school that he wishes. He had the necessary knowledge: the *Life* records numerous visits to galleries and exhibitions, at home and abroad, beginning with his apprentice years in London, when he used to pay regular visits to the National Gallery, 'confining his attention to a single master on each visit' (p. 52). These visits would be supplemented, no doubt, by the study of plates and engravings. Some of the knowledge thus acquired is imported too directly into his novels, leading readers to complain of his pedantry and self-exhibition. Certainly some of his allusions seem more helpful to the author than the readers: to be told of Jude's great-aunt, for instance, that she turned upon Jude and Sue 'a countenance like that of Sebastiano's Lazarus' is not of much use if one does not know the painting in question. Often, however, the point of comparison is made explicit, and the justification of the allusion then depends on its subtlety and relevance. Thus, if one knows anything of Dürer at all, it is helpful to be told that the bonfire (*RN*, 45) caused the 'lineaments and general contours' of the heath-folk 'to be drawn with Düreresque vigour and dash'. We know Liddy

Smallbury better for learning that she had a 'perfection of hue which . . . was the softened ruddiness on a surface of high rotundity that we meet with in a Terburg or Gerard Douw' (*FFMC*, 101): the association with the Dutch School is itself suggestive. Most powerful of all is the comparison of Angel Clare and 'Liza-Lu, as they walk with clasped hands and bowed heads out of the city of Wintoncester on the morning of Tess's execution, to 'Giotto's' *Two Apostles*.[6] There is a reticence about this that makes it all the more compelling: the bowed heads are the only stated point of comparison, but more perhaps is hinted at. Wintoncester, with its towers and spires and pinnacles 'showing as in an isometric drawing', set against 'the rotund upland of St. Catherine's hill' with the sweeping 'landscape beyond landscape' behind, becomes by association a modern Jerusalem, resembling that seen in the background of so many Renaissance religious paintings, and its gaol thus becomes a new Calvary, where Tess is made a Christian sacrifice. If this interpretation is correct, and if there is, as I have suggested, a recollection, conscious or unconscious, of Bellini's *Agony in the Garden* in Tess's arrest at Stonehenge, then we might associate with these two passages yet a third, that in which Angel walking with Tess to the early morning milking is reminded of the Resurrection hour. What he (or his creator) is reminded of, in all probability, is some *painting* of the Resurrection hour – the chill morning light in Piero della Francesca's fresco, perhaps, or perhaps again of Bellini's; the 'almost regnant power' which Angel feels in Tess certainly has its counterpart in the triumphant risen Christ of either of these. 'He little thought', says Hardy, 'that the Magdalen might be at his side.' Indeed not: the comparison points to a different identification. *Tess* is arguably the most deeply felt of all Hardy's novels, and what these parallels, if correct, reveal is the almost religious sense he has of Tess as victim.

Such understatement and implicit suggestion, however, is rare in Hardy's art-allusions, which normally have the explicit directness of Scott (in, for example, *The Antiquary*), rather than the sophistication and subtlety of Proust. Collectively they may be thought of in relation to Hardy's creative activity as a word-painter, as a kind of *repoussoir* figure, drawing us into the main picture. It is in his own creations that the really significant allusiveness, wide-ranging, complex, and sometimes profound, occurs.

The habit and skills are there from the start, in Hardy's first published novel, *Desperate Remedies*. Hardy was bitterly wounded

by the *Spectator* reviewer's quip about desperate remedies 'for an
emaciated purse', but remained sufficiently composed to notice also,
and to quote in a letter to Alexander Macmillan, his statement
that he had been irresistibly reminded in places 'of the paintings
of Wilkie, and still more, perhaps, of those of Teniers', and that
such scenes 'indicate powers that might and ought to be extended
largely in this direction'.[7] Another reviewer (possibly Horace Moule),
writing in the *Saturday Review*, found in the cider-making scene
'the same sort of thing in written sentences that a clear fresh
country piece of Hobbema's is in art'.[8] With this encouragement,
Under the Greenwood Tree followed, and was announced on its title-page
as 'A Rural Painting of the Dutch School'. *Desperate Remedies* was
provided with a sensational plot to satisfy, as Hardy thought, public
taste, but at the core of it is the youthful author's own record
of experience: both his uncertainties in love and his sensuous response
to the world about him find an outlet and a first tentative artistic
expression here. In *Under the Greenwood Tree* the sensationalism is
discarded and the sensuous response takes over entirely. In both
novels Hardy portrays a rural world which he knows at first hand,
so freshly that the paint seems scarcely dry. A similarity in subject
and feeling (a love of ordinary people engaged in their ordinary
pursuits, a delight in the objects of the home or of trade simply
as objects) would in itself suggest a resemblance to Dutch art,
but there are also more specific links. The cider-making scene
commended by the *Saturday Review*, for example, suggests a Dutch
painting by its arrangement and detail. The cider-mill and press
are set on 'a green plot' beneath 'two or three large, wide-spreading
elm-trees', from which the inn-sign of the Three Tranters is sus-
pended, and round them is gathered a miscellaneous group, including
not only Mr Springrove and his men but also

> two or three other men, grinders and supernumeraries, a woman
> with an infant in her arms, a flock of pigeons, and some little
> boys with straws in their mouths, endeavouring, whenever the
> men's backs were turned, to get a sip of the sweet juice issuing
> from the vat.

The trees, the busy interested crowd, even the cheeky little boys,
all evoke recollections, not so much of similar scenes seen elsewhere,
as of similar scenes seen painted elsewhere – perhaps by Jan Steen
(his *Skittle Players*, for instance). Some details of colour are introduced

later, in the description of Mr Springrove in his leather apron
and the 'brown-faced peasants' in their smock-frocks, and the action
of the shovel in catching the rays of the declining sun and reflecting
them 'in bristling stars of light' is mentioned, but the effect is
rather diffuse, and it could be that at this stage Hardy's imitation
of the Dutch masters is unconscious, not deliberate, as it was to
become after a nudge from the reviewers. Later in the book, the
description of the disorderly home of Mrs Higgins, with the roll
of baby-linen, the 'pap-clogged spoon' and 'overturned tin pap-cup'
prominent on the floor, a baby crying against every chair-leg,
and Mrs Higgins herself showing rather too much bosom, suggests
less a direct acquaintance with the life of the London poor than
a knowledge of Steen's series of paintings of 'dissolute families',[9]
or even of Hogarth. But here again the resemblance is one of
subject; nothing is said of either colour, light or shade. Hardy's
interest in these is already evident in *Desperate Remedies* – in the
early scenes in Budmouth, with their descriptions of the effect
of sunlight on the heather and the sea; in various candle-light
scenes; and in the spectacular fire-scene – but he has not yet combined
them with content so as to heighten the painterly manner of his
writing and make the pictorial analogy inescapable. In *Under the
Greenwood Tree* he takes this further step – in, for instance, the reflected
sunlight on Mr Day's staircase (discussed earlier) or the picture
of the choir grouped around Mr Penny's open shop-window, illuminated by the setting sun, and each 'backed up by a shadow
as long as a steeple'. Hardy perhaps had his Gerard Douw hat
on when he 'painted' this scene (despite the allusion to Moroni)
and also the earlier one of Mrs Dewy sitting by the fire, with
her children Charley and Bessy engaged in characteristic pastimes
beside her. Life going on at open windows is a feature of Douw's
paintings, and his *Young Mother* is somewhat akin in mood to Hardy's
picture of the Dewy household.

The 'Dutch' style remained thenceforward readily available to
Hardy: most of his later novels have passages in which he recognisably
'goes Dutch'. One of the most highly finished of these is the
description of Thomasin gathering apples in the loft, the sun shining
in upon her through a semi-circular hole 'in a bright yellow patch',
the pigeons flying around her head, and the face of her aunt
'just visible above the floor of the loft, lit by a few stray motes
of light, as she stood half-way up the ladder' (*RN*, 131). In a
different vein, there are the scenes of debauchery, like that in

the barn in *Far from the Madding Crowd*. This, being static, invites
the same kind of long perusal we give to a picture and has a
quality of almost hypnotic realism in its detail (the over-turned
water-jug, for instance) such as occurs in the tavern scenes of
Steen or of the Flemish artists, Brueghel, Brouwer or Teniers. Another
version of the domestic interior of 'muck and muddle' seen already
in the Higgins household is the 'one-candled spectacle' of Mrs
Durbeyfield balancing on one foot beside the wash-tub and rocking
the cradle with the other, which Hardy describes as one of 'yellow
melancholy'.

This last example, however, may remind us of the strong family
likeness existing between the *genre* painting of seventeenth-century
Holland and its descendant, the *genre* and narrative painting of
nineteenth-century Britain. The *Spectator* reviewer had referred to
Wilkie as well as Teniers, and Wilkie's cottage-interiors may well
be recalled by the Durbeyfields' humble home. The cross-fertilisation
between painting and the novel during the Victorian period has
been a subject for investigation recently by a number of critics.[10]
The pictures tell stories. The stories are told, to a large extent,
in pictures. Both stories and pictures, moreover, share a common
ground and common interests, even a common sensibility. Domesticity
at all levels, but particularly a humble one; the humorous and
pathetic incidents of everyday life; the joys and sorrows of love;
sick-beds, death-beds, and graveyards – these are the favourite subjects
and themes of painters and story-tellers (in prose and verse) alike.
Scenes and characters from novels often provided subjects for a
painting – Goldsmith, Sterne and Scott, for example, were favourite
sources. Later novelists seem often to be anticipating the transfer,
by painting the scene in words themselves first. And, indeed, many
scenes that did not achieve the distinction of being painted were
illustrated, often strikingly and beautifully, for this was the great
age of book illustration.

The critical commonplace of the novel as a 'picture', a commonplace fully substantiated by the practice of Victorian novelists themselves, found ready acceptance by Hardy. In 1863 he sends his
sister some brotherly advice on the 'pictures' painted by Thackeray,
and his worry when he came to write novels himself was that
his works were 'not novels at all, as usually understood — that
is pictures of modern customs and observances' (*Life*, 104). The
emphasis presumably is on the last five words: his novels are pictures,
but not of urban society or the fashionable life. *The Hand of Ethelberta*

and to a lesser extent *A Laodicean* and *Two on a Tower* were attempts to remedy this imagined deficiency, but the best and most characteristic of his novels are still, as *Under the Greenwood Tree* had been acknowledged to be, 'rural pictures'. As such they are also *genre* pictures. This too Hardy seems eventually to acknowledge, when he refers in his Preface to *The Mayor of Casterbridge* (1896) to 'my Exhibition of Wessex life'. He chooses in each novel a different aspect of that life to portray – sheep-farming, furze-cutting, corn-selling, tree-planting, timber-felling, cider-making, dairy-farming, pig-breeding. The whole constitutes a portfolio of pictures such as Hardy's contemporaries delighted in. For, if he felt that the representation of urban life, high or low or both, was *de rigueur* in the novel, he had only to look around him at the South Kensington Museum (now the Victoria and Albert) or the Royal Academy exhibitions to see that in *genre* painting this was not so. From the beginning of the century country life, both within doors and without, had been a highly popular subject. At the start of the century Sir David Wilkie is the outstanding example, but he was followed by William Collins, Thomas Webster, William Maw Egley, Thomas Faed, Myles Birket Foster and many others, including at times such Pre-Raphaelites as Brown, Hunt and Millais. The actual *work* of the countryside comes also, and perhaps more frequently, into landscape-painting (which I shall be considering later), and, when that too is taken into account, Hardy's fears of not meeting the public taste begin to look very unfounded.

Each of Hardy's major novels, however, besides forming as a whole a kind of composite *genre* picture, contains within it a number of individual *genre* paintings, or elements reminiscent of *genre* painting. The most *genre*-conscious of them all (*Under the Greenwood Tree* being assigned, on the whole with good reason, to 'the Dutch School') seems to be *Far from the Madding Crowd*. The *Spectator* reviewer listed most of the scenes portrayed –

> The reader sees in turn the life of the shepherd in lambing-time, of the bailiff and his out-door labourers at the homestead, of the mistress on her pay-day, the interior of the malt-house and its gossip, the corn-market at the county town, the thunder-storm which breaks up the fine harvest weather, the rural inn and its company, the sheep-fair on the downs . . .

– and comments that they 'are painted with all the vividness of a powerful imagination'.[11] Hardy's *genre* manner, however, is also equally striking in passages depicting incidents arising out of the story itself – passages, that is, in which the narrative, dramatic and emotive interest is uppermost. One such is our first picture of Bathsheba, when the ornamental spring waggon conveniently stands still so that we and Gabriel may look at her. The picture brings all the clutter of a cottage interior out into the open – the tables and chairs, the settle, the pots of geraniums, myrtles and cactuses, the caged canary, the cat in a willow basket – and on top of the load sits Bathsheba, gazing at herself in a swing looking-glass, while the sun lights up her crimson jacket and paints 'a soft lustre' upon her face and hair. This combines together the elements of three potential pictures to form a fourth. There is the out-door, waggon-with-pretty-girl picture; the indoor, cottage-kitchen one; and the young-lady-at-her-mirror one (as in C. R. Leslie's *The Toilette* in the Sheepshanks collection in the Victoria and Albert Museum – an important collection for us, because it must have formed the bulk of the pictures studied by Hardy in the South Kensington Museum in 1869). The picture thus created has something of the strangeness and slight oddity of, say, Ford Madox Brown's *Pretty Baa-Lambs*, although unlike Brown Hardy moralises it for us: 'Woman's prescriptive infirmity had stalked into the sunlight, which had clothed it in the freshness of an originality.'

As even this picture, fresh and original as it is, may suggest, it is their fidelity to *objects* and to the 'simple primary human affections and passions' that authenticates Hardy's *genre* paintings. The shelves across the corner, the other shelf on which are ranged the bottles and canisters necessary to Gabriel's calling, the sheep-crook, the flute lying beside the bread and cheese and cider as in a still-life – it is these that suggest the relationship to *genre* of the description of Gabriel's hut, significantly given the chapter-heading 'An Interior'. (Some of the details recall those in one of the most celebrated of the Sheepshanks pictures, Landseer's *The Old Shepherd's Chief Mourner*.) Victorian *genre* painting, like the Victorian way of life, deals largely with substantial things. And Hardy loved things, especially old and homely things, finding in them a 'beauty of association' entirely superior to 'beauty of aspect' (*Life*, 120). By reference to things he is able to evoke the character, the very smell and temperature, of a country home, as his counterparts among the painters do by depicting them. He has no need to compose the picture formally: often he does so, but often too it is enough simply to suggest. We know the Yeobrights' living room or kitchen through its flowers on the window-sill and its sanded flagstone floor, so that the simple statement 'She was sitting by the window as usual when he came downstairs' is sufficient to create a poignant picture of Mrs Yeobright in her grief and melancholy; a picture comparable in mood and generally in its background with yet another in the Sheepshanks collection, Thomas Duncan's *The Waefu' Heart*, in which a woman sits gazing (not, certainly, out of the window but into the fire), in an attitude of pensive sadness such as we may imagine to have been Mrs Yeobright's. Later we learn more about the furnishings of the Yeobright household, including its 'gaunt oak-cased clock', its corner cupboard with the glass door, its dumb-waiter and its wooden tea-trays. These are just the sort of details the Victorian painter likes to record: they help to give the true 'feel' of the background he is depicting. They are as 'right' as are the pembroke table, the fringed mantelpiece, the bellows, the tray, the tressel-stool and the corner shelves of Haynes King's *Jealousy and Flirtation* (1874, now in the Victoria and Albert). Hardy had included a rough version of those corner shelves in his account of Gabriel's hut, but he generally prefers the corner cupboard – the Lovedays, the Caros, Shepherd Fennel and even the Durbeyfields have one.

The lines of demarcation between *genre* painting and narrative painting in the Victorian period are sometimes difficult to draw. A scene involving people, after all, however 'typical', almost inevitably appears to have a story to tell; a picture setting out to tell a story, on the other hand, usually has some generic characteristics. In this way the situations Hardy depicts, and not merely their backgrounds, have at times their pictorial counterparts. Thus, the situation in *Jealousy and Flirtation* is not unlike a humbler version of that in *The Mayor of Casterbridge* in which Elizabeth-Jane looks on while Lucetta flirts with Farfrae. In King's picture a young carpenter sits with his chair drawn up close to a mischievously smiling servant girl, while in the corner by the window another girl looks on sadly. Although Hardy does not attribute jealousy to Elizabeth-Jane, he does make clear both her awareness of the situation, and her pain at it. The two artists use the same visual means to enforce the contrast. The flirtatious young minx is gaily and loosely clad, low-bodiced, and wearing earrings: a sewing-basket is beside her on the table, her knitting on the floor. The other girl is much more soberly clad, in dark clothes, with a striped

apron and a bonnet: she evidently does the hard work. Compare
this with the first occasion on which Farfrae sees Elizabeth-Jane
and Lucetta together, when they run out to inspect the horse-drill,
Lucetta resplendent in a new gown of a 'deep cherry colour',
Elizabeth-Jane with her bonnet and shawl 'pitchforked on in a
moment'. I introduce this parallel not to suggest that Hardy's
episode actually derives from King's, but as an illustration of the
kind of affinity existing between him and the Victorian narrative
painters in their choice of the human relationships and emotions
they depict, and the means employed. This particular parallel can
in fact be supported by another painting, John Callcott Horsley's
Showing a Preference, in which the personages represented are socially
on the same level as Hardy's trio. This shows a man walking
with two women along a country lane: he holds a parasol over
one woman and leans towards her, totally ignoring the other.[12]

  The Mayor of Casterbridge, however, is interesting on another count:
it is the first of Hardy's novels in which an element of 'social
realism' occurs in the pictures. 'Social realism' was the term used
to describe the work of a group of artists associated during the
1870s with *The Graphic* (founded in 1870) and the *Illustrated London
News*. Their subjects were usually though not exclusively urban
and industrial: they portrayed, forcefully and without glamour,
the lives of the working-classes at work – in the mills, the factories,
the pits – and outside it – in the work-houses, the lodging-houses,
and on the streets. Hubert Herkomer, one of the leading members
of the group, was later to paint Hardy's portrait (in 1908), and
to contribute several illustrations for *Tess of the d'Urbervilles* when
it was serialised in *The Graphic* in 1891. His *Agricultural Labourer*
and *Brewer's Drayman*, which appeared in the *Graphic* series 'Heads
of the People' in October and November 1875, are impressive
studies. He also produced two celebrated engravings of Chelsea
pensioners, *Sunday at Chelsea Hospital* and *The Last Muster* (later
also a painting), which must surely have appealed to Hardy. In
1885 he painted the picture *Hard Times*, now in the Manchester
City Art Gallery. It presents a family group resting exhausted
by the roadside: clearly they are tramping in search of work (the
man and woman carry a bundle; the man's pick-axes lie in the
road). Again, it is not suggested that there is any direct relationship
between the picture and the novel. But it is instructive, I think,
to compare this with the opening of *The Mayor*, where again we
see a man carrying the tools of his trade, walking with his wife

and child in search of work. Although Henchard rises for a time to prosperity, this novel faces the problems of poverty, work and the economics of work much more directly than any of its predecessors. It is also relatively unpictorial, probably because of the absence of landscapes, and its memorable images tend to be those which enforce this theme: Elizabeth and her mother making fish-nets, in the days of their poverty, or trudging along the road to Weydon-Priors, Elizabeth carrying a withy-basket, her mother a blue bundle; Henchard in the shabby clothes that symbolise his decline. Wearing 'the remains of an old blue cloth suit of his gentlemanly times, a rusty silk hat, and a once black satin stock, soiled and shabby', he recalls the central figure in Luke Fildes's truly graphic *Houseless and Hungry*, who stands, top-hatted and shabby, the lines of authority still marked in his brooding, down-cast face, isolated and incongruous among the other destitutes.[13] Hardy's account of Mixen Lane, where 'Vice ran freely in and out of certain of the doors', seems also to be being offered as a kind of rural equivalent of the slum-quarters, gin-palaces and opium dens of the *Graphic* artists, although it is a considerably toned-down version: the vices are not specified; theft apparently occurs only 'in times of privation'; and the only crime mentioned is a bit of harmless poaching. Even so, the description is something new in Hardy's work, which has hitherto avoided the sordid. In 1883 Hardy had recommended the engravings in 'the *Graphic*, *Illustrated News*, etc.' to a correspondent as suitable for use in art-education in elementary schools (*Life*, 159). By that date the *Graphic*'s great period of social realism was over: nevertheless, it seems probable that when two years later Hardy began writing *The Mayor*, his experience of its engravings and the paintings they engendered affected his presentation.

Social realism remained henceforth an ingredient of Hardy's art. Work as a harsh economic necessity is stressed in the picture of Marty South sitting by the fire making spars, or holding up the young fir trees for Giles with a hand 'chill as a stone' and still more in the depiction of Tess's labours at Marlott and Flintcomb-Ash. Here the thoroughly rural nature of the occupations brings Millet to mind: I suppose no one ever read Hardy's description of the Marlott women binding the corn, wearing their 'drawn cotton bonnets with great flapping curtains', without thinking of Millet. As Van Gogh recognised, the *Graphic* artists were artists in Millet's style: what he had done for the peasantry, they did for the urban manual workers.[14] Hardy's turn in this direction in his last four

major novels shows him moving with the times. His 'painting'
method tended always to be expansive: he incorporated new styles
in successive works, but without abandoning the old. The realism
he sought to achieve was always basically the realism of 'inscape',
what he called in a note of January 1881 (*Life*, 147) 'seeing into
the *heart of a thing*', through the power of 'the imaginative reason'.
This remained his objective even in the later novels, but the imaginative reason had by then led him to see the socially realistic facts
at the heart of his subject, the life of rural Wessex – not forming
the whole of that heart, for life remained a 'hobble' simply by
being life, but certainly a significant part of it. Although still
strongly pictorial and still 'painterly' in manner, his representation
of that life becomes at this point less 'picturesque', in so far as
that word connotes the quaint and the charming. In his essay
'The Dorsetshire Labourer' (1883) he notes the declining 'artistic
merit' of this class with the growth of mechanisation, how, 'like
the men, the women are, pictorially, less interesting than they
used to be', but adds that loss of 'personal charm' is scarcely
a reason for keeping them permanently backward: 'it is only the
old story that progress and picturesqueness do not harmonise'.[15]
Such 'personal charm' and picturesqueness had been well to the
fore in the early novels, because at that time they were for Hardy
the essence of the way of life he was depicting, the pattern in
the carpet 'his idiosyncrasy moved him to observe' (*Life*, 153).
He was not idealising, nor sentimentalising: he was expressing the
'object' as he saw it, at a time when his natural artistic pleasure
at 'the goings-on of the Universe' still remained relatively robust.

The abandonment of novel-writing and its plot-requirements after
the publication of *Jude* in 1895 brought Hardy a new freedom.
His 'watching eye' was now free to roam where it would and
to record in verse any circumstance, incident, or scene whatsoever
which it found significant or affecting. It was not confined to
rural Wessex: although Wessex scenes and folk still held a central
position, the sense in the poems of a larger world stretching behind
and around them is strong. City streets, railway stations, the Victorian
parlour, dining-room or ballroom often provide a background to
the action. It is a life-time's experience that Hardy has now taken
as his province, and of that experience these have all formed part.
The presence of Max Gate, so to speak, is felt in these poems,
along with that of Upper Bockhampton. As a result, there is an

extension of range in his *genre* painting: the middle-class world of Augustus Egg or James Tissot and the modern world of Frith appear alongside the older, more rural world of Wilkie and Webster.

As we have already noticed (p. 22), Hardy has a number of poems which form complete verbal paintings. Most of them (for example, 'No Buyers', 'A Light Snow-Fall after Frost', 'Last Look round St Martin's Fair') are clearly of the *genre* type. Others, although sparser in detail and colour, resemble narrative painting in their subjects. 'At the Railway Station, Upway', for instance, seems asking to be painted, perhaps by Mulready: in it a little boy plays his violin to comfort a hand-cuffed convict 'till the train [comes] in', while the constable in charge looks smilingly on. 'At the Aquatic Sports' belongs to the same category: here two fiddlers and a man singing stand with their backs to the sea, unheeding the crab-catchings and laughing crowds behind them. The matter-of-fact tone of these and similar poems (the reader being left to see their point for himself) makes them sound almost like the description of, or prescription for, a painting, if they are not paintings themselves. Others are somewhat more overt in their expression of and appeal to emotion, as narrative painting itself often is. 'A Parting-Scene' provides an example. Here a soldier is seen parting from his young wife and his mother at a railway terminal. The poem speaks of their misery, which they try to hide from the eyes of the world by staying behind the waiting-room door, thereby revealing it to the spectator–reader. This scene is of the very essence of Victorian narrative painting: its setting inevitably recalls Frith, but in theme it is closer to Abraham Solomon's *Second Class – The Parting* (1854), in which a mother sorrowfully says goodbye to her son, who is emigrating. Narrative painting of this kind – the compassionate observation of some incident of common life – forms a distinct strain in the *Poems*. Its presence is felt not only in the short, descriptive poems, but also in many of the longer, narrative ones, such as 'The Chapel-Organist' and 'The Widow Betrothed'.

As a moralist and ironist, Hardy also found the 'companion pieces' favoured by the *genre* or narrative painter very suitable to his purpose. The fashion goes back to Hogarth, not only to his larger narrative sequences, such as *The Rake's Progress* and *Marriage à la Mode*, but also to smaller sets, such as *The Four Times of Day* and the *Before* and *After* engravings. In view of the subject of the last – a distinctly sleazy seduction, in which the couple are

an eighteenth-century version of Eliot's typist and young man carbun-
cular – it is amusing to notice Hardy's fondness for the 'Before
and After' title, signifying the contrasting scenes the poem either
paints or suggests – 'The Coquette and After' (this comes closest
to Hogarth in theme, though still far removed from it in tone),
'First Sight of Her and After', 'Before and After Summer', 'Her
Death and After', even 'Before Marching and After' and 'Before
Life and After'. Closer than Hogarth to Hardy are the contrasting
scenes painted by nineteenth-century artists. Abraham Solomon's
Second Class – The Parting, mentioned earlier, is, for example, a com-
panion-piece to *First Class – The Meeting*, the pain of one picture
contrasting with the happiness of the other. Cruikshank's *Born a
Genius* and *Born a Dwarf* offer a sharp piece of social comment
after Hardy's own heart. Still more relevant is the *Past and Present*
of Augustus Egg. This triptych of paintings, dated 1858, shows,
first, a woman flinging herself at her husband's feet after his discovery
of her infidelity; secondly, the same woman several years later,
an outcast sheltering under the Adelphi Arches by the Thames;
lastly, her two daughters seated at an open bedroom window praying
for their lost mother. Here the 'Before and After' theme is combined
with the irony of contrasting presents, for the moment of the last
two pictures is identical – this is indicated by the presence of the
moon, with the same thin strip of cloud beneath it, in each. Such
'satires of circumstance' appeal greatly to Hardy. The moon, by
virtue of its 'Overworld' viewpoint, is well qualified to become
a Spirit Ironic, and it does so in several poems, one of which,
'The Moon Looks In', in which a lover lies in bed imagining
his beloved dreaming of him, while actually she is preparing to
go to a dance and never giving him a thought, is structurally
close to Egg's painting. Other poems which have the character
of companion-pieces are 'A Wife in London', in which in the
first part the wife receives news of her husband's death in action,
and in the second part receives, next day, a letter from him,
full of plans for his 'hoped return'; 'The Voice of the Thorn';
'Seventy-Four and Twenty'; 'Where They Lived'; 'The Second
Visit'; even perhaps 'Weathers'. In 'Life and Death at Sunrise'
and 'Plena Timoris' the contrasting pictures are combined in one,
rather as in Hardy's own illustration to 'Her Dilemma' in *Wessex
Poems*. Such simple but striking ironies and contrasts are a feature
of Victorian paintings, both single and companion. Even 'The Convergence of the Twain' has its counterpart in Landseer's *Man*

Proposes, God Disposes,[16] in which a group of polar bears plays among icebergs with a union jack: change 'God' to 'the Immanent Will', and this could have captioned Hardy's poem too.

To return, however, from the ice-floes to the Victorian drawing-room. I said earlier that the Hardy who wrote the poems was the Hardy of Max Gate as well as of Mellstock. As a result there is a kind of composite *genre* picture of late Victorian middle-class life running through them. There are the settings – 'At the Dinner-Table', 'In the Marquee', 'Where the Picnic Was', 'Henley Regatta', 'The High-School Lawn'; inns, railway-carriages, hansom-cabs. There are also the properties – the candles and lamps ('the common lamp-lit room', 'the candles mooning each face'), the mirrors, windows, and letters, the sunshades that appear so often in representations of the comfortable, elegant life of this section of society. There are the elegant ladies – the Agnes of 'Concerning Agnes', 'The Rejected Member's Wife' waving her white-gloved hand, the charming lady (said to be Florence Henniker) who 'wore a new "terra-cotta" gown'. Above all, there are the ladies at the piano. To end this section, I shall set the poem 'At the Piano' beside Sir Frank Dicksee's painting *A Reverie*, exhibited at the Royal Academy in 1895 and now in the Walker Art Gallery, Liverpool. The poem runs,

A woman was playing,
  A man looking on;
  And the mould of her face,
  And her neck, and her hair,
  Which the rays fell upon
  Of the two candles there,
Sent him mentally straying
  In some fancy-place
  Where pain had no trace.

A cowled Apparition
  Came pushing between;
  And her notes seemed to sigh;
  And the lights to burn pale,
  As a spell numbed the scene.
  But the maid saw no bale,
And the man no monition;
  And Time laughed awry,
  And the Phantom hid nigh.

In the painting a woman sits at the piano, the lamplight falling on her face and shoulders; a man sits in a chair near her, listening, with closed eyes. Behind the woman stands a ghostly figure. The catalogue entry has the quotation,

In the years that are fled
Lips that are dead
Sang me that song.[17]

The situations are clearly not identical: the man in the poem has his eyes open, and the menacing Apparition seems to belong to the future rather than to the past. But the resemblance is sufficient, I think, to suggest the strong ties of sympathy linking Hardy the poet with the painters of his day. Dicksee's painting in fact epitomises a whole group of Hardy's poems, closer to it in spirit and theme, though less close in design, than the one quoted. These include the semi-narrative 'The Wistful Lady', 'The Last Performance', 'A Duettist to Her Pianoforte', 'The Prophetess', and the opening of 'The Strange House (Max Gate, A.D. 2000)':

'I hear the piano playing –
    Just as a ghost might play.'
'– O, but what are you saying?
    There's no piano to-day.'

These are all, except, presumably, the first, poems about Hardy's first wife Emma, who from the moment of her death never ceased to haunt his poetry. His second wife, Florence, must often have found herself in the situation of the woman in Dicksee's picture.

III

We have so far considered the chameleon painter in two of his roles – as an artist of the Dutch School, and as a Victorian *genre* and narrative painter. Hardy's delight in the human scene found in these its appropriate form of expression. Most readers, however, probably think of him primarily as a landscape artist, and of his characters, pictorially considered, as 'figures in a landscape'. This is understandable and justifiable. Yet his characters, as we have seen, may be 'in' other settings than a landscape. They may also be other than 'figures': they may be seen in close-up as well as at a distance. Hardy, in other words, is also a portrait-painter.

Portrait-painting, of course, is a part of any novelist's art, and a description of a character's physical appearance is bound to be in some degree a verbal picture, even though there may be wide variations in the method employed, from the occasionally laborious cataloguing of Scott to a more suggestive use of comparison and allusion and of the significant detail. If Hardy's descriptions do not immediately suggest the portrait-painter to us, this is partly because their manner does not at first glance differ greatly from that of other novelists: it is not markedly more pictorial than theirs – than, for example, Dickens's or George Eliot's (both of whom are, indeed, frequently highly pictorial). But it is also because he is here exercising the art that conceals art (the painter's art) – not entirely concealing it, because he still wishes to preserve the aesthetic distancing which for him is a part of life as well as of art, but concealing it sufficiently to prevent the portrait from acquiring the fixity of its painted counterpart: *this* picture must be able to get up and walk away. People may be 'figments' for Hardy, but, seen at close quarters especially, they have 'real vitality, real warmth'; prick them, and they bleed. The painted portrait present within the literary description may be a reminder to us, sometimes explicit, sometimes subliminal, that faces are, ultimately, 'but a gallery of pictures', but it is also there because Hardy has found instructive the portrait-painter's methods of achieving vivid visualisation and hence a heightened sense of life.

In Hardy's novels everybody is a picture for somebody, and this is sometimes explicitly acknowledged. Thus John Lackland, returning to Longpuddle after thirty-five years, learns that 'Old figures have dropped out of their frames, so to speak, and new ones have been put in their places' (*SS*, 427). The frames are frequently a door or a window: Henchard at the King's Arms, Fancy acknowledging the carol-singers. In Fancy's case, Hardy is quite explicit: like the numerous 'Girls at a Window' painted by Douw, she is 'framed as a picture by the window architrave'. Sometimes the type of picture is particularised. Dick Dewy first appears in profile against the sky 'like the portrait of a gentleman in black cardboard' (*UGWT*, 33); Mrs Yeobright shows 'whitely, and without half-lights, like a cameo' (*RN*, 58); Tess's profile too, as she sits milking Old Pretty with the sun shining directly

upon her, is rendered 'keen as a cameo cut from the dun background
of the cow' (*TD*, 177). In Tess's case, the picture is regarded
appreciatively by Angel Clare, sitting under his own cow. But
for Angel it is more than a picture: he reflects that all here
'was real vitality, real warmth, real incarnation'; the curves of
those lips which he has studied so often 'that he could reproduce
them mentally with ease' are now confronting him 'clothed with
colour and life'.

'Clothed with colour and life': this duality is the governing
principle of Hardy's art of portraiture. Portraits are not simply
'from the life': they *are* the life. Hardy might have signed them
'Pygmalion'. Take Elizabeth-Jane's first view of Farfrae. The subject
is posed as in a picture: Farfrae is seen 'idly reading a copy
of the local paper'. Hardy does not describe him, but tells us
the things Elizabeth-Jane noticed:

> how his forehead shone where the light caught it, and how
> nicely his hair was cut, and the sort of velvet-pile or down
> that was on the skin at the back of his neck, and how his
> cheek was so truly curved as to be part of a globe, and how
> clearly drawn were the lids and lashes which hid his bent eyes.

This seemingly random collection of observations is in fact a coherent
portrait. It is composed in a series of curves – the bent-down head,
the curving cheek, the curves of the eyelids – the eye of the observer
being carefully led from one to the other. The light which draws
attention to the forehead is continued, more faintly, in the 'velvet-pile
or down' on the skin at the back of the neck. As in a good
portrait, character is communicated through the deft handling of
light and colour and line: the light falls fittingly on the forehead
of this clever young man who knows how to turn grown wheat
into wholesome wheat; the 'velvet-pile or down' suggests an almost
feminine refinement and delicacy, in contrast with Henchard's
swarthiness; while the perfectly rounded cheek and clearly drawn
lids and lashes perhaps bespeak the self-sufficiency, self-complacency
almost, that is 'bred in the bone'. The portrait is instinct with
life, and ready to spring into action at the drop of the supper-tray.

As this example illustrates, Hardy looks at his characters' facial
characteristics with the eye of a painter. He notices line, curve,
and colour, and is alert to what they can tell us of the personality
within. Henchard 'showed in profile a facial angle so slightly inclined

as to be almost perpendicular' (*MC*, 37), a perpendicularity expressive as much of his stubbornness as of his rectitude. Boldwood has 'full and distinctly outlined Roman features, the prominences of which glowed in the sun with a bronze-like richness of tone' (*FFMC*, 120). Although both men are 'reddish-fleshed' (*FFMC*, 146), Boldwood's 'bronze-like richness of tone' suggests the patrician, in contrast with the coarser 'red and black visage' (*MC*, 108) of Henchard. Hardy notices mouths: he knows Tess's 'mobile peony mouth', for instance, as thoroughly as Angel Clare does. Grace Melbury's 'small, delicate mouth' suggests her immaturity: it 'had hardly settled down to its matured curves' (*W*, 69). Facial curves are often indicative to him of maturity or its lack: thus in Elizabeth-Jane's face there was 'an under-handsomeness . . . struggling to reveal itself through the provisional curves of immaturity' (*MC*, 57), while in Marty, by contrast, 'the provisional curves of her childhood's face' have been forced by poverty 'to a premature finality' (*W*, 43). He sees the transformation of the child's face into that of the adult as normally much more gradual. Of Tess he says,

> Phases of her childhood lurked in her aspect still. As she walked along to-day, for all her bouncing handsome womanliness, you could sometimes see her twelfth year in her cheeks, or her ninth sparkling from her eyes; and even her fifth would flit over the curves of her mouth now and then.

He says much the same of the twenty-eight-year-old Gabriel Oak: 'In his face one might notice that many of the hues and curves of youth had tarried on to manhood: there even remained in his remoter crannies some relics of the boy.'

The finality of the adult face is itself only relative, since in terms of expression it is subject to changes of mood, and, as Hardy comments in *The Return of the Native* (79), 'In respect of character a face may make certain admissions by its outline; but it fully confesses only in its changes', while shape and structure themselves are subject to 'Time's transforming chisel' (*CP*, 194). Poor Lady Constantine, though only in her mid-thirties, appears another woman 'and not the original Viviette' to Swithin when he returns from his travels. 'Her cheeks had lost for ever that firm contour which had been drawn by the vigorous hand of youth' (*TT*, 273). The sixty-year-old Marcia in *The Well-Beloved* is forced by the removal of her make-up into an act of self-exposure which has all the

grimness of a 'Memento mori'. In the poems the recognition of
'wasted skin', 'wrenched wrinkled features', 'a rag drawn over
a skeleton / As in El Greco's canvases' becomes explicit, and, looking
back, Hardy's sensitiveness to the 'phases' of the human face appears
alarmingly similar to Rowlandson's grim vision of the 'Eight Ages
of Woman', in which a line of gradually enlarging and lengthening
faces demonstrates the transformation from the tiny child's face
to the final grinning death's-head.[18] It is not suggested that Hardy
knew the Rowlandson sketch, but the resemblance strengthens the
impression that a study of artistic anatomy, or at least a draughts-
man's interest in the subject, underlies Hardy's concern with the
'curves' of maturity and immaturity.

The phases may stop short, however, before the ugliness of the
death's-head, or of old age. They do so for Eustacia, who as
she lay still in death 'eclipsed all her living phases'. The 'eternal
rigidity' that has seized her is an eternity of art: the expression
on her 'finely carved' mouth is pleasant, and her 'stateliness of
look' has 'at last found an artistically happy background'. In
fact, one would have said that Egdon, that 'near relation of night',
provided an *artistically* happy background for this 'Queen of Night',
although a personally unhappy one. If death provides a happier,
it is through the marble repose it brings. (Sculpture rather than
painting is the relevant art here.) It thus completes Hardy's vision
of her, which has been predominantly in aesthetic terms. In this
novel Hardy becomes, in part, the aesthetic adventurer, and the
adventure is mainly concentrated on Eustacia. Generally speaking,
her personality is inadequate to support her image, which remains
stranded in the world of art – of painting and sculpture. Her Pre-Ra-
phaelite origins seem unmistakable: her statuesque dignity and brooding intensity inevitably recall Rossetti's heroines, especially Jane
Morris; with her hair closing over her forehead 'like nightfall extinguishing the western glow' and her 'Pagan eyes, full of nocturnal
mysteries', she is a rival to the *Astarte Syriaca* (1877). But she
is also a dweller on what William Gaunt has called the Victorian
Olympus, one of the creators of which was Hardy's close friend,
Alma-Tadema: 'On Olympus she would have done well with a
little preparation' (*RN*, 89). A later remark makes clear the artistic
associations, somewhat unkindly, since we are told that, with the
new moon behind her head, an old helmet upon it, or a diadem
of dewdrops round her brow, she could have 'struck' the note of
Artemis, Athena or Hera respectively 'with as close an approximation

to the antique as that which passes muster on many respected canvases'
(*RN*, 90).

Yet 'our Eustacia', however queenly and goddess-like in Hardy's
eyes and her own, is underneath 'no more but e'en a woman',
and at times portrayed as such. Against the 'celestial imperiousness'
and firm outlines of that imagined helmet-clad portrait should be
set a later portrait (p. 268) of her in her bonnet. Her 'rebellious
sadness', Hardy tell us,

> was cloaked and softened by her outdoor attire, which always
> had a sort of nebulousness about it, devoid of harsh edges anywhere;
> so that her face looked from its environment as from a cloud,
> with no noticeable lines of demarcation between flesh and clothes.

Even in the 'Queen of Night' chapter he had described her as
'soft to the touch as a cloud'. This softness establishes her femininity:
even Eustacia cannot escape the legend of 'The Weaker' which
Hardy sees written on the 'tender feminine faces' in the Melchester
Training College (*JO*, 160). We see that weakness in action when
Eustacia's 'little hands' quiver so violently that she cannot tie
the strings of her bonnet after Clym's denunciation of her. Hardy's
picture of her in her bonnet (though unlikely, at this date, to
have been influenced by him) has something of the tenderness
(and the technique) of a Renoir, even of such a study of innocence
as *La Première Sortie*; it perhaps looks back to such artists as Gainsborough, Fragonard and Murillo, all of whom delighted in that 'liquefac-
tion of her clothes' by which femininity is expressed and enhanced.
Hardy had early achieved such expression, when in *Under the Greenwood
Tree* (165) he had written of Fancy floating down the school steps
'in the form of a nebulous collection of colours inclining to blue'.
His keen eye for woman's 'infirmities' was matched by a highly
appreciative one for her beauties, and repeatedly, when a woman
is his subject, he attempts to capture her essential femininity, as
did the painters I have mentioned. In doing this he often seeks
the help of actual painters. Elizabeth-Jane, Charlotte De Stancy,
and Elfride all suggest comparisons with Correggio. In 'the most
elaborate of all Hardy's experiments in what might be called pictorial
definition',[19] the description of Elfride in the opening pages of
A Pair of Blue Eyes, Raphael and Rubens are added for good
measure.

Hardy's favourite single model for feminine portraiture, however,

certainly in his early novels, is 'Greuze's' *Head of a Girl*.[20] Likening
Cytherea to it in *Desperate Remedies* (84), he comments archly,

> It is not for a man to tell fishers of men how to set out their
> fascinations so as to bring about the highest possible average
> of takes within the year; but the action that tugs the hardest
> of all at an emotional beholder is this sweet method of turning
> which steals the bosom away and leaves the eyes behind.

The comparison appears again in *A Pair of Blue Eyes* (103) – 'With
her head thrown sideways in the Greuze attitude she looked a
tender reproach at his doubt' – and, again, though without direct
allusion, in *Far from the Madding Crowd* (282), on an occasion when
'the tenderest and softest phases of Bathsheba's nature were prominent':

> Few men could have resisted the arch yet dignified entreaty
> of the beautiful face, thrown a little back and sideways in the
> well-known attitude that expresses more than the words it accom-
> panies, and which seems to have been designed for these special
> occasions.

Greuze, who was highly praised by Diderot as a moralist, has
frequently been condemned for a rather prurient sentimentality
in his pictures of young girls in ambiguous situations – weeping
over a dead bird or a broken mirror, holding in their lap the
fragments of a broken pitcher. Tess Durbeyfield is far removed
in her robust integrity from these china dolls, but it could be
that they (in particular, *La Cruche Cassée*, which Hardy could have
seen in the Louvre) are recalled in the picture of Tess as she
returns from her first visit to the d'Urbervilles, adorned with roses,
one of which, symbolically, pricks her chin.

Tess of the d'Urbervilles is also remarkable for a passage which
unites Rubens and Botticelli, without naming either. This is Hardy's
comment on his own marvellous picture of Tess coming downstairs
yawning and still heavy with sleep, on the afternoon of Clare's
return from Emminster. He writes, 'It was a moment when a woman's
soul is more incarnate than at any other time; when the most
spiritual beauty bespeaks itself flesh; and sex takes the outside
place in the presentation.' The thought seems to be linked with
an observation Hardy noted down in March 1889, when he was

already planning *Tess*: 'In a Botticelli the soul is outside the body, permeating its spectator with its emotions. In a Rubens the flesh is without, and the soul (possibly) within. The very odour of the flesh is distinguishable in the latter' (*Life*, 217).

As in the above example, Hardy's portraits often extend beyond the face or profile to include the full figure. Where his women are concerned, artistic standards appear to operate in combination with normal male appreciativeness. 'In Englishwomen', he tells us (*FFMC*, 54), 'a classically-formed face is seldom found to be united with a figure of the same pattern, the highly-finished features being generally too large for the remainder of the frame', while 'a graceful and proportionate figure of eight heads usually goes off into random facial curves'. The 'figure of eight heads' is the 'classical ideal' traditional in art. Bathsheba comes near to fulfilling it, so that criticism (no doubt both artistic and common-or-garden male) 'looked at her proportions with a long consciousness of pleasure'. This is usually the case with Hardy's heroines, whether they are 'fine women', as Bathsheba and Eustacia, or 'graceful and slender', as Anne Garland and Sue Bridehead. At one end of the spectrum – the Rubens end, where 'the flesh is without and the soul (possibly) within' – stands Arabella, 'a fine dark-eyed girl . . . a complete and substantial female animal – no more, no less' (*JO*, 62); at the other, the Botticelli end, stands Sue, 'so ethereal a creature that her spirit could be seen trembling through her limbs' (*JO*, 204). The others all come somewhere in between, with Tess, that 'soul incarnate', perfectly balanced at the centre. Marty alone (and Elizabeth-Jane when young) stands outside the circle, in that unforgettable picture of her at Giles's grave, 'the contours of womanhood so undeveloped as to be scarcely perceptible in her'. As a rule, the contours of womanhood are decidedly perceptible, and perceived, in Hardy's portraits, whether it is Pennyways whetting Troy's appetite for returning to Bathsheba by his description of her at the cider-wringing when 'her bosom plimmed and fell' plain to the eye, or Jude comparing the 'small, tight, apple-like convexities' of Sue's bodice with Arabella's 'amplitudes' (*JO*, 205).

It is notable too how elegant Hardy's women generally are. The 'picturesque country girl, and no more' such as Tess appears to be (deceptively) at the start of her story is rare. It is not only Eustacia who is 'lady-like'. Bathsheba begins as a country-lass, a milk-maid even, but soon uses her sudden prosperity to transform her image, donning a 'new riding-habit of myrtle-green, which fitted her to the waist as a rind fits its fruit', to ride with Boldwood, and wearing to walk with Troy in Bath 'a beautiful gold-colour silk gown, trimmed with black lace, that would have stood alone 'ithout legs inside if required'. Elizabeth-Jane undergoes a similar transformation. Hardy seems greatly to enjoy giving accurate and detailed accounts of his heroines' attire, and generally speaking they seem to belong much more to the world of the fashion-plate or of Du Maurier's drawings than to that of the sheep-fold or the barn. Anne Garland in 'her celebrated celestial blue pelisse, her Leghorn hat, and her muslin dress with the waist under the arms' (*TM*, 243) is a Kate Greenaway figure. Even Tess seldom appears 'a fieldwoman pure and simple': at the beginning she is a Whistler *Little White Girl* or *Miss Alexander*, especially at her second appearance in her white frock, when she is leaving home to join the d'Urbervilles, and her hair has been washed and brushed so that 'it looked twice as much as at other times', and the 'airy fulness' of her frock supplements this 'enlarged *coiffure*'; and after her marriage she appears from time to time in outfits appropriate to her changed station, culminating, alas, in that 'bewilderingly' unexpected attire Clare finds her in when he comes to claim her a second time.

Fewer particulars are given concerning the figure and dress of Hardy's men-characters. Often Hardy finds it enough simply to state, or imply, that they are 'finely formed', as Fitzpiers, or 'well-shaped', as Bob Loveday. In this respect, his portraits of his men-characters are facial portraits, rather than full-length, since attention is normally concentrated upon the features. One memorable exception is Boldwood: mention is early made of his 'square-framed perpendicularity' (*FFMC*, 146), a quality which is turned to almost tragic use later when Gabriel, himself grief-stricken at the discovery of Bathsheba's rash marriage, sees the farmer riding past, full of repressed sorrow: 'He saw the square figure sitting erect upon the horse, the head turned to neither side, the elbows steady by the hips, the brim of the hat level and undisturbed in its onward glide.' Boldwood's squareness is here expressive of the tensions of suffering within him, and a figure which could come from a collection of prints of 'country types' has become almost Spenserian in its capacity to incarnate an emotion.

Finally, it is to be noted that Hardy has another style of portraiture, suggestive of line-drawing or pen-and-ink. Usually, though not invariably, it is employed for comic purposes, and thus is most often a means of characterising the rustics. It reduces faces to flat circles: Maryann Money, for instance, 'for face had a circular disc' (*FFMC*, 103). It uses the conventions of the style to express emotional reactions, such as surprise or dismay, as when Christian Cantle, confessing to being the man whom no woman will marry, turns upon his companions 'his painfully circular eyes, surrounded by concentric lines like targets' (*RN*, 52). No one's eyes ever *really* looked like that, any more than they ever looked like 'little straight lines like hyphens' (Mrs Penny's 'chronic smile' while danc-ing – *UGWT*, 68), or became 'wider vertically than crosswise' (David registering astonishment at Matilda's flitting – *TM*, 162). The images suggested to our minds by such statements are the images of drawings, and it is from them that our sense of the vividness and humour, even the lifelikeness, of the picture derives. This is a sign-language we are familiar with – familiar from childhood, it would seem at times, for the drinkers at the Buck's Head, looking like 'a fiddle and a couple of warming-pans' (*FFMC*, 297), Martin Cannister stamping into the doorway 'in the form of a pair of legs beneath a great box' (*PBE*, 233), and Cartlett with his 'globular stomach and small legs, resembling a top on two pegs' (*JO*, 302) all seem to belong to the illustrated pages of a book of nursery rhymes or stories. Others could have been drawn by Cruikshank or 'Phiz' – Christian's 'great quantity of wrist and ankle beyond his clothes', for example, recalls the picture of 'Oliver asking for More', and the 'new-moon-shaped grin' on Henchard's mouth as he reads aloud to Farfrae passages from Lucetta's letters, could easily find a place in the illustrations to, say, *Sketches by Boz*, or those of Leech to *Handley Cross* and other Surtees novels. There is also an association with caricature. Hardy acknowledges this when he describes the corners of Mrs Swancourt's mouth as turning upwards 'in precisely the curve adopted to represent mirth in the broad caricatures of schoolboys' (*PBE*, 141). More sophisticated examples suggest a parallel rather with genuine artists such as Rowlandson and Gillray. The effect is achieved through simile: Hardy gives us verbally the kind of grotesque or fantastic simile that artists such as these render visually. Festus Derriman, that red-headed giant, his white teeth showing 'like snow in a Dutch cabbage' when he speaks, and with, when angry, a glare 'like a turnip-lantern' (*TM*, 66, 126), could have stepped out of a Gillray drawing. So too, perhaps, could the jovial miller, with those mobile 'fleshy lumps' that compose his face, 'a roll of flesh forming a buttress

to his nose on each side, and a deep ravine lying between his
lower lip and the tumulus represented by his chin' (*TM*, 46).
(Hardy had, we know, studied Gillray in preparation for this work
and for *The Dynasts*, although, except possibly in the 'unnatural
Monster' Devastation, his influence is not discernible in the latter.)
Another type of nose is seen at Ethelberta's story-telling, 'noses
of the prominent and dignified type, which when viewed in oblique
perspective ranged as regularly as bow-windows at a watering-place'
(*HE*, 126). Again, the impression appears familiar, not as a direct
experience from life but as something seen in caricature – a *Punch*
cartoon perhaps? (The choice of Du Maurier as the illustrator
of *Ethelberta* was a happy one, since it is largely his world that
is portrayed there. Ethelberta herself, 'a plump-armed creature,
with a white round neck as firm as a fort' (p. 62) is a perfect
Du Maurier type.) Casterbridge Market Square on Market Day,
on the other hand, with its 'gibbous human shapes' – 'a little
world of leggings, switches, and sample-bags' (*MC*, 171) – is pure
Rowlandson.

IV

Although, however, Hardy's characters may approach so close, to
each other and to us, that they see into each other's pupils, as
both Henchard and Elizabeth-Jane are said to do, or we see into
theirs, as when with Angel we plumb the depths of Tess's, 'with
their radiating fibrils of blue, and black, and gray, and violet'
(*TD*, 198), such closeness is not sustained: sooner or later they
recede to become at the furthest distance mere spots or specks;
or, less distantly, the 'figures in a landscape' they are generally
considered to be. Hardy seldom portrays an *empty* landscape: even
Egdon Heath required the figure on the top of Bulbarrow to give
'a perfect, delicate, and necessary finish' to its 'dark pile of hills'.
His landscapes are never simply topography; even 'views' and
'prospects', such as the description of Blackmoor Vale ('untrodden
as yet by tourist or landscape-painter') at the beginning of *Tess
of the d'Urbervilles* are relatively rare. He presents the countryside
as something experienced, not just passively seen, and particularly
as experienced by those who live and work there (including himself).
His peasants, like those of Barnes as he describes them, live a

life of 'absolute dependence on the moods of the air, earth, and sky'. Although Hardy's realisation of these moods is not effected by means of the painter's (or landscape-painter's) art alone, its contribution is, nevertheless, of vital importance. It involves mainly light and shade, colour, and atmosphere. Hardy's treatment of these shows him as the disciple of many masters, the most pervasive being Turner.

Turner's influence is already felt in *Desperate Remedies*, which displays a rather self-conscious concern with the modifications of local colour produced by light, reflection, and shadow, a feature of Turner's work which had been much stressed by Ruskin in *Modern Painters*, Volume 1. The statement 'The light so intensified the colours that they seemed to stand above the surface of the earth and float in mid-air like an exhalation of red' (*DR*, 57) could come from a Turner catalogue. In this novel too occurs (p. 234) the first of Hardy's colourful skies (later repeated, word for word, in *The Return of the Native*). Its 'copper-coloured and lilac clouds, stretched out in flats beneath a sky of pale soft green' recall both Turner himself and Turner as expounded by Ruskin.

Under the Greenwood Tree, being homely and 'Dutch', is correspondingly less atmospheric, but in *A Pair of Blue Eyes* the vivid colouring returns, with an actual allusion to Turner. The reference in this instance is not to landscape but to the 'lumps of flesh' on the butchers' stalls below Knight's London chambers, illuminated by the gas-jets 'to splotches of orange and vermilion, like the wild colouring of Turner's later pictures' (p. 150). Vermilion is, however, one of the dominant colours of the novel, seen in the centrally-placed, elaborate picture of Elfride as Knight saw her looking 'towards the sun, hanging over a glade just now fair as Tempe's vale' (p. 174), and repeated at the end in the 'crowns of orange fire' which decorate the 'eminences of the landscape' as the train bearing Knight, Stephen, and Elfride's body steams towards Camelton. This novel is full of pictures; reading it is like turning the pages of an album, which is perhaps what it was for Hardy – a record of his Cornish courtship. It is self-consciously pictorial, as in its handling of perspective in the following (p. 231):

A leaf on a bough at Stephen's elbow blotted out a whole hill in the contrasting district far away; a green bunch of nuts covered a complete upland there, and the great cliff itself was outvied by a pigmy crag in the bank hard by him.

It is *felt* in terms of colours – Elfride's blue eyes, the golden sun, silver moonlight, the blackness of the after-sunset, the coffin, and death. We know from the poems how strong for Hardy is the link between emotion, experience and colour; such strong emotional colouring in a novel associated so closely with the most lyrical episode of his own life is therefore not surprising.

If *Far from the Madding Crowd* has a dominant colour, it is surely green, the green of trees and ferns and hedgerows, but especially of grass. This is the first of Hardy's novels in which the poetry of the life of the 'modern peasant' as Hardy described it in his essay on Barnes is fully realised. The violence of the elements – of fire, air and water – produces spectacles of Turnerian grandeur, and Turner's vivid morning and evening skies appear again. Nevertheless, it is a gentler English landscape tradition that is suggested by the book as a whole; in fact, the central tradition represented by Gainsborough, Constable, some of Turner's own water-colours, and by lesser artists such as Cox, Cotman, De Wint and Linnell, to say nothing of the legion of amateurs and RAs down to our own day, whose work Hardy summed up in his poem 'At the Royal Academy':

These summer landscapes – clump, and copse, and croft –
Woodland and meadowland – here hung aloft,
Gay with limp grass and leafery new and soft . . . .

The scene in the haymead, where 'gnarled and flexuous forms' are busy respectively scything or tossing the hay (p. 190), or the one at the oat-harvest, when 'all the men were a-field under a monochromatic Lammas sky, amid the trembling air and short shadows of noon' (p. 234), could be matched many times in nineteenth-century landscape-painting.[21] But for me the painting closest in spirit, of all those I have seen, to Hardy's novel is Richard Redgrave's *Sweet Summer Time – Sheep in Wotton Meadows*, in the Victoria and Albert Museum (dated 1869). There are not only sheep but also people at work in the meadows, and the sweetness of the summer-time is conveyed chiefly through the delicious softness of the grass – the 'limp grass' of Hardy's poem, or of his sheep-washing scene.

Hardy's exquisite description of the sheep-washing pool observes the principles of pictorial composition in an unobtrusive manner which allows the reader to visualise it directly from Nature (rather

than as 'a picture of a picture') and yet to feel that it embodies
memories of all the tranquil painted landscapes he has ever seen.
The circularity of the pool, with its clear water reflecting the
light sky and its margin of moist grass, is repeated in the 'rounded
and hollow pastures' which form the outskirts of the meadow;
the river continues the curving line, the reeds and sedge which
form 'a flexible palisade upon its moist brink' providing an equivalent
to the moist grass around the pool; the trees to the north, with
their 'new, soft, and moist' leaves repeat the theme again, while
the colour of the leaves, 'yellow beside a green – green beside a
yellow', partly picks up that of the pastures, 'where just now
every flower that was not a buttercup was a daisy'. Thus the
picture is unified by means akin to those of the painter. The
trees to the north even serve to cut off the scene, as they would
in a painting. The scene's tranquil beauty may, of course, remind
us of other paintings besides English ones – of nineteenth-century
French painters such as Corot and Rousseau; even, a little, of
Claude.

Claude might be described, it seems to me, as one of the unseen
presences of this novel. No scene is markedly Claudian, yet beyond
the Englishness of the setting and the 'blame – fury' of the story
there is the idyllicism of the classical pastoral world which is the
work's archetype. This becomes explicit in the account of the shearing-
supper, with its references to Silenus, 'the swains Chromis and
Mnasylus', and the merry gods in Homer's heaven, and here if
anywhere perhaps is Claude tangibly present, when the sun is
described in 'the beaming time of evening' creeping round 'the
tree' and beginning to sink, touching as it does so the heads
and shoulders of the shearers 'with a yellow of self-sustained bril-
liancy' while their lower parts are 'steeped in embrowning twilight'.
'The tree' has not been mentioned earlier: its presence here for
the sun to creep round suggests the tree or trees that generally
figure prominently in Claude's landscapes. Yet it would be wrong
to think only of Claude: when the sun goes down 'in an ochreous
mist', we are reminded that Turner too painted peaceful classical
scenes, and in the Claudian manner; and, when Oak (who 'could
pipe with a truly Arcadian sweetness') adds his 'dulcet piping'
to Bathsheba's song, while 'the shearers reclined against each other
as at suppers in the early ages of the world', the 'suppers' Hardy
is thinking of may have been seen on some Grecian urn or classical
frieze, if not in some other Renaissance painting, such as Bellini's

Feast of the Gods. The detail of posture makes it probable that they have been *seen*, and not merely invented.

To turn from this to Egdon Heath is according to Hardy to exchange the past for the future, when 'the new Vale of Tempe may be a gaunt waste in Thule' (*RN*, 34). Yet, however *avant-garde* may be the tastes and perceptions the Heath represents, considered simply as a specimen of landscape-painting it is no great novelty. Its ancestry goes back to the Dutch landscape painting of the seventeenth century, particularly that of Jacob van Ruisdael, in which the extensive, gloomy plains of Holland are surmounted by huge, cloudy skies answering gloom with gloom in a 'counterpoint-like movement'[22] closely corresponding to the 'black fraternization' described by Hardy (except that the areas of relative light and darkness are reversed, the earth being lighter than the sky in Ruisdael). The resemblance is most striking in Ruisdael's *View of Haarlem* (in Zürich), where the meeting-line of earth and sky on the horizon is clearly marked, again as in Hardy. Other comparable paintings of the same period are the *Landscape* by Koninck in the Victoria and Albert Museum, his *Dunes and River* in Rotterdam, and some of Van Goyen, notably his *View of Leiden* (Northampton, Massachussets). Moving to Hardy's own century and country, there is John Crome's *Mousehold Heath, Norwich*.[23] This has as a central feature an 'aged highway', 'quite open to the heath on each side', like that on Egdon, and like that 'diminishing and bending away on the furthest horizon'. T. S. R. Boase says of this painting that 'it deals with immensity and there is poetic alchemy in it; it stands with Hardy's "Egdon" as the final distillation of English waste land'.[24] Crome's Norwich School was of course influenced by the art of neighbouring Holland, and it is interesting to note that Van Gogh links his name with those of Van Goyen and the early-nineteenth-century French artist Georges Michel.[25] Michel's painting *The Plain of St Denis* is intensely Egdonish in both appearance and atmosphere, a 'vast tract of unenclosed wild' communicating like Egdon a sense of brooding, infinite loneliness.[26]

The parallel that Hardy draws between Egdon and 'the sand-dunes of Scheveningen' as types of the preferred landscape of the future suggests that he has an at least instinctive awareness of the affinities I have outlined. One artist at least confirmed his insight: in the early 1880s, only a few years after the publication of *The Return of the Native*, Van Gogh was living at The Hague and enthusiastically painting the neighbouring Scheveningen: a scene 'strikingly gloomy and serious ... over the landscape a simple gray sky with a light streak on the horizon', 'nothing but a bit of sand, sea, sky – gray and lonely'.[27]

The typical landscape of *The Return of the Native*, however, is not so much a painting as an engraving, a study in black and white. The Heath's character as 'a near relation of night' is impressed upon us by the action, much of which takes place at night. It appears as 'an amplitude of darkness reigning ... almost to the zenith' (p. 75). Contrast is provided by a human face or hand: a 'whitish something' – Johnny Nunsuch's hand feeding Eustacia's bonfire; by the 'faint shine' from a window; and by the relative lightness of the sky. The latter keeps 'sky-lines' visible even when 'thick obscurity' prevails on the heath (p. 67), and against these lines human figures are often seen in silhouette: Diggory watches a 'sky-backed pantomime of silhouettes' on Rainbarrow (p. 42); the villagers approaching the hut where Mrs Yeobright lies dying appear as moving figures animating 'the line between earth and sky'. When Diggory, after eavesdropping on Eustacia and Wildeve, sees them walking away, we read, 'Their black figures sank and disappeared from against the sky. They were as two horns which the sluggish heath had put forth from its crown, like a mollusc, and had now again drawn in.' Here the emphasis on line, simple and almost stylised, makes the resemblance to an engraving clear, especially when set beside, say, the description of Tess looking like 'a fly on a billiard-table of indefinite length' (*TD*, 133), where, though there is the same insistence on human insignificance, the visual effect is very different. The comparison with the mollusc succeeds, it seems to me, precisely because it is reinforced by the silent and unconscious comparison with an engraving: our minds convert the image first into Art and then back into Nature, and so apprehend its rightness. The fly on the billiard-board, which lacks this artistic reinforcement, is less convincing.

When Eustacia leaves her grandfather's house on her last, tragic journey, Hardy writes, 'The gloom of the night was funereal; all nature seemed clothed in crape. The spiky points of the fir-trees behind the house rose into the sky like the turrets and pinnacles of an abbey.' As Tess and Angel drive to the station with the milk, Egdon Heath is visible in the distance: 'On its summit stood clumps and stretches of fir-trees, whose notched tips appeared like battlemented towers crowning black-fronted castles of enchantment.' They are evidently the same fir-trees, and the similes employed, although in each case appropriate to the occasion and the characters, are alike in their romantic, even Gothic, associations. But, again, I think there is at work Hardy's memory not only of actual fir-trees, actual abbeys and castles he has seen, but also of engravings, engravings of fir-trees, abbeys, battlemented towers and 'black-fronted castles of enchantment'. ('Notched tips' suggests a wood-cut, like the 'notch of sky and plantation' in which Mrs Dollery's van looms up at the beginning of *The Woodlanders* or the 'dark polygonal notch' which the Swancourts' house cuts out of the sky to Stephen's gaze (*PBE*, 249).) Together the passages suggest that Hardy's engraved landscapes *as* engravings may owe something, consciously or unconsciously, to his recollection of illustrated fairy stories and romances, including, perhaps, the Cruikshank etchings for the novels of Harrison Ainsworth, which he read with great enjoyment in his boyhood.

Night has of course a natural affinity with the art of engraving, both in its blackness and in its sharp contrasts of light and shade. A writer so sensitive to picture as Hardy could hardly fail to perceive and render it in this way. The same is true of winter, when trees and hedges are bare: as Hardy notes on 7 December 1886, 'Winter. The landscape has turned from a painting to an engraving' (*Life*, 184). When night and winter combine, the effect is enhanced. Thus, to Dick Dewy, glancing upward as he walked through the winter woods, the various trees appeared 'as black and flat outlines upon the sky' (*UGWT*, 32). Some of the poems explicitly recognise the analogy: thus 'Lying Awake' opens,

> You, Morningtide Star, now are steady-eyed, over the east,
>   I know it as if I saw you;
> You, Beeches, engrave on the sky your thin twigs, even the
>   least;
>   Had I paper and pencil I'd draw you.

'The tangled bine-stems' which 'scored the sky' in 'The Darkling Thrush' embody the same perception, while behind the lines

> The land's sharp features seemed to be
>   The Century's corpse outleant

there seems to lie another kind of engraving, that of the political cartoon, later to appear in the vision of Europe as a 'prone and emaciated figure' at the beginning of *The Dynasts*.

Moonlight too can suggest an engraving: indeed, some of the most magical engravings – Blake's in his illustrations to Virgil's *Pastorals*, some of Calvert's – are concerned, as Palmer so often is, with moonlight. The magic of Hardy's moonlight scenes is generally a *natural* magic, but on one occasion at least he achieves a haunting, elusive quality that approaches the visionary. This is in his description of Bathsheba driving home from Greenhill Fair. 'The moon having risen,' he tells us, 'and the gig being ready,'

> she drove across the hill-top in the wending ways which led
> downwards – to oblivious obscurity, as it seemed, for the moon
> and the hill it flooded with light were in appearance on a
> level, the rest of the world lying as a vast shady concave between
> them.

The simplicity and fluidity of line here seem to link it with the work of the artists I have mentioned – the contrast between the light of the moon and hill above and the darkness of the valley below; the series of softened curves suggested by moon, hill, 'wending ways' and 'shady concave', even by the gig itself. The effect is enhanced by the later statement that, as Bathsheba and Boldwood ('her outrider') descended into the lowlands, 'the sounds of those left on the hill came like voices from the sky, and the lights were as those of a camp in heaven'.

The Woodlanders too has its transfiguring moonlight; it has its brilliant colours – of sunset, orchards in blossom, autumn woods; and it has its *chiaroscuro*. The new element in its treatment of landscape, however, is its emphasis on disease and decay, 'the Unfulfilled Intention', expressed through images which turn the woods into an eery, haunted place, full of Gothic horrors. There are old trees 'wrinkled like an old crone's face and antlered with dead branches' (p. 217); trees that appear as 'haggard, grey phantoms' (p. 243); 'a half-dead oak, ... its roots spreading out like claws grasping the ground' (p. 231). When we read of the 'smooth surfaces of glossy plants' coming out like 'weak, lidless eyes', of 'strange faces and figures from expiring lights', of 'low peeps of the sky between the trunks' looking like 'sheeted shapes', and of 'faint cloven tongues' sitting on the tips of boughs (pp. 310–11), we seem to be in the surrealist world of Max Ernst. In fact, we are probably in the world of Ernst's ancestor, Grünewald. In *Two on a Tower* (80) Hardy had written, in reference to the fir-trees

surrounding the tower, of 'twigs scratching the pillar with the
drag of impish claws as tenacious as those figuring in St Anthony's
temptation'. Various artists have represented St Anthony's temptation, but the most violent representation is Grünewald's, on the
Isenheim Altar panel. If Hardy saw this on his Rhine tour, he
is hardly likely to have forgotten it, and certainly the fantastic
images he introduces into *The Woodlanders* seem designed to create
a similar sense of horror and menace, one which reaches its climax
in the man-trap, which 'when set, produced a vivid impression
that it was endowed with life', combining aspects of 'a shark,
a crocodile, and a scorpion'. The horror, though intermittent, is
real: Hardy's despair in the face of the struggle for existence combines
with the forest gloom of German folk-tradition to engender it.
The imps reappear in 'multitudes' in *Tess of the d'Urbervilles* (368),
as Tess walks at night through a part of Blackmoor Vale which
had once been forest, 'every tree and tall hedge making the most
of its presence'.

Hardy's art is at its richest in *Tess*. 'Eye and heart' are deeply
engaged; his own imaginative fecundity matches that of Var Vale.
Pictorially his imagination in its rendering of Tess's experience
draws nourishment and aid from many sources, some of which
we have already considered. At the heart of the work, however,
helping to shape its vision from within, are, I believe, the combined
influences of Impressionism and Turner.

Already, in *The Woodlanders*, Hardy had presented

> an impression-picture of extremest type, wherein the girl's hair
> alone, as the focus of observation, was depicted with intensity
> and distinctness, while her face, shoulders, hands, and figure
> in general were a blurred mass of unimportant detail lost in
> haze and obscurity.

This is a description of Marty South, as seen by the barber anxious
to cut off her hair. Hardy is evidently applying the principle
which he had deduced from the examples of 'the impressionist
school' he had seen on a visit to the Society of British Artists
Exhibition in December 1886, at a time when he was engaged
in writing *The Woodlanders*:

> [But] their principle is, as I understand it, that what you carry
> away with you from a scene is the true feature to grasp; or
> in other words, *what appeals to your own individual eye and heart*

in particular amid much that does not so appeal, and which you therefore omit to record. (*Life*, 184)

Although this is inadequate as a description of the aims of the Impressionists, the combination of blur and sharp focus in the 'impression-picture' of Marty does correspond to the effect achieved in some of the most familiar works of the school – Renoir's *La Première Sortie*, for example, or his *Le Moulin de la Galette*, Manet's *Un Bar aux Folies-Bergère*. In the next few years, before the writing and completion of *Tess*, Hardy would have the opportunity of extending his knowledge of Impressionism both in London and in Paris, where in 1888 he visited the Salon, by then accepting the work of some of these artists. Since the governing principle of the movement as he understood it was identical with that which he had earlier discovered to be proper to the 'seer' (to 'watch that pattern among general things which his idiosyncrasy moves him to observe, and describe that alone' – (*Life*, 153), he probably did study it further, especially since he had recognised its relevance to his own work: 'It is even more suggestive in the direction of literature than in that of art' (*Life*, 184). *Tess of the d'Urbervilles*, in the Preface to which (in the 1895 edition) Hardy enunciated the principle 'A novel is an impression, not an argument', bears the mark of that study.

The Impressionists are primarily, although by no means exclusively, landscape-painters. They painted in the open air and usually in full daylight, their aim being to catch as in a net the evanescent colours that at any given moment form the component parts of light as it is glimpsed in the scene before them. Thus their pictures are truly moments of vision, of 'prismatic vision'.[28] 'Chromo-luminarism', the name Signac would have preferred for the movement, defines this essential quality awkwardly but well. *Chiaroscuro*, black and white, and to a large extent brown, are banished: colour is limited to the colours of the spectrum. Firm outline is rare: forms themselves tend to dissolve, objects to lose their solidity, all caught in the mesh of colours and dappled light which is the true subject of the picture. The dominant 'impression' is one of atmosphere, of the very 'feel' of the moment, most frequently the warmth of a summer afternoon by the river or in field or orchard.

Tess of the d'Urbervilles, despite the cruel story it tells, is the most iridescent of all Hardy's novels. There is only one word

to describe the 'impression' created by its central part, a word
often used by Hardy himself there: radiant. Much of the action
takes place in the open air and in full daylight. Effects of *chiaroscuro*,
so frequent in the earlier novels, are almost non-existent: from
the 'violet or pink dawn' to 'the last red rays of the west' the
sun beams down on 'the impassioned, summer-steeped heathens
in the Var Vale'. Not on them only: earlier in the book, after
the birth of Tess's baby, there is that memorable 'hazy sunrise'
on the day of the reaping, when the sun, referred to (significantly,
I think – he is being consciously thought of as the source of light)
as 'the luminary', appears as 'a golden-haired, beaming, mild-eyed,
God-like creature, gazing down in the vigour and intentness of
youth upon an earth that was brimming with interest for him'.
Earlier still, there is that 'fine September evening, just before sunset'
when Tess makes her fateful journey to Chaseborough, a time
'when yellow lights struggle with blue shades in hair-like lines,
and the atmosphere itself forms a prospect without aid from more
solid objects, except the innumerable winged insects that dance
in it'. This in itself reads almost like a description of an Impressionist
painting: the 'blue shades' especially are worth noting, for the
blueness of their shadows is one of the familiar characteristics of
the Impressionists. At the dance in the Chaseborough outhouse
artificial light replaces that of the sun, as 'there floated into the
obscurity a mist of yellow radiance', observed by Tess from the
garden outside. When Tess comes closer and looks in she sees
'indistinct forms racing up and down to the figure of the dance'.
Later still, on a nearer view, a young man with 'his straw hat
so far back upon his head that the brim encircled it like the
nimbus of a saint' addresses Tess. All these features – the 'blurred'
radiance, the indistinctness of the figures, the straw-hatted young
man – combine to suggest a rustic version of Renoir's *Le Moulin
de la Galette*, although, when the whole description is taken into
account, a decidedly more bacchanalian one. Much later in the
novel that 'mist of yellow radiance' is both recalled and counter-
pointed in the 'pollen of radiance' the sun forms over the landscape
as Tess and Angel wander together through the meads in an October
'of wonderful afternoons'. The blue shades also reappear, in the
form of 'tiny blue fogs in the shadows of trees and hedges'. The
description is both true to the actuality of autumn and reminiscent,
in its radiance, blueness, and blur of 'pollen' and 'fog', of Impressionist technique as we meet it in a variety of canvases celebrating

'wonderful afternoons'.

There is indeed a pollen of radiance over all the early books of the novel. Even the reprehensible share it (Tess herself wonders 'why the sun do shine on the just and the unjust alike'): the boozy Trantridge work-folk walking home have each 'a circle of opalized light' like a halo round their head-shadow, and the weeds in the garden where Tess overhears Angel's harp-playing have 'red and yellow and purple hues' forming 'a polychrome as dazzling as that of the cultivated flowers' and sending forth 'waves of colour'. Hardy himself seems to have become hypersensitive to colour and light and atmosphere. Blackmoor Vale as seen from the chalk ridge, its hedgerows 'a network of dark green threads overspreading the paler green of the grass', has a langorous atmosphere tinged with azure even in its 'middle distance' and a horizon 'of the deepest ultramarine'. The atmosphere of the Froom Valley hangs 'heavy as an opiate over the dairy-folk, the cows, and the trees'. Yet in this heavy atmosphere the milk-maids appear in delicate-shaded gowns of pink, white and lilac, gauzy-skirted and of 'transparent tissue'. When Clare carries Tess over the flood-water, he likens her to 'an undulating billow warmed by the sun', with all the 'fluff of muslin' around her as the froth. Later, as he gazes into her eyes, he is to see the 'radiating fibrils of blue, and black, and gray, and violet' of their ever-varying pupils. And at the moment of her seduction Tess had been described as 'this beautiful feminine tissue, sensitive as gossamer'.

In all this, I would suggest, an Impressionist sensibility is at work. Hints of such a sensibility had appeared before, even as long ago as *Desperate Remedies*, with its 'pale-blue sheep' and 'livid red clover flowers', but only now has it found full release through Hardy's absorption of Impressionist example, working in combination with the deep emotional pressure exerted by his subject. Hardy's appreciation of femininity seems to me always akin to that of Renoir, but over the years the affinity grows stronger as his heroines progressively lose that slight touch of 'mannishness' Bathsheba feared she possessed, and we reach the totally feminine Tess and Sue. (Actually the most completely Renoir-like single description he ever wrote of a woman comes, to my mind, in the short story 'The Withered Arm', where Gertrude's complexion is said to be 'soft and evanescent, like the light under a heap of rose-petals'.) Tess's 'beautiful feminine tissue', like that of Renoir's women, is a mixture of the ethereal, the delicately refined, and the voluptuous; her

'brimfulness of nature' is a quality possessed by them too. Not
only in Tess's person, however, but in her experience too, do
we find the Impressionist vision. Tess's experience often has the
effect of making her appear to live like an Impressionist painter,
or to see as he sees. The radiance of the landscape without is
reflected in the landscape within, and *vice-versa*. Landscape and
heroine are one.

Tess's move from Marlott[29] is undertaken in a spirit of great
hopefulness, which becomes almost exuberance as she looks down
on the Froom Valley from the Egdon uplands. We read, 'Her
hopes mingled with the sunshine in an ideal photosphere which
surrounded her as she bounded along against the soft south wind.'
The photosphere is to become actual in the hot summer days
at Talbothays, and that actual radiance is to be internalised again,
in the mingled joy and hope (albeit clouded at times by fear)
of her love for Clare. Tess's emotions from the time of Angel's
first proposal to the conclusion of the wedding ceremony turn the
world about her into 'an impression-picture of extremest type'.
Thus, after their rapturous embrace on his return to the dairy
after visiting his parents, we read, 'Tess was in a dream wherein
familiar objects appeared as having light and shade and position,
but no particular outline.' Again, during those October walks of
pollen-like radiance, 'Her affection for him was now the breath
and life of Tess's being; it enveloped her as a photosphere, irradiated
her into forgetfulness of her past sorrows ....' At the time of
the wedding, 'In dressing, she moved about in a mental cloud
of many-coloured idealities, which eclipsed all sinister contingencies
by its brightness'; and, on the way to church, 'She knew that
Angel was close to her; all the rest was a luminous mist.' After
the ceremony, the 'vibrant air humming round them from the
louvred belfry matched the highly-charged mental atmosphere in
which she was living'; and, Hardy adds, 'this condition of mind,
wherein she felt glorified by an irradiation not her own' persisted
'till the sounds of the church bells had died away'. There is
no more sunshine after that, internal or external. When Tess and
Angel return to pay a fleeting farewell visit to the dairy before
they part, 'The gold of the summer picture was now gray, the
colours mean, the rich soil mud, and the river cold.' Not until
Tess's execution 'in all the brightness and warmth of a July morning'
does the sun come back, the horizon behind the gaol 'lost in

the radiance of the sun hanging above it'.

There is nothing particularly Impressionist, of course, in finding something golden in youth and hope and love. What is Impressionist is the creation, throughout the entire Talbothays section of the novel, of a single physical and emotional 'photosphere' by which Tess's experience is expressed. Tess, 'the pulse of hopeful life still warm within her' as she sets off for Talbothays, becomes for Angel and, one suspects, for Hardy himself, virtually identical with 'Life ... the great passionate pulse of existence' (p. 187), and Life itself is warmth and light, colour and perfume. It is also fluid, compounded, a succession of moments. Hardy's sense of the changing 'phases' of Tess's face, repeated in the 'phases' of her life which structure the novel, has its parallel in the Impressionist awareness of the instability of impressions which led Monet to paint in series Rouen Cathedral, the Gare Sainte-Lazare, or an avenue of poplars, as they change from moment to moment. That Hardy conceives of Tess's life as light broken into colours is indicated by his description (p. 66) of Alec d'Urberville as 'one who stood fair to be the blood-red ray in the spectrum of her young life'.

Light itself in the novel, although predominantly shadowless, is usually blurred: it comes mixed with the autumnal haze or the 'scroff' of the barn to form a pollen or mist of radiance. Moonlight too, on the night of Tess's seduction, is modified by 'a faint luminous fog' which seems to hold it 'in suspension, rendering it more pervasive than in clear air'. The Impressionists did not often paint mist directly, although their technique of dissolving form in atmosphere did lead to misty effects or 'blur'. Monet's *Impression: Sunrise*, from which the movement took its name, is dominated by blue fog, and in his *Westminster Bridge* (1871) the grey fog is lit from within by a faint golden glow. (Oscar Wilde commented that it was Monet who taught us to see that the London fog grows iridescent around bridges.) The persistence of fog, however, in Hardy's light-pictures, the combination of the luminous and the misty, whether in the 'low-lit mistiness' through which Tess walks to Chaseborough, the 'faint luminous fog' of the Chase, the blue fogs of autumn, or the 'luminous mist' surrounding Tess during the months of courtship, leads us beyond the Impressionists to Turner (with whom the Impressionists themselves acknowledged an affinity). Hardy's two notes on Turner show a wonderful sympathy with him, and great insight into the work of his 'maddest and greatest days'

(*Life*, 216). In January 1887, following closely on his note of the previous month concerning the Impressionists, he associates Turner with the portrayal of Nature as a mystery, the revelation of 'the deeper reality underlying the scenic' (p. 185). A year later, at the Old Masters, Royal Academy, he notes, 'Turner's water-colours: each is a landscape *plus* a man's soul.... What he paints chiefly is *light as modified by objects*' (p. 216), and comments perceptively on a number of the 'mad, great' pictures.

In *Tess of the d'Urbervilles* Nature is portrayed as a mystery through the mixture of light and mist, in true Turnerian fashion. The summer fogs at the early-morning milkings, when 'the meadows lay like a white sea, out of which the scattered trees rose like dangerous rocks', have all the mystery of a Turner – of *Norham Castle: Sunrise*, for example, or *Sunrise with a Boat between Headlands*. And Tess herself is made mysterious by them, acquiring a 'strange and ethereal beauty', like the Venice of Turner's Sunrises. Her own later experience, as she moves through the 'luminous mist' of her love for Clare, gives her all the dreamy quality of a figure or object in the water-colours of Venice or Switzerland of Turner's final period. When she emerges from her dream, moreover, it is to enter at Flintcomb-Ash a Turnerian nightmare, working in a 'cloaking gray mist' or in snowstorms suggesting by their spinning 'an achromatic chaos of things', and watched by 'strange birds' whose eyes bear witness to the scenes of Turnerian 'cataclysmal horror in inaccessible polar regions' they have seen, the 'crash of icebergs and the slide of snow-hills', 'the whirl of colossal storms and terraqueous distortions'. Equally Turnerian is the succession of scenes preceding Tess's seduction, already referred to: the 'yellow lights' and 'blue shades' of the September evening; the mist from the barn which Tess at first thinks is 'illuminated smoke' (compare Constable's phrase 'tinted steam' to describe *Norham Castle*); the 'nebulosity that involved the scene' within and the description of it as a 'luminous pillar of cloud'; and the foggy moonlight of the ride.

By these means the novel becomes a picture of a landscape *plus* a man's, or rather a woman's, soul. Light obscured by mist, mist irradiated by light: these embody and reflect the character and experience of Tess's soul, as, like the gnats of November, it wanders across the shimmering pathway of life, is 'irradiated' as if it bore fire within, then passes out of the line and becomes 'quite extinct' (p. 229).

V

Light and colour, and with them any inclination on Hardy's part to 'paint' the scene in detail, have very largely departed in *Jude the Obscure*. Nature has lost that 'luxuriance of aspect' which in Var Vale (and in most of the earlier novels) it shared with Tess: the whole world has become, like Flintcomb-Ash, a 'starve-acre place'. Landscape *as* landscape has virtually disappeared. It has become simply a background, reflecting and harmonising with the emotions and experiences of the characters, but otherwise aloof from them. Its colours are predominantly brown and grey, colours of earth and air. Mist or fog is, as in *Tess*, a prominent feature, but, except when lit up by Jude's vision of Christminster, it is not luminous: it is 'clammy', 'chilly', and eventually a killer. Its function is to obscure Jude from the world; to blind him to the futility of his dreams and Christminster to the futility of itself. It is felt as a presence, rather than seen as part of a picture. Its presence indeed partly accounts for the relative absence of picture: wrapped in its folds, the characters and their surroundings alike grow ghost-like. On its first appearance it is associated with Jude's breath: 'The morning was a little foggy, and the boy's breathing unfurled itself as a thicker fog upon the still and heavy air.' This is appropriate in a work which could be said to be *about* Jude's breath, his fight for life and for a place in the sun. On his first arrival in Christminster he is to be 'encircled as it were with the breath and sentiment' of the city, but he is to find in the end that it is an atmosphere that denies breath to him.

Hardy has not lost, nor abandoned entirely, his old skills and habits as a painter. They reappear in, for example, the grouping of Jude, Sue and Phillotson at their first meeting under 'a lamp with a paper shade' in Phillotson's parlour, which is as dramatic in its contrasts as a Rembrandt; or in the careful re-creation of the tavern where Arabella first presents herself to Jude simply through 'the reflection of her back in the glass behind her' – inevitably, though perhaps accidentally, suggestive of Manet. Such passages, however, are no longer characteristic.

It seems that in *Jude the Obscure* we have reached the 'new artistic departure' predicted in *The Return of the Native*. 'The reign of orthodox beauty', there said to be approaching its last quarter, is now definitely over, at any rate for Hardy. The reason lies not in the subject alone, but in Hardy himself, who chose the

subject. His early pictures were created out of love. This must
be so: no one could create scenes of such precisely observed natural
and human detail, so brilliant and colourful, so carefully selected
and composed, it he did not love both the objects observed and
the art that embodied them. Such love became increasingly difficult
and painful for him as his mind awoke 'to the tragical mysteries
of life' (*Life*, 185), and as science uncovered 'the defects of natural
laws' (*RN*, 185), yet still, up to and including *Tess*, an 'old-fashioned
revelling' of senses and emotion fuels much of Hardy's art, certainly
the pictorial part of it. Indeed *Tess*, in its Talbothays section,
is almost the apotheosis of this revelling, its final fling. With *Jude*,
it has gone. Hardy himself, as well as Jude, is a disappointed
lover – of the universe (though perhaps also of Mrs Henniker, and
the memory of Tryphena). His position is thus strikingly analogous
to that of the modern artist, as Lord Clark has described it in
his eloquent 'Epilogue' to *Landscape into Art*, unable to create landscape because of his 'loss of intimacy and love with which it was
possible to contemplate the old anthropocentric nature'.[30] Indeed,
Hardy *is* the modern artist, as he recognises. Jude and Sue feel
themselves to be in advance of their time, and, as for Little Father
Time, one of those boys who 'see all [Life's] terrors before they
are old enough to have staying power to resist them' (p. 346),
he could be the forerunner or epitome of ourselves. To see *Jude*,
in its combination of geometrical sub-structure (two 'eternal triangles'
within a quadrilateral of characters, enclosing a balanced series
of contrasts and linear relationships) and chaotic surface, as actually
anticipating later artistic developments such as Cubism or Futurism
would perhaps be fanciful. Yet the experience of modern life imaged
at the start of the novel in Jude's (literally vorticist – he is called
'the whirling child') suffering at the hands of Farmer Troutham,
afterwards generalised by him into 'something glaring, garish, rattling' all around you that 'hit upon the little cell called your
life, and shook it, and warped it', certainly suggests a context
similar to that out of which such art movements have sprung.
   Alfred Alvarez has called *Jude* 'a supremely vivid dramatization
of the state of mind out of which Hardy's poetry emerged'.[31]
This overlooks both the variety of Hardy's poetry and the affinities
existing between it and the earlier novels, all of which in their
varying ways dramatise his state of mind. Nevertheless, it is substan-
tially true. In the poems themselves that state of mind projects
itself through landscapes and figures both actual and imagined.

Hardy the painter of the external world reappears here in all his roles and styles, some of which we have already considered. His Gibbon – 'And far lamps fleck him through the thin acacias' – is in the Impressionist manner, as is also 'A Countenance':

> And her lips were too full, some might say:
> I did not think so. Anyway,
> The shadow her lower one would cast
> Was green in hue whenever she passed
>   Bright sun on midsummer leaves.

'Once at Swanage' ('The spray sprang up across the cusps of the moon') recalls the Japanese artist Hokusai. 'The Harbour Bridge' invites comparison with Whistler's *Battersea Bridge*. But, although, as in the novels, the outer world is thus made 'vividly visible', one is also conscious of an inner world, a world that is at once both painting and gallery, hung, as a gallery, with images of past events and persons and places, but as a painting endlessly combining the colours and shapes in which emotions come to Hardy into a fluid, changing landscape-with-figures, in which the pictorial arts of the novels have their emotional source and spring. It is a landscape of sunshine and shadow, 'gleam' and 'gloom'. Thus it paints the *chiaroscuro* of life: the contrast between life and death (the actress seen in 'The Two Rosalinds' as 'a creature / Hovering mid the shine and shade as 'twixt the live world and the tomb' typifies man in general); hope and 'unhope'; illusion and reality. When the gleam predominates, as in the memories of youth when 'everything glowed with a gleam', the colours are bright – green, golden, rosy, 'iris-hued', glorious with all the 'hope-hues' of the rainbow. When the gloom takes over, the colours fade into greyness as the poet's visions 'waste to fog' (*CP*, 439). And beyond the fog lies 'blur and blot' (*CP*, 315), and the final blankness, when the image that has been created is expunged, the canvas – of existence, memory, or both – wiped clean. Tess, in 'Tess's Lament', may desire this state, praying for a time that will 'turn my memory to a blot', but the contemplation of it depresses Hardy:

>   in darkening dankness
> The yawning blankness
> Of the perspective sickens me!
>   (*CP*, 338)

The perspective there is both actual and metaphorical, a feature of both space and time. It is a characteristic of this inner world that it converts temporal perspectives into visual ones. Days are apprehended in terms of colour – 'mornings beryl-bespread' contrast with 'a joyless-hued July' or with 'this diurnal unit, bearing blanks in all its rays – / Dullest of dull-hued Days!' (*CP*, 115). Time becomes place, as in the image of the Present as a garden where the gates close at sunset in 'When the Present has latched its postern behind my tremulous stay' (*CP*, 553). Past relationships and experiences are translated into landscape, weather and seasons – most strikingly in the poem 'The Five Students', where, for example, in the line 'The home-bound foot-folk wrap their snow-flaked heads', we could be looking at a picture by Millet or Pissarro, yet are actually reading a statement about old age. This poem is typical too of Hardy's inner landscape in that, although 'five of us' stride out together in the morning, by the end of the poem and the day and the poet's life, only 'one of us' 'still stalk[s] the course', and that is 'I'. Of the 'figures in a landscape' which still characterise Hardy's art, he himself is the central figure, and one as lonely in his 'pilgrimage' as Mrs Yeobright, Tess or Jude. The 'onward earth-track' of 'The Temporary the All' leads him for a time to 'paths through flowers' (*CP*, 349), but his common complaint is that 'Life's bare pathway looms like a desert track to me' (p. 269): 'Ever the road!' (p. 742).

In his poem 'The Two Houses' Hardy describes a house so 'packed' and 'obsessed' with the presences of its former occupants that it has taken on their character:

> Where such inbe,
> A dwelling's character
> Takes theirs, and a vague semblancy
> To them in all its limbs, and light, and atmosphere.

The picture of Wessex Hardy has created in his novels is such a house: it too is stamped with his own presence 'in all its limbs, and light, and atmosphere'. Its colours reflect the colours of his inner world, both its greens and its greys; its mists and fogs are his. Its perspectives and horizons are his: the characters who 'small' to mere 'moving specks', spots, 'two grains of corn', do so because this is for Hardy an inescapable 'aspect' of the human picture. For Hardy, as, according to Alison Fairlie, for Baudelaire, 'the recurring fascination of effects of perspective is intimately related to themes of human limitation and longing'.[32] The relationship between earth and sky and their meeting-point on the horizon are contemplated repeatedly, for they represent the conditions and limits of both our outer and inner vision, the skyline, but also 'the horizon of circumstances' (*FFMC*, 304). When, towards the end of *A Pair of Blue Eyes*, Smith and Knight leave the 'yellow glow' of the blacksmith's shop after reading Elfride's name on the coffin-plate there, 'the chill darkness', we read, 'enclosed them round, and the quiet sky asserted its presence overhead as a dim gray sheet of blank monotony'. Hardy's inner world is generally backed by such a sky. Sometimes, especially in snow, as on two occasions in *Far from the Madding Crowd*, earth and sky become confused, as do sea and sky in some of Turner's paintings, and, as in Turner, this seems to epitomise man's condition, his confusions and uncertainties. It contrasts with that other 'moment of evening' described in *Tess of the d'Urbervilles* and elsewhere,

> when the light and the darkness are so evenly balanced that the constraint of day and the suspense of night neutralize each other, leaving absolute mental liberty. It is then that the plight of being alive becomes attenuated to its least possible dimensions. (*TD*, 114)

Hardy's thought seems close to that of John Dewey:

> Only when the past ceases to trouble and anticipations of the future are not perturbing is a being wholly united with his environment and therefore fully alive.[34]

The juxtaposition may suggest why such moments of equilibrium were not often experienced by Hardy, although he valued their existence.

3 Theatrical Arts

One of Hardy's earliest ambitions was to write plays in blank verse. As a young man in the 1860s, he even sought experience as an actor on the London stage, believing that this would teach him the techniques of drama. Forty years later he fulfilled his ambition in a manner he could hardly have anticipated, in his epic-drama, *The Dynasts*. In the intervening years, certainly from 1875 onwards, this work was being dreamed over, planned, prepared, and finally written – the *magnum opus* compared with which Hardy seems to have felt, like Milton similarly setting his sights on *Paradise Lost*, that in his prose works he had the use of his left hand only. Meanwhile, however, the dramatic talents which had to wait so long to burst out into sudden blaze found an outlet in the despised prose itself.

It is not surprising that this should be so. In literature Hardy was always a devotee of the great tradition (though not exactly in F. R. Leavis's sense). 'Good fiction', he declared, 'may be defined . . . as that kind of imaginative writing which lies nearest to the epic, dramatic, or narrative masterpieces of the past'.[1] In his own fiction he constantly measures himself against his favourite dramatists, Shakespeare and the Greeks. He thinks of both life and literature in terms of the dramatic categories, 'tragedy, comedy, farce' (*JO*, 139). The metaphor of the *theatrum mundi* is scarcely a metaphor for him: it is a fact. The visual nature of experience ensures that; so does its ephemerality. Looking back after Emma's death, for instance, he saw not only the pictures mentioned in his letter to Benson, but plays too, as in the

> sweet soft scene
> That was once in play
> By that briny green . . . .

('The Phantom Horsewoman')

All the great Shakespearian commonplaces were Hardy's also: 'All the world's a stage', the 'insubstantial pageant', the 'walking shadow'. The poems especially, along with *The Dynasts*, make that clear: they present innumerable 'human shows' and 'far phantasies'. But always there is the sense of an ending: 'Exeunt Omnes', 'And then, the Curtain'.

The Dynasts, of course, was intended for 'mental performance' only. Defending this aspect of the work in a letter to *The Times* in February 1904, Hardy asserted that 'this play-shape is essentially, if not quite literally, at one with the instinctive, primitive, narrative shape'.[2] To write 'Scene so-and-so, Time so-and-so' instead of 'Once upon a time, At such a place', is, he suggested, 'a trifling variation that makes no difference to the mental images raised'. Four years later (May 1908), in a letter rejecting an invitation to join a committee to consider the erection of a memorial theatre to Shakespeare, he expressed the view that it was a mere 'accident of his social circumstances' that Shakespeare, whom he describes as a 'seer of life', wrote plays to be acted rather than 'books to be read' (*Life*, 341). This rather disdainful repudiation of the actual theatre may owe something to Hardy's disappointment at the failure of his ventures into it (with adaptations of *Tess* and *Far from the Madding Crowd*); more to his distaste for the over-elaborate productions and misguided 'realism' of the contemporary theatre; but most of all to a partisan preference for the alternative type of drama which the nature of his material had driven him to create. His identification of the 'play-shape' with 'the instinctive, primitive, narrative shape' is nevertheless worth remembering, for it underlines a truth about Hardy's own narratives. In a sense, all his novels aspire to the condition of *The Dynasts*. To establish a firm setting of time and place and then to move rapidly into an action: this is his chosen method. His short poem 'An August

Midnight', in which the title itself is a stage direction, epitomises
his approach:

> A shaded lamp and a waving blind,
> And the beat of a clock from a distant floor:
> On this scene enter – winged, horned, and spined –
> A longlegs, a moth, and a dumbledore . . . .

Hardy adopts this 'play-shape' because, like Conrad, he wishes
'to make you see', and obviously the dramatic mode, like the
pictorial, assists this. But this is not the only reason. The drama
also appealed to him, it is clear, for its excitement, its heightening
of emotion and situation. Hence, just as he finds 'the high-relief
of the actions and emotions' to be the proper function of the
stage-play, so 'the highest province of fiction' lies for him in 'the
portraiture of scenes in any way emotional or dramatic'.[3] Dramatic
techniques, in other words, are another way to that intensifying
of the expression of things which Hardy notes to be the essence
of his art. And in this respect the dramatic embraces the theatrical.
The techniques Hardy employed to raise up his 'mental images'
came to him from the theatre itself, not merely from the study.
In his novels, no less (though less obviously) than in *The Dynasts*,
he creates not merely drama but theatre. The *theatrum mundi* is
just that – a *theatrum*.

The sense of a theatre is created in the first place by our now
familiar friend, the watcher. Paradoxically, this largely unseen presence in the novels materialises in *The Dynasts* in the form of
abstract intelligences, the Spirits of the Overworld. They make
the theatrical performance explicit. All the world, quite literally,
becomes a stage:

> Hence to the precinct, then,
> And count as framework to the stagery
> Yon architraves of sunbeam-smitten cloud

says the Spirit of the Years. Stage-curtains are provided by the
elements: 'A nebulous curtain draws slowly across'; 'Curtain of
Evening Shades'; 'The sun sets, and the curtain falls.' Actual
scenes are shown as, even in their actuality, play-scenes: men simultaneously act and play-act. Seated above in (as we might say)
'the Gods', the Spirits form an attentive audience, exchanging

lively comments in the intervals.

The spectator in the novels is equally attentive, although more elusive. His presence is often implied rather than stated. When, for instance, Elfride visits Mrs Jethway's deserted cottage and 'a light footstep was heard' and later 'the dancing yellow sheen' of the fire 'revealed the fair and anxious countenance of Elfride', it must be his observations that are being recorded: no one else is around in the quad. At other times his presence is proposed hypothetically: he is the 'thoughtful person' who might have seen Gabriel Oak 'walking across one of his fields on a certain December morning' (*FFMC*, 42), or the 'looker-on' who, had he been posted 'in the immediate vicinity of the barrow' (*RN*, 43), would have been able to identify the heath-folk carrying up their bonfire material. But, whether defined or undefined, his presence always operates, like that of the Spirits, to direct and focus the reader's vision. It is with him and through him that we watch the actions of the characters, closely following their movements, gestures, and changes of expression, and listening to their words.

The visual concentration thus created is, or closely resembles, the concentration of the theatre. Hardy's characters, as is generally recognised and as we noticed in the last chapter, often appear as 'figures in a landscape'. When they move and speak, however, they are better regarded as actors in a scene. And, however extensive the background, the scene itself usually occupies a fairly restricted area: with the whole of dark Egdon around her, for instance, Eustacia beats upon a single narrow footpath between Rainbarrow and Mistover, and that accordingly is where our gaze also is directed. As 'Another Part of the Heath' the footpath, with Eustacia, demands and receives all our attention; we may feel the rest of the heath as a surrounding presence, but it is at this that we look. Visual immediacy and visual control are of the highest moment in Hardy's art, and the very clarity of definition has the effect of creating a sense of theatre. In *The Dynasts*, where he is depicting actual events, Hardy, faithful to his theatre-image, will write 'Enter from the west a plain, lonely carriage . . .' (2.v.vi) or 'Exit King Joseph on horseback; afterwards the hussars and dragoons go out fighting' (3.II.iii). The scene in the first passage is the village of Courcelles; in the latter it is 'The Road from the Town' (Vitoria). Where exactly do King Joseph and the hussars 'exit' and 'go out' *from* and *to*? In so far as the Spirits are watching actual events (and not merely a representation of them) we would expect to read

'King Joseph proceeds along the road, followed later by the hussars', or something like that. It is the use of the stage convention that confines the action to a limited area, blocked as it were by wings; in fact, we are being asked to *make-believe* that the road is a stage. A similar ambivalence between (a fictitious) actuality and a theatrical presentation (implied rather than stated) exists in the novels. For all its breadth and size, Egdon Heath is such a limited area or stage: the action never removes from it, and, although Venn, Wildeve and Thomasin 'enter' from Anglebury and Clym 'returns' from Paris, these places, never being seen by us, exist for us only off-stage or in the wings. *The Return of the Native*, since it is clearly deliberately constructed on dramatic principles, may seem a special case, but in fact examples of this moulding of the natural to a theatre (not merely play) shape occur throughout the novels.

There are, most obviously, the openings of the novels. Here Hardy almost invariably follows the Horatian principle of beginning not *ab ovo* but *in medias res*. Even if an introductory description of a personage is given, as in *Far from the Madding Crowd*, it is short, and attention is quickly directed to the action – here Gabriel's walk across the field, followed by the incident of Bathsheba and the mirror, described by Hardy as 'a performance' before an audience of 'sparrows, blackbirds, and unperceived farmer', though we may add to that number both the unseen observer and ourselves (who, unlike Bathsheba, 'perceive' Gabriel too). The description of the deserted highway at the beginning of *The Woodlanders* makes it appear like an empty stage upon which a man (the barber) enters 'from a stile hard by'. The opening chapter of *Tess of the d'Urbervilles* is a miniature play in itself, a curtain-raiser or prologue (in a present-day film or television drama it would appear before the credit-titles), comprising two scenes, the first between Durbeyfield and Parson Tringham, the second between Durbeyfield and Fred, Fred entering (as it were) from the wings after the Parson has crossed the stage and 'exited' on the same side. The scene or scenes consists mainly of dialogue, but action and gesture are indicated with the precision and brevity of stage directions, even to the positioning of parson and haggler at the start of their conversation. The sounds of the brass-band heard as Fred departs and Durbeyfield remains resting on the daisied bank, awaiting the carriage to take him home, are like 'noises off'.

The first chapter of *Tess* is remarkable in Hardy's work for the directness of its presentation. There is no intermediary hypothetical observer or other 'watcher': the reader simply uses his own eyes, as he would at a theatre – the stage is there before him. More often a presenter of one kind or another is employed. Sometimes it is the author himself in his capacity as 'showman', as in a later chapter of *Tess*:

> From the foregoing events of the winter-time let us press on to an October day more than eight months subsequent to the parting of Clare and Tess. We discover the latter in changed conditions;... we see her a lonely woman with a basket and a bundle in her own porterage.... (p. 297)

The sense of the curtain rising here is faint, but unmistakable: 'Eight months later. When the curtain rises, Tess is discovered, etc.' – the transposition is easy. At other times, the hypothetical observer is employed, as in the opening of *The Mayor of Casterbridge*, to direct our gaze and interpret the evidence. At still other times, it is the watching personages within the story itself who focus our vision. Sometimes they do no more than *remind* us of the theatre, because eavesdropping is a very stagy device: this is the case with, say, Venn's spying on Eustacia's and Wildeve's meeting on Rainbarrow, where his hiding under the turves of heather irresistibly recalls the episode involving Caliban and Trinculo in *The Tempest*. But they may also, and particularly near the beginning of a novel, provide not merely a reminder but also an actual illusion of theatre. *The Woodlanders* may serve as an example. Here, with Marty South watching from the shadows, a complete scene is acted out between Melbury and his wife. Their garden becomes a stage, upon which they 'enter' from the back door of the house. Again, as in the opening scene of *Tess*, their position and movements are indicated, and the greater part of the scene is in dialogue, with Marty 'starting', as good eavesdroppers always do, at what she overhears about Giles Winterborne. At the end of the scene the speakers exit by the way they came, and Marty too 'withdraws', though pausing to comment that 'Giles Winterborne is not for me!' The purpose of the scene is to give us (and Marty) some necessary information about Melbury's plans for Grace and Giles. In other words, it is a piece of exposition, as undisguised as (again to think of *The Tempest*) Prospero's 'briefing' of Miranda and Ariel, with Melbury 'reminding' his wife of what she knows already (and which even Marty has 'heard before'). In action and setting the scene recalls the celebrated garden scene in Kyd's *Spanish Tragedy*, in which Hieronimo enters 'in his shirt', followed by the anxious Isabella. The comparison is not wholly incongruous, for although the situations are very different, Melbury's devotion to his child resembles Hieronimo's in its intensity and is to prove in its way just as destructive. The resemblance is increased by the presence of watchers. Marty has nothing in common with Revenge and the Ghost of Don Andrea in form, but she has in function, for just as they frame and define the entire action of Kyd's play, so does she this shorter action. And, generalising from this particular example, I would suggest that it is always in this way that Hardy's watchers create a sense of theatre. They operate unconsciously as a kind of Prologue or Induction, revealing to us 'the play within the play'. It may seem a far cry from Revenge to Marty South (or Gabriel, or Diggory, or Elizabeth-Jane, good watchers all), but not if we go by way of the Overworld or of the poem 'The Moth-Signal', which seems to dramatise the triangular situation between Clym, Eustacia and Wildeve and incorporates its own watcher:

Then grinned the Ancient Briton
  From the tumulus treed with pine:
'So, hearts are thwartly smitten
  In these days as in mine!'

In scenes such as the one just discussed, the area of action acquires the character of a stage by being limited in extent, boxed in or enclosed in some way, inset or framed. Thus the stage in this particular scene is backed by the timber-merchant's house, with the garden hedge forming the wings, reinforced on either side by stables and outbuildings, including the waggon house where Marty stands. The boxing-in does not necessarily require physical objects for its creation: the universe may be crammed, or appear to be crammed, within a wooden O, as happens in *The Dynasts*, and the spacious expanse of Egdon Heath may temporarily be bounded like a nutshell. Thus at the bonfire on Rainbarrow the stage is created by the very darkness surrounding it: it seemed, says Hardy, 'as if the bonfire-makers were standing in some radiant upper storey of the world, detached from and independent of the dark stretches below'. 'On this scene enter', from opposite sides, first Venn (preceded by 'noises off') and then Mrs Yeobright. Another instance of an area of indefinite size being actually reduced, for our vision, to stage-proportions occurs in chapter 11 of *Far from the Madding Crowd*, 'Outside the Barracks'. Here Hardy specifically draws our attention to the 'left-hand' and 'right-hand' characteristics, but also makes use of the elements to box-in the scene, almost claustrophobically: 'the vast arch of cloud above was strangely low,' we are told, 'and formed as it were the roof of a large dark cavern, gradually sinking in upon its floor'. The scene which follows between Fanny and Sergeant Troy, consisting almost entirely of dialogue, reinforces the dramatic impression. In *The Mayor of Casterbridge* the market-place, of which Lucetta's house provides a 'raking view' (convenient for watchers) is explicitly compared (p. 182) to 'the regulation Open Place in spectacular dramas, where the incidents that occur always happen to bear on the lives of the adjoining residents'. Earlier scenes – the wife-selling in the circus-tent, the reconciliation in the amphitheatre – had suggested, rather, the arena, theatre-in-the-round, and it is noteworthy that when Henchard, whose life has had a similar circularity, finds himself back where he started, Hardy tells us (p. 320), 'He had no wish to make an arena a second time of a world that had become a mere painted scene to him.'

Other aspects of presentation conform to and thus reinforce this intermittent and elusive yet persistent sense of a stage-setting – the grouping of the characters, the arrangement of 'props', the episodic nature of much of the action. The action advances largely through a succession of scenes or dialogues between two characters; seldom more – except, of course, in the conversations of the rustics. Troy and Fanny, Bathsheba and Boldwood, Bathsheba and Troy, Eustacia and Clym, Clym and Mrs Yeobright – the couples are as distinct and the points at issue between them as clearly rendered as in French classical drama. If more people are present (generally the rustics), their subordinate role in relation to the principals is made plain: as has often been noticed, they surround them like a Chorus, whether of Greek tragedy or of opera and operetta. In the scene between Troy and Fanny an unseen chorus of soldiers rounds off the action with their 'Ho – ho – Sergeant!' This is followed immediately by the scene in the Casterbridge Corn Exchange where a chorus of farmers – 'hot men who talked among each other in twos and threes' – cavort and pirouette with their ground-ash saplings, bending them round their backs, forming arches of them between

their two hands, overweighting them on the ground till they reach
'nearly a semicircle', thus providing a suitable foil for the 'feminine
figure' gliding amongst them. (It would be no surprise if they
were to burst into 'Tell me pretty maiden' or some such ditty;
indeed, the surprise is that they don't.) In the wife-selling episode
in *The Mayor of Casterbridge* the show is skilfully stage-managed
by Henchard himself, who rather likes an audience; although it
is his creator who brings in Newson at the last moment and poses
him 'in the triangular opening which formed the door of the
tent' to achieve a dramatic climax. At a comic level, Festus Derriman
similarly comes most carefully upon his cue when he adds a final
stentorian 'Rollicum rorum' to Sergeant Stanner's song from outside
the window shutter, to the astonishment of all within (*TM*, 64).
The precise detail 'outside the window *shutter*' (rather than simply
'outside'), followed by the opening of the door and Festus's entrance,
enhances the theatrical effect, turning the Mill momentarily into
a stage-house. The framing of characters in doorways and windows
often has the same effect – Fancy looking down from a high open
window upon the crown of Dick's hat, for example; even Henchard
presiding at the mayoral banquet.

   At times too, Hardy explicitly invites us to think of his novels
in terms of theatre. *The Hand of Ethelberta* is described as 'A Comedy
in Chapters', and that 'Comedy' means stage comedy is made
clear by the chapters, each of which presents a fresh 'scene'. (Rather
than to the novels of Meredith, the work seems indeed to owe
its inspiration to the stage comedies of the time, with their preoccupa-
tions with wealth and the class system, and their rather brittle,
self-conscious dialogue. Apart from the plays of Robertson and
the earlier but still thriving *Money* of Bulwer Lytton, Tom Taylor's
New Men and Old Acres, which ran for 196 performances at its
revival in 1876, the year of *Ethelberta*'s publication, seems relevant.[4])
A Pair of Blue Eyes begins with a list of 'dramatis personae'. In
his 1895 Preface to this novel Hardy refers to 'those convenient
corners wherein I have ventured to erect my theatre for these
imperfect dramas of country life and passions'. And in the General
Preface to the Wessex edition of 1912 he justified 'the geographical
limits of the stage here trodden' primarily by citing the precedent
of Greek classical drama. It would be a mistake to dismiss such
language as merely hackneyed or conventional. The idea is repeated
often enough to be taken seriously, particularly as it is supported
by the novels themselves.

II

Hardy's affinity with the Greek tragic dramatists is not a mere
matter of stage dimensions. Like them, he raises on his narrow
stage questions that are as large as the universe, eternal questions
of suffering and justice, and of the fate not just of men but of
man. We recognise in his work a certain classical ambience, created
partly by particular analogies but even more by outlook and tone.
These are familiar matters, requiring no fresh rehearsal here. My
concern is with theatre rather than drama, the play seen rather
than the play read, and Hardy's experience of Greek tragedy was
probably limited to the play read. It would be interesting to know
how far, if at all, he actually visualised his action in terms of
the Greek stage. The question seems unanswerable, yet simply to
raise it may be to qualify the commonly accepted notion that
the rustics represent 'a kind of Greek Chorus'. Although the rustics
do gossip about the actions of the main protagonists, they are
seldom present at the tragic climaxes, and accordingly cannot be
said to act either as witnesses of or commentators on them. Nor,
despite their folk wisdom, have they the capacity for tragic comment.
Much closer to the Chorus in all these respects is that unseen
observer, truly 'the spectator idealised', whose eyes and voice are
often one with those of the author himself. His presence throughout
the action does provide a visual (even if at the same time invisible)
analogue with the Chorus, asserting, so to speak, a stage-presence.
The narration itself is thus a truer Chorus than are the rustics.

Shakespeare, that other inescapable dramatic presence, haunts
Hardy's fiction like an ancestral ghost. Shakespeare's plays were
for Hardy first and foremost 'a book to be read', and most of
his Shakespearian reminiscences are sufficiently accounted for by
his reading. His mind must, however, have been well stocked with
memories of actual stage performances. 'During Phelps's series of
Shakespeare plays at Drury Lane' in the 1860s, he tells us, 'he
followed up every one', text in hand (*Life*, 53), and the theatre-going
he records in his periodic visits to London in later years must
have included many Shakespearian productions. The *Life* also recalls
(p. 336) Helen Faucit's performances at Drury Lane. In the season
1864–5, in a highly successful production of *Cymbeline*, she acted
Imogen to Phelps's Posthumus. When Hardy in *Desperate Remedies*
describes Manston's wife, overhearing the conversation of Cytherea
and Owen, as standing 'as precisely in the attitude of Imogen

by the cave of Belarius, as if she had studied the position from the play', it seems likely that he had Helen Faucit in mind, for this particular part of her performance was singled out for praise, *The Times* (20 October 1864), for instance, commenting, 'As for the timid approach of the disguised Imogen to the cave of Belarius, it is a study for the painter.'[5] The comparison seems strained, however we regard it, but scarcely makes sense at all if Hardy had *not* some particular performance in mind. And, if this supposition is correct, it may perhaps be inferred that some of Hardy's other Shakespearian moments have recollections of actual performances behind them. Such performances may also have helped to fix certain scenes and images more firmly in his mind.

In *Far from the Madding Crowd*, for example, the delineation of Boldwood's jealousy owes something to *Othello*. The 'blame – fury' he unleashes upon Bathsheba at their encounter on the highway after her rejection of him have the ring of Othello in them, particularly when he curses Troy for stealing his 'treasure' and laments, 'I have lost my respect, my good name, my standing – lost it, never to get it again. . . . Heaven – heaven – if I had got jilted secretly and the dishonour not known, and my position kept!' With Bathsheba's reflection, 'Such astounding wells of fevered feeling in a still man like Mr Boldwood were incomprehensible, dreadful', we might compare Lodovico's 'Is this the nature / Whom passion could not shake?' Although there is nothing in the characterisation here that could not have been suggested by Shakespeare's text alone, it may also owe something to Hardy's recollection of Phelps's Othello, which the critics agreed in praising for its strong contrast between the grave and dignified Moor of the first two acts and the violence of the later ones, the effect of which upon an audience was said to be electrifying.[6] Hardy's gradual build-up to the 'furious' climax, from the moment Boldwood enters with downcast eyes and changed countenance to the point when 'the impending night appeared to concentrate in his eye', is consistent with this interpretation.

Later, with the aid of the unwitting Bathsheba, Troy enacts before Boldwood (in hiding) a variant on the scene between Iago and Cassio which convinces Othello of Desdemona's unchastity. Troy is mischievously leading Boldwood on to the same view of Bathsheba, and in doing so he assumes an Iago-like character: he is 'ironical', 'derisive', and 'contemptuous'. 'Devil, you torture me!' cries Boldwood.

In this scene a Shakespearian stage-setting, it seems to me, is imposed upon the 'natural' setting of the Weatherbury village street. The action is recognisably 'stagy'; in a sense, it is only through recognition of its staginess that it is made plausible. In his desire for emotional heightening Hardy constantly asks us to accept dramatic conventions, especially the conventions of the Elizabethan stage, in place of the more 'realistic' narrative method associated with the novel. Such acceptance does not always come easily: in scenes such as that between Bathsheba and Boldwood or, in *The Return of the Native*, that of Clym's Lear-*cum*-Hamlet-like ravings (with a dash of Oedipus) after the death of his mother, the dialogue has at times a sub-Shakespearian tumescence that is almost embarrassing. Yet undoubtedly Hardy sought through his apprenticeship to Shakespeare to find means of making the novel poetic as Shakespeare's plays were poetic, and especially was encouraged by his example to present emotional confrontations and crises in their most naked and concentrated form. The endeavour after a Shakespearian form of utterance has its successes as well as its failures: Mrs Cuxsom's epitaph on Susan Henchard, beginning, 'And she was as white as marble-stone', will stand comparison with Mistress Quickly's on Falstaff, which it resembles ('Ah, poor heart!' exclaims one of Mrs Cuxsom's listeners; Mistress Quickly had used the same expression in announcing Falstaff's illness); and such passages as Henchard's last will and testament or Marty's eulogy of Giles Winterborne are both a vindication and fulfilment of Hardy's Shakespearian longings, achieving as they do a comparable sublimity, though without specific echoes or borrowings.

The emotional intensity and dramatic heightening of Hardy's novels bring to mind also the Jacobean dramatists, especially Webster and Ford. The resemblance was noticed by Hardy's contemporaries: Havelock Ellis, for example, described Ford (whose plays he had recently edited for the Mermaid series) as 'a great seventeenth-century predecessor of Mr Hardy in the knowledge of the heart'.[7] The comment was made in relation to *Jude the Obscure*. In this novel Hardy is clearly following a new dramatic master, Ibsen. The earnest discussions of personal and social relationships and the 'emancipated' opinions expressed in them reflect unmistakably his recent experience of Ibsen on the stage, along with his general awareness of the Ibsen 'debate' then going on. But the appeal of the new drama cannot annul the bonds of affinity with the old. Sue's strained feelings about her adulterous condition, for instance, are closer to those of Penthea in Ford's *The Broken Heart* than to anything

in Ibsen. She tells Phillotson, 'For a man and woman to live
on intimate terms when one feels as I do is adultery, in any
circumstances, however legal' (*JO*, 239). Similarly, Penthea feels
that her marriage to Bassanes, after her earlier engagement to
and continuing love for Orgilus, has made her 'a spotted whore'.
The idea is reversed when Sue later returns to Phillotson, convinced
now that it is her life with Jude that was adulterous. Penthea
goes mad, while Sue becomes for Jude 'the most melancholy wreck
of a promising human intellect that it has ever been my lot to
behold' (p. 394). More generally, the emotional chaos into which
the characters are plunged in the violent last Book, 'At Christminster
Again', resembles that following the separation of Giovanni and
Annabella in Ford's *'Tis Pity she's a Whore*, with Sue embodying,
like Annabella, a sense of sin and repentance, Jude a continuing
scepticism, and poor Phillotson cast for a grim Soranzo-like role
as Sue's virtual gaoler. When on her return to Phillotson Sue
'rends' her 'adulterous' embroidered nightgown, 'the tears resounding through the house like a screech-owl', we feel a shudder from
the world of Webster. Somewhere in the depths of his imagination
Hardy is surely remembering

> Hark, now everything is still
> The screech-owl and the whistler shrill
> Call upon our dame aloud,
> And bid her quickly don her shroud.
>
> (*The Duchess of Malfi*, IV. ii)

The 'absolutely plain garment, of coarse and unbleached calico'
which Sue selects *is* a sort of shroud, appropriate to the living
death she faces with Phillotson.

III

The example of Ibsen shows, and that of Shakespeare to some
extent suggests, that Hardy's work could be affected directly by
his experience in the theatre. We have little knowledge of what
he actually saw over many years of theatre-going, but as well
as Shakespeare and Ibsen we can be sure that it included many
melodramas.

Hardy's novels, or at any rate parts of them, have often been described as melodramatic, usually in the derogatory sense of 'crudely sensational' or 'emotionally exaggerated'. The injustice of seeing melodrama itself *only* in these terms is now increasingly being recognised. Like most forms of art, melodrama is of kin to the little girl who had a little curl: horrid as it might be when bad, it could also be when good, very, very good. But, again like other arts, it was good in its own way: its form was appropriate to its own quite valid vision. If Hardy employs many of the conventions of melodrama, this is because in some fundamental respects he shares that vision. The melodramatic elements in his work go right through, like the name of a seaside town through a stick of rock. His imagination itself is melodramatic. His sympathy with the Victorian theatre is in this sense innate, and is reflected in the melodramatic mode in which his 'plays' are fashioned.

This is apparent even in his characters. Hardy's 'casts' are surprisingly small, and the roles he creates tend to be repeated from novel to novel, almost as if he were writing for a repertory company. A dark, passionate woman is contrasted with a gentler, usually fair-haired type: Bathsheba/Fanny; Eustacia/Thomasin; Lucetta/Elizabeth-Jane; Mrs Charmond/Grace. The male 'leads' show a similar contrast of opposing types (complicated sometimes by the addition of a third man). Dark-haired is opposed to fair-haired; solid worth to flashy charm; good egg to bad, as may be seen variously in Boldwood/Troy; Henchard/Farfrae; Winterborne/Fitzpiers; Angel/Alec. The supporting cast is made up of assorted parents, an unusually large number of comic countrymen (and occasionally women), and very few others. (The similarity between Leaf, Poorgrass and Christian Cantle even gives them the air of being character-parts created for the same actor.) There is a suggestive resemblance between these character-patterns and the organisation of the nineteenth-century Permanent Company Playing Repertory, as described by Martin Meisel in his *Shaw and the Nineteenth-Century Theater*. Meisel's account, which derives from Shaw himself, lists among the constituents of the company the Juvenile Lead and Ingénue, first and second Light Comedians, first and second Low Comedians, Heavies of both sexes, 'for villainy, tragedy, blood and thunder etc.', and first and second Old Man and Old Woman. Characters corresponding to these stereotypes were created by dramatists over and over again; so well established were they that 'long after the passing of the particular type of stock company . . . the theatrical stereotypes persisted in the minds of actors and dramatists as the image of nature

itself'.[8] The parallels in Hardy are clear: Eustacia as the female
Heavy (characterised by Meisel as dark, volcanic, tempestuous and
passionate), in contrast with Thomasin's Ingénue role; Bathsheba
another Heavy, ligher than Eustacia certainly, but still a Heavy
when set beside Fanny; Boldwood, Henchard, and Alec d'Urberville
distinctly Heavies.

To recognise that Hardy's characters begin as melodramatic stereotypes is not to imply that they end there. Melodrama provides
him with a basic pattern or frame, within which he weaves his
own delicate tissues of sympathy and insight, creating those unique
personages who could be no one but themselves. Occasionally the
stereotype dominates a character: this is notoriously the case with
Alec d'Urberville, who, apart from his role as the seducer of rural
innocence, bears all the insignia of the part, a swarthy complexion,
black moustache with curled points, flashy clothes, a cigar, and
a diamond ring. Cigar-smoking brings a whiff of decadence to
those lesser 'Heavies' Wildeve and Fitzpiers. A cigarette does the
same for Mrs Charmond: cigarettes, according to Michael Booth,
'indicate a villain or villainess'.[9] Mrs Charmond and to a lesser
extent Lucetta come from the world of high-society melodrama
that developed in the second half of the century to meet the
tastes of fashionable West End audiences: their habit of receiving
visitors reclining voluptuously on a sofa, with one arm thrown
upward, establishes their origins, and their character as dangerous
women.[10] At the other extreme, Fanny Robin recalls the earliest
and most popular type of heroine, the seduced and long-suffering
village girl: her first big scene, in the snow before the barracks,
stamps her character unmistakably. 'The poor starving heroine,
huddled in a corner of the stage, with the pitiless paper snow
falling'[11] was well known to audiences. Tess Durbeyfield too undergoes
her ordeal by snow. Tess embodies the stereotype just as clearly
as Fanny; in fact there is in her a merging of two types, the
simple village girl, popular in the melodramas of the early nineteenth
century, such as *Clari, Maid of Milan*, and the magdalen figure
(the Dame aux Camélias, or Lady Isabel in *East Lynne*) who later
became fashionable. But Tess, by the depth of personal life Hardy
has given her, also shows how the stereotype may be transformed
without being destroyed.

Events and situations in the novels and Hardy's handling of
them often recall those of melodrama. The endless flow of incident
(partly due to serialisation), rapid changes of scene, and unflagging

pace in themselves establish the resemblance. This is particularly noticeable in *Far from the Madding Crowd*. Here, as the chapters, some of them very short, whisk us from scene to scene, the chapter-titles indicate the scene-changes. One could imagine them on a play-bill:

The Sheep-Washing – The Offer
Perplexity – Grinding the Shears – A Quarrel
Troubles in the Fold – A Message
THE GREAT BARN AND THE SHEEP-SHEARERS
Eventide – A Second Declaration

My selection should perhaps have included 'The Fair – The Journey – The Fire' and 'The Storm – The Two Together', for in the fire and the storm we have the novel's two sensation scenes, sure to receive a big billing. As an essentially spectacular form of drama, melodrama had always relied heavily on natural disasters and man-made terrors to provide its excitements, but the sensation scene in its most elaborate and characteristic form was an innovation of Boucicault's which by the 1860s had become extremely popular. Fire was an especial favourite: it was used in Boucicault's *Streets of London* (originally *The Poor of New York*, acted in London in 1864) and his *Lost at Sea* (1869), and also in the adaptation of *Lady Audley's Secret*, put on in May 1863. The fire in *Desperate Remedies* (which Hardy in his Preface of 1912 called 'this sensational and strictly conventional narrative') clearly comes from the same drawer as these. As in these plays it is a human dwelling – a country inn, as in *Lady Audley's Secret* – not simply a rick, that is burning, with in addition the threat or promise of a charred corpse to be found among the ashes. In another of Boucicault's plays, *The Wicklow Wedding*, performed at the Princess's Theatre in 1864, there is a remarkable scene in which the hero, Shaun, escapes from prison by climbing the front of the 'fortress'. At one point 'the ivy above his head gives way, and a large mass falls, carrying him with it; leaves and matted branches cover him. His descent is checked by some roots of the ivy, which hold fast.'[12] At the top of the tower sits his sweet-heart, Arrah, 'leaning over the abyss'. Henry Knight's adventure on the cliff in *A Pair of Blue Eyes* awesomely sets the thin-spun life of man against the remorseless longevity of Nature. Nevertheless it is, quite literally, a cliff-hanger, and Hardy manages the suspense by similar means – the

quartz that slips, the tuft of sea-pink that comes out by the roots
as Knight holds it, the 'lowest tuft of vegetation' that miraculously
holds firm and arrests his fall. Earlier in *The Wicklow Wedding*
there is a scene in which the 'traitor' Beamish disappears through
a trap-door in the roof to escape a search-party of soldiers. Bob
Loveday's escape from the press-gang through the trap-door in
the Mill (in *The Trumpet-Major*) roughly parallels this, although
the chase at the Mill is much more elaborate and prolonged.
Assuredly the chase had stage-antecedents of some kind: for the
modern reader it may recall the brilliant mad chase up in the
flies at the end of the Marx Brothers' film *A Night at the Opera*.

As these examples may suggest, there is at times a family resemblance between Hardy's material and specific plays. *Desperate Remedies*
recalls *Lady Audley's Secret* not only in its inn-fire, but also in the
subterfuge by which a supposedly dead spouse is advertised for
in the newspapers. As Manston's remedies become increasingly desperate, his role as a masculine counterpart to Lady Audley becomes
increasingly obvious. (Of course, the 'debt' in this case, if debt
there be, is not necessarily to the play: it could be to the novel
itself.) Manston's confession from the condemned cell allies him
to William Corder in *Maria Marten*; his burying of the body also
suggests Corder, and contemporary readers would perhaps have
visions of Maria's last frenzied struggles to escape as they followed
his pursuit of Cytherea round and round the table. The challenge
to Manston's ingenuity presented by the need to recover incriminating
documents from a post-box is also in the melodramatic tradition.
James L. Smith describes how the villain in the play *London Pride*,
faced with the same problem, solved it with the help of a fish-hook.[13]

Hardy may thus deliberately have sought help from the stage,
as well as, as is usually suggested, from the novels of Wilkie Collins,
in 'constructing the eminently "sensational" plot of *Desperate Remedies*' (*Life*, 63). Echoes of specific plays in later novels seem less
deliberate; more a matter of imaginative sympathy than of narrative
necessity. One can never be sure, of course, about what plays
Hardy actually saw. Yet there is one play which he can hardly
have failed to see and enjoy: Boucicault's *The Colleen Bawn*, one
of the great successes of the 1860s. (It was available as both a
play and an opera: the operatic version, Benedict's *Lily of Killarney*,
was in the repertory of the Royal English Opera Company during
this period.) The central situation of the drama, that of the upper-class
Hardress Cregan secretly married to the lowly Eily O'Connor, has

a very general affinity with that of *Tess*. What makes the affinity
worth noticing is the adoring, self-sacrificing nature of Eily's love:
like Tess, she is willing to forego the marriage, offering, as Tess
does, to become her husband's servant merely, anxious not to 'be
a shame to him an' a ruin', ready even to die to prevent such
shame, and willingly forgiving him the attempt on her life. The
play, it seems, may have lingered in Hardy's memory to lend
a touch here. In *The Return of the Native* the resemblances are
more considerable. There is firstly the same use of a localised
and impressive natural setting: the action of *The Colleen Bawn* takes
place at various points around Lake Killarney, and like that of
The Return achieves a sense of spaciousness within well-controlled
limits. There are a number of similarities in the action itself, each
in itself slight but quite remarkable when taken together. Eily
and Hardress, for instance, arrange their meetings by means of
a 'signal light' from Eily's cottage: compare Eustacia's and Wildeve's
use of the bonfire. Hardress's mother is a strong, domineering person,
a little like Mrs Yeobright: like her, she wants her son to marry
his cousin, Anne, with whom he has been brought up. Most notable,
however, is the watchful care of Eily shown by her disappointed
lover Myles-Na-Coppaleen. In this he is very like Diggory Venn:
'Oh Eily,' he soliloquises, '. . . as the stars watch over Innesfallen,
and as the wathers go round it and keep it, so I watch and
keep round you, mavourneen!' (i.ii). Like Diggory he is a solitary,
living alone in his hut, from which, as from Diggory's van, strange
sights and sounds proceed which make people think the place is
haunted. (He keeps a whisky-still there.) It is Myles who rescues
Eily from drowning, in the great sensation scene when she is pushed
off a rock by Danny Mann. This too is worth remembering in
relation to *The Return of the Native*. Lastly, when Myles after rescuing
Eily hands over his hut to her, locking her in and retiring to
his bed 'on the mountain above', we are reminded of a later
novel, *The Woodlanders*, and Giles's similarly chivalrous behaviour
towards Grace. Myles was, incidentally, the outstanding character-
creation of Boucicault's play, certain to be remembered by those
who saw it.

Elsewhere there is the occasional interesting parallel: the cobbler
Watchful Waxend, for instance, who in *My Poll and My Partner
Joe* (first produced in 1835), preaches religion in a public house
and is known as the Bishop of Battersea (compare Jude's scornful
soubriquet, 'Tutor of St Slum's'); or the itinerant barber in *Ark-*

wright's Wife (the Globe, 1873) waiting to buy 'the profuse auburn tresses' of Margaret Hayes[14] (compare Percomb's pursuit of Marty South). Generally speaking, however, where plot and incident are concerned the links between Hardy's work and stage melodrama are better regarded as generic rather than specific. His country settings and humble heroes and heroines provide the basis, for the trials and tribulations of villagers, usually at the hands of an oppressive squire or landlord, often a *parvenu*, themselves consti-tuted one of the basic forms of melodrama. Seduction, though the most popular, is not the only theme: other forms of oppression, such as rack-renting and eviction (often combined with seduction), also occur, as in Jerrold's *Black-Eyed Susan* (1829) and *The Rent Day* (1832) or Buckstone's *Luke the Labourer* (1826). The hardships of the Industrial Revolution led to plays of social protest such as John Walker's *The Factory Lad* (1834) and Charles Reade's powerful *It's Never Too Late to Mend* (1864), about prison life, plays which in their exposure of real ills (setting aside their exaggerations of plot) provide a dramatic counterpart to the *Graphic* illustrations discussed in the previous chapter. From this point of view, *Tess of the d'Urbervilles* may be seen to be related to melodrama through its picture of 'the agricultural community in decline' as well as through its persecuted heroine. The villain of the piece in this sense is the cruel Farmer Groby, with Tess's sufferings on the threshing-machine presenting a memorable image of oppression. *Jude the Obscure* too embodies its own melodrama of protest in its excessively black picture of its hero, the Poor Man, struggling within the prison of the marriage laws against the grim bullies, Church and Society.

Tess, combining in herself, as we saw, the village maiden and the magdalen figure, also fills simultaneously the roles of wronged and of erring wife, popular in the domestic melodrama of the middle and late nineteenth century. Hardy's clearest exemplar of the wronged wife, however, is obviously Grace Melbury. Hardy's sympathy with the ethical assumptions of melodrama comes out clearly in *The Woodlanders*: aristocratic (or well-to-do) vice is opposed to rural virtue, and Giles and Marty make it plain that kind hearts are more than coronets, as melodrama always did.

Hardy's habit of dramatising the action of his novels – that is, of giving them not merely a play-shape but a stage-play shape – ex-tends to such details as gesture, movement, and facial expression. There are many occasions when one feels that what Hardy is seeing in his mind's eye is not simply the scene in itself, but the scene on a stage. And, when he does so, the stage is often the melodramatic stage. When Bathsheba, tormented by the rumour she has heard about Fanny, 'locked her fingers, threw back her head, and strained her hot hands rigidly across her forehead', the action is distinctly theatrical, in the grand manner of the tragedy queen. So is her later gliding 'rapidly up and down the room . . . her hands clasped in front of her'. Paula Power pulling out her jet necklace, 'extending it with the thumb of her left hand' (*L*, 83), may be employing a bit of 'stage business' Hardy has actually observed in one of his women friends, but Bathsheba he has surely seen on the stage and nowhere else. Probably the same is true of the action he gives to Henchard when Elizabeth-Jane introduces him to Lucetta, with whom, of course, he is already well acquainted: 'Henchard put his hand to his hat, which he brought down with a great wave till it met his body at the knee.' On Henchard's part it is a deliberately theatrical gesture, mockingly exaggerated: Hardy himself was perhaps recalling a familiar feature of the costume drama of the day (the ever-popular Dumas, for example). One almost imagines Henchard's hat as plumed.

There are many such occasions on which Hardy seems to double the role of playwright with that of play-producer. The scenes thus created may have varying degrees of 'staginess'. Mrs Charmond (who has been an actress) at her first meeting with Fitzpiers follows a stage-routine as familiar perhaps to her creator as to herself. Every gesture, both here and in the subsequent 'temptation scene', is carefully studied: the 'thin stream' of cigarette smoke sent towards the ceiling; the glance up at Fitzpiers 'across her brows and forehead'; the lingering glance hastily withdrawn, followed by the 'mechanical' application of the cigarette again to her lips. Hardy has sought help from the theatre, but so has Mrs Charmond. By contrast, the scene between Troy, Bathsheba and the dead Fanny succeeds by its sheer *dramatic* power. Yet, though it transcends 'staginess', it probably owes as much to the stage as do the scenes between Fitzpiers and Mrs Charmond. The almost unbearable tension of the scene is achieved largely by careful control of movement, of the features as well as the limbs. As Bathsheba 'with dilated eye' pushes past Troy to get out, he seizes her hand and together they approach the coffin. The shock Troy receives on seeing Fanny is expressed through the suspension of movement, 'congealed immobility'. We can imagine an audience holding its breath, its eyes

riveted on him as his are on the coffin. It is like the moment in
a film before a shot man reels and falls. Troy then gradually
sinks forward to a kneeling position and begins kissing the dead
Fanny, his expression modulating from dismay 'to illimitable sadness'.
Meanwhile Bathsheba regards him from the other side, 'still with
parted lips and distracted eyes'. Few words are spoken in this
scene: it speaks for itself. Hardy has revealed his characters' emotions
through movement and facial expression. Melodrama would do
it in precisely the same way.

The sustained high tension of much of *Far from the Madding
Crowd*, combined with its unflagging pace and variety of scenic
and dramatic interest, makes it Hardy's most complete and perfect
melodrama. It includes at its climax, the shooting of Troy, one
of the most familiar of melodrama's big scenes: violent action in
a ballroom or drawing-room, where the guests crowd in or throng
the stairs and the principals make a striking tableau in the centre
of the stage. *The Colleen Bawn* ends in this way; so did *The Duke's
Motto*, which Hardy could have seen at the Lyceum in January
1863; and there is a fine version in Watts Phillips's *Lost in London*
(1867). It is also common in opera. Bathsheba 'sitting on the floor
beside the body of Troy, his head pillowed in her lap', presents,
it could be said, one of melodrama's central images. It may be
compared, for instance, with the illustration to Boucicault's *The
Trial of Effie Deans* in the *Illustrated London News* for 7 February
1863, which shows Jeannie Deans kneeling on the court-room floor
beside the prostrate body of her father, who has collapsed on
hearing the verdict.

Bathsheba's first reaction to Troy's reappearance had been to
sink down 'on the lowest stair' (the party was taking place in
the hall, conveniently ensuring that all the dramatic events 'converge'
on the same spot). A staircase (preferably with newel) seems to
be a necessary piece of indoor scenery in Hardy's novels, for use
by the characters at moments of high emotion. (One is reminded
a little of Stephen in Ben Jonson's *Every Man in his Humour*: 'Is
there a stool to be melancholy upon?') Picotee, after learning
the truth about Ethelberta and Christopher (*HE*, 144), leans against
the stair-newel, with parted lips. Grace Melbury, softened by the
sight of Suke's and Felice's grief after Fitzpiers's accident, 'went
out to the balustrade, bent herself upon it, and wept'. Phillotson
after Sue's leap from the bedroom offers another variation of the
same action: he 'sat down on the lower stairs, holding the newel

with one hand, and bowing his face into the other'. This repeated effect could be a piece of 'theatre' Hardy is recalling: it has a theatrical look about it.

Another image that exercised a powerful hold over Hardy's imagination is readily identifiable as one of the dominant images of the melodramatic stage. This is the image of a woman lying prostrate, looking like a mere bundle of drapery. In melodrama it is often the repentant wife, stretched at her husband's feet: so Tess 'crouched in a heap' before Angel after making her confession. Bathsheba sinks down and becomes 'a shapeless heap of drapery' after laying out Troy. Sue, lying beneath the chancel cross in St Silas's church, appears to Jude at first as 'a heap of black clothes'. Earlier, after her leap to escape from (as she thought) Phillotson's embraces, she had been a white heap: 'there on the gravel before him lay a white heap'. This strikingly resembles one of the most dramatic and horrifying moments in nineteenth-century literature, the fall of Amy Robsart at the end of Scott's *Kenilworth*: '"I see only a heap of white clothes, like a snowdrift" said Foster. "O God, she moves an arm!"' Hardy knew *Kenilworth*;[15] he may have known Yeames's painting of this incident; he may also have seen the stage version, *Amy Robsart*, which in 1870 'attracted crowds to Drury Lane' with Adelaide Neilson in the name-part.[16] The poignancy of Hardy's use of such images derives, I think, from a view of life akin to and perhaps partly suggested by the 'philosophy of clothes' expounded by Carlyle in *Sartor Resartus*. The form the images take, however, is more likely to have been suggested by melodrama.

At this point the nature of the affinity between Hardy's art and that of melodrama should be becoming clear. The language of melodrama is primarily not one of words, but one of action and spectacle. Michael Booth quotes Percy Fitzgerald: 'We go not so much to hear as to look. It is like a gigantic peep-show, and we pay the showman, and put our eyes to the glass and stare.'[17] Emotions were communicated by movement, gesture, and facial expression, all of which had to be 'telling'. This, indeed, was a requirement of nineteenth-century acting generally – 'Every movement, every look of the eye, should *tell* to some purpose', Ellen Terry advised aspirants to the profession[18] – and was itself a legacy from the eighteenth century. The importance of visual experience to Hardy has already been sufficiently stressed throughout this book. He too in his rendering of it is at pains to make it 'telling'. He practises the art (or science) of physiognomy constantly, in relation both to Nature and to man. An expressive countenance is, he seems to feel, especially characteristic of the countryman. *The Woodlanders*, perhaps because of its still, meditative character, is particularly rich in examples, from 'the physiognomy of a deserted highway', which 'expresses solitude to a degree that is not reached by mere dales or downs', to the 'fulness of expression' developed in Marty's face, on which Hardy comments (*W*, 43),

> Where the eyes of a multitude continuously beat like waves upon a countenance they seem to wear away its mobile power; but in the still water of privacy every feeling and sentiment unfolds in visible luxuriance, to be interpreted as readily as a printed word by an intruder.

As Angel Clare is transformed into a farmer, the muscles of his face grow more expressive: 'his eyes looked as much information as his tongue spoke, and more'. Even Joseph Poorgrass knows how 'tell-tale' the features can be at moments of stress: 'Just eye my features, and see if the tell-tale blood overheats me much, neighbours', he begs, when asked to sing at the shearing-supper. Characters such as these, in whom 'the infinitesimal movement of muscle, curve, hair, and wrinkle' is 'watched and translated' by their comrades (*W*, 134), are already unconscious and natural actors. Put them in those 'scenes in any way emotional or dramatic' the portraiture of which Hardy declared to be 'the highest province of fiction'; continue to watch and translate; and their 'nerves and muscles' are 'seen as in an *écorché*'[19] – or as in a melodrama.

Thus the melodramatic mode in Hardy's novels brings out the written marks of the 'habits, vices, passions and memories' of his characters, much as Hardy had observed cold weather to do on faces. Events provide the equivalent of the cold weather: it is in their response to them that these characters reveal themselves, no less than in the 'tomb-like stillness' and 'still water' of the environment itself. Hardy's melodramatic imagination thus provides an excellent example to add to those of Balzac and James in Peter Brooks's important essay on this subject. Brooks relates melodrama to 'a novelistic enterprise where transcribed gesture, the world described, will be totally significant and legible, and totally expressive of emotional and moral conditions', and suggests that 'the melodramatic mode arises in an era which demands rediscovery

of the spiritual within and behind a phenomenal realm which
seems to have been deprived of possibilities for transcendence'.[20]
He sees the writer of melodrama as 'ever conscious of standing
over a void, dealing in conflicts, qualities and quantities whose
very existence is uncertain'.[21] His argument is strikingly relevant
to the 'phenomenal realm' Hardy's art explores, and suggests how
the apparent contradiction in Hardy's artistic principles, between
his assertion 'Art is concerned with seemings only' and his description
of his own art as a way of making 'the heart and inner meaning
vividly visible', may be reconciled. Life is for Hardy a palimpsest
which Art attempts to read. The melodramatic imagination provides
the 'warmth' required (as in the bringing out of a writing in
sympathetic ink). The inner being of the sentient creatures who
are his subject is brought to the surface in the 'transcribed gestures'
by which their emotion, their very sentience itself, is expressed.

Hardy's 'reading' of his characters' stories also has much in
common with melodrama. Despite recent scepticism about this, it
still seems to me that Hardy saw his characters very largely as
victims, certainly in the sense that he chose to emphasise suffering
rather than sin in them, and was thus more inclined to pity than
to blame them. Granted that men could do more to ameliorate
their own and their neighbours' condition and that circumspection
may provide a measure of protection against the hostility of circumstance, yet still that hostility remains for him a central, inescapable
fact. Hardy's essay on 'Candour in English Fiction' opens,

> Even imagination is the slave of stolid circumstance; and the
> unending flow of inventiveness which finds expression in the litera-
> ture of Fiction is no exception to the general law. It is conditioned
> by its surroundings like a river-stream.[22]

The implication, taken for granted as part of 'the general law',
clearly is that man himself is such a slave. Hardy felt this all his
life. 'Crass Casualty obstructs the sun and rain', he wrote in 1866
in the poem 'Hap', and forty years later, in September 1926,
commenting on a proposed dramatisation of *Jude*,

> Would not Arabella be the villain of the piece? – or Jude's personal
> constitution? – so far as there is any villain more than blind
> Chance. Christminster is of course the tragic influence of Jude's
> drama in one sense, but innocently so, and merely as crass
> obstruction. (*Life*, 433)

Thus Hardy's novels seldom need any human villain to establish their relationship to melodrama. In their 'brief transit through a sorry world' his characters all find their paths obstructed by the villain Circumstance or blind Chance, and their endeavours mocked. Henry Knight, speaking what is almost Elfride's epitaph, puts the matter clearly: 'Circumstance has, as usual, overpowered her purposes – fragile and delicate as she – liable to be overthrown in a moment by the coarse elements of accident.' The villain has almost materialised here, and in a form palpably close to that of Alec d'Urberville when he 'traced such a coarse pattern' upon Tess's 'beautiful feminine tissue, sensitive as gossamer'.

Hardy's perception of the villainous role of Circumstance gives him a strong sense of the vulnerability of his characters, indeed of all forms of life. And such a sense is the very foundation of melodrama, of its excitements and its tears. As James L. Smith writes, in reference to such melodramas as Aeschylus's *The Persians*, Euripides's *The Trojan Women*, Webster's *The Duchess of Malfi*, and others of like calibre,

> These plays do not attempt to bypass the essential structure of an innocent protagonist overthrown by outside forces; they succeed because they give that framework a validity and truth which makes it answerable to our own experience. . . . The melodrama of defeat chronicles all those miseries which drift towards us on the tide of hostile nature, fate or politics, war or accident or desperate men. . . . This is one part of our experience of reality, and the melodrama of defeat presents it truthfully as art.[23]

The 'melodrama of defeat' is one of the three categories proposed by Smith in his fine essay in rehabilitation, the others being the melodrama of triumph and of protest. Following distinctions made by Robert Heilman in his *Tragedy and Melodrama* (Seattle, 1968), Smith sees melodrama itself as a form in which an undivided protagonist fights only against external pressures, not like the tragic hero against forces within himself. Thus defined, melodrama is, he suggests, 'the dramatic form which expresses the reality of the human condition as we all experience it most of the time', and 'most of the serious plays ever written' have in fact been melodramas, not tragedies.[24] The relevance of this to Hardy's novels seems plain. Although the mental sufferings of his protagonists do include an element of self-questioning and self-reproach, this is not, with the

exception of Henchard, where the emphasis falls. *Jude the Obscure*
attempts to tell, Hardy says, 'of a deadly war waged between
flesh and spirit'. In so far as it does so, Jude may be seen as
a tragic hero. Yet the parallels drawn between his situation and
that of Job, the much-afflicted, long-suffering, righteous man; the
novel's view of marriage as a steel trap; Hardy's statement in
his 'Postscript' of 1912, 'Artistic effort always pays heavily for
finding its tragedies in the forced adaptation of human instincts
to rusty and irksome moulds that do not fit them'; and the various
suggestions he makes in 1926 for identifying 'the villain of the
piece' – all point rather towards a 'melodrama of defeat'. As for
Tess, although Hardy is careful to give her 'faults' and weaknesses,
his insistence on her essential innocence is clear, from the title-page
('Poor wounded name!') onwards. During her engagement to Clare,
Tess suffers inwardly, experiencing 'doubt, fear, moodiness, care,
shame', but Hardy comments,

> It was no mature woman with a long dark vista of intrigue
> behind her who was tormented thus; but a girl of simple life,
> not yet one-and-twenty, who had been caught during her days
> of immaturity like a bird in a springe.

The very emotions that beset her are represented as hostile forces –
spectres persistently attempting to touch her, wolves waiting 'just
outside the circumscribing light', 'shapes of darkness'. 'Once victim,
always victim – that's the law!' declares Tess to Alec, and,
one must believe, with the approval of her author. Attempts to
prove her in any seriously blameworthy way responsible for her
own tragedy seem, therefore, as much misguided as is the argument
that the Duchess of Malfi brought her fate on herself through
her sin against 'degree'. The comment of Cariola, the Duchess's
waiting-woman, 'I owe her much of pity', is equally applicable
to both.

IV

The coinage 'the melodrama of defeat' may, according to Smith,
take 'upwards of a century' to establish itself. It had, of course,
no place in Hardy's critical vocabulary. The Pities, representative

of 'the spectator idealised' or 'Humanity, with all its weaknesses' (*Life*, 321), see the action of *The Dynasts* essentially as 'terrestrial tragedy': it is to the Spirit Sinister that it appears an 'excellently high-coloured drama'. For the Spirit Ironic it is comedy. His own 'unadjusted impressions' allow Hardy to recognise the existence of such alternatives. He liked to quote Ruskin's statement 'Comedy is tragedy if you look deep enough', and reversed it in 'All tragedy is grotesque – if you allow yourself to see it as such' (*Life*, 296). When tragedy is seen as something grotesque, it becomes not tragedy but melodrama in its crude popular sense, comedy, farce, burlesque. Above all, it becomes pantomime, a form ample and elastic enough at its most expansive to include all these.

Pantomime in its basic sense of a mode of expression and communication through bodily movement and gesture clearly has a place in Hardy's art. The dramatic techniques of his novels, as we have seen, reflect the essentially pantomimic techniques of melodrama. By a quite logical development the Dumb Show becomes in *The Dynasts* an indispensable feature, more important perhaps on the human plane than the dialogue.

My concern at this point, however, is with the form of entertainment we know as English pantomime. This had its hey-day in the nineteenth century, with spectacular productions each Christmas at Covent Garden and Drury Lane, and many of the smaller London theatres besides. It presented, as it still does, a familiar nursery story or fairy tale, elaborately staged in a succession of colourful and varied scenes. But it had one fixed feature that has now been largely lost: it ended with a grand transformation in which the principal characters turned into the traditional characters of the Commedia dell' Arte – Harlequin, Columbine, Clown, and Pantaloon – and went through a series of fantastic or hilarious antics known as the 'harlequinade'.

Hardy's familiarity with pantomime was not that of a spectator merely. He had also been a performer. In the season of 1866–7 he appeared as one of the 'countless supernumeraries'[25] in the Covent Garden production *Ali Baba and the Forty Thieves*; *or Harlequin and the Genii of the Arabian Nights*, by Gilbert Arthur à Beckett. This had as Ali Baba and later Clown the celebrated W. H. Payne, whom A. E. Wilson describes as 'the supreme pantomime artist in the post-Grimaldi period'.[26] His son Fred Payne was Harlequin. The harlequinade seems to have had a medical slant: the play-bill announces

Wine Vaults. Private House. Doctor's Shop.
Mrs Strongnerve, the new M. D., F. R. S. – Wonderful Cures. –
A Head at discount. – In high spirits. –
Quiet lodgings. – A Flying Knocker.[27]

The Oxford and Cambridge Boat Race, with the River Thames
at Putney, was also represented, along with a Grand University
Revel. In both of these scenes, doubtless, Hardy formed one of
the crowd. Although another pantomime-writer, E. L. Blanchard,
dismissed *Ali Baba* as 'all legs and limelight',[28] *The Times* praised
it for its excellent ballets and gorgeous scenery, finding the Dryads'
Sylvan Home 'as true to nature as it is picturesque' and the
Fairy Transformation 'one of those marvels of scenic contrivance
to which the public has long been accustomed by Mr T. Grieve'.[29]

In *The Dynasts* the action in its absurd destructiveness and cruelty
is occasionally explicitly seen as a harlequinade. Waterloo, for instance, is so described (3. vi. viii). At the Bridge of the Beresina
(3. i. x), when the bridge gives way beneath the retreating French,
throngs of whom 'roll shrieking into the stream and are drowned',
the Pities comment

So loudly swell their shrieks as to be heard above the roar
of guns and the wailful wind,
Giving in one brief cry their last wild word on that mock life
through which they have harlequined!

Much earlier, at the death of Pitt, the Spirit of the Years had
commented (1. vi. viii)

Time and time,
When all Earth's light has lain on the nether side,
And yapping midnight winds have leapt on roofs,
And raised for him an evil harlequinade
Of national disasters in long train,
That tortured him with harrowing grimace,
Have I communed with that intelligence.

Significantly, these explicit allusions come from the Pities and the
Years: they recognise the form of drama they are watching, but
are able to look deep enough to see the tragedy underlying its

comedy. Thus, at Talavera, when at a pause in the battle the 'inimic hosts' drink from the same stream, even shaking hands across it, the Pities cry (2. IV. v),

> What more could plead the wryness of the times
> Than such unstudied piteous pantomimes!

They may see comedy before them, but they 'read' it as tragedy. The Spirits Ironic and Sinister react in exactly the opposite way. Even when to the eye of the Pities and of the reader the action is clearly tragic, they persist in seeing it as comedy. They acknowledge the horrors, but find their fun in them. 'Ho-ho', laughs the Spirit Sinister as, at Ulm, 'The Will throws Mack again in agitation.' And to the Pities' protest, 'Nay, hard one, nay', his response is 'It's good antic at a vacant time!' Later, while the Pities lament the failure of the negotiations for peace during Fox's administration, the Spirit Sinister considers it fortunate 'for the manufacture of corpses by machinery', in his view doubtless an entertaining panto-mime trick, while the Spirit Ironic, relishing 'this remarkable little piece', finds 'the remainder of the episode . . . frankly farcical'. At Waterloo these two 'wry-formed phantoms' are comparatively silent, but the comment of the Spirit Sinister as he moves invisible about the battle-field and the balls of both sides 'scream brisk and breezy tunes' through him,

> It's merry so;
> What damage mortal flesh must undergo!

is again in the spirit of pantomime.[30] This is the 'merriment' of the harlequinade, which, like that of its relatives the Punch and Judy show and slapstick comedy, has its basis in physical violence and cruelty: for the Spirit Sinister, Waterloo's cannon-balls are custard-pies.

In Hardy's novels too it is frequently suggested that life is a series of bad (or good) practical jokes, perpetrated by, or for the amusement of, some indefinable mocking presence or presences. The joker may be variously identified as destiny, chance, circum-stance, or Heaven, even as the President of the Immortals. In the poems it is, rather, Time who makes laughingstocks of us. In *The Well-Beloved* it is Hymen, and here the comparison with the harlequinade is explicit: Hymen, we are told (p. 135), 'seemed

to haunt Pierston . . . with undignified mockery which savoured rather
of Harlequin than of the torch-bearer'. 'The sad buffoonery that
fate, fortune, and the guardian angels had been playing with Ethelberta of late' (*HE*, 117) also seems close to the harlequinade,
although Ethelberta was lucky to get off with mere buffoonery.
Other characters suffer 'buffetings' (Henchard) and 'scourgings'
(even the tender Grace Melbury). Above all, the child Jude, whirled
round and beaten by Farmer Troutham, suffers like a harlequin
victim, his own clacker serving as harlequin's bat. Experience itself
presents itself thereafter to Jude in these terms, with 'the little
cell called your life' shaken and warped by the noise and glare
of the attack.

One striking feature of the world of pantomime is its plasticity:
demarcation lines between the human and the non-human are
blurred; objects cease to be, in Coleridge's words, fixed and dead,
and become mobile and alive. A review of Henry J. Byron's *Harlequin
Beauty and the Beast* (Covent Garden, 1862), for example, mentions
a scene 'the trees in which are literally alive with action. So
likewise are the chairs and tables in the next scene.'[31] Objects
thus liberated might exercise their powers benevolently or malevolently, but in the harlequinade itself it was usually malevolently.
Existence became a hazardous and bewildering thing for the Clown
as trick followed trick: chairs and sofas walked away when sat
upon, or turned into wheelbarrows; fire-irons and chimney-ornaments
flew about the room; vegetables and kitchen utensils walked about
grinning broadly.[32] Hardy's animism ('In spite of myself,' he
said – *Life*, 285 – 'I cannot help noticing countenances and tempers
in objects of scenery, *e.g.* trees, hills, houses') creates a similar
world about his characters. The 'malicious leer' of the jack in
All Saints' Church, the gargoyle that 'had for four hundred years
laughed at the surrounding landscape' and that now destroys Troy's
handiwork on Fanny Robin's grave, the 'ironical smile' that Bathsheba earlier had seen on 'all things' about her by Fanny's coffin
are all in the spirit of pantomime. So are the 'sly and wicked
leer' on the face of Shiner's house; the 'drunken leer' of the
sun as Henry Knight clings to the cliff-side; the lamps of Christminster, winking their yellow eyes dubiously at Jude on his arrival
in the city. The animated objects of Hardy's world are less mobile
than those of the harlequinade, but they are at one with them
in their mischievous mockery. When on one occasion he has something
that moves to deal with – the wind at Giles's death in *The Woodlan-*

ders – he introduces what is virtually a complete harlequinade in miniature, describing the wind as 'trampling and climbing over the roof, making branches creak, springing out of the trees upon the chimney, popping its head into the flue, and shrieking and blaspheming at every corner of the walls'. The Spirit of the Years was later to envisage Pitt enduring just such a harlequinade. (See above, p. 97.)

Sometimes in Hardy the harlequinade is brought about by a transformation, as is the rule in pantomime. Since Hardy's harlequinades are in fact images expressive of his characters' reactions to hostile, and often changed, circumstances, this it not surprising. *Tess of the d'Urbervilles* provides the clearest example. Here, as Tess makes her confession to Angel on their wedding-night, we read,

> But the complexion even of external things seemed to suffer transmutation as her announcement progressed. The fire in the grate looked impish – demoniacally funny, as if it did not care in the least about her strait. The fender grinned idly, as if it too did not care. The light from the water-bottle was merely engaged in a chromatic problem.

This contrasts with the friendliness household furniture may show in more comfortable circumstances, as when in Henchard's parlour a 'restless acrobatic flame, poised on a coal, called from the shady walls the smiles of all shapes that could respond', including 'the old pier-glass . . . , the picture-frames, sundry knobs and handles . . .'. But it also contrasts with the earlier experience in the pantomime mode of Angel Clare, when, after his and Tess's first embrace, the dairy-house suddenly becomes animated: 'The aged and lichened brick gable breathed forth "Stay!" The windows smiled, the door coaxed and beckoned, the creeper blushed confederacy.'

Tess herself seems from the start to be conscious of the pantomime world through which she moves. In their first sustained conversation she tells Clare, 'The trees have inquisitive eyes, haven't they? – that is, seem as if they had. And the river says, – "Why do ye trouble me with your looks?"' The 'luminous mist' that surrounds her during their engagement turns her existence into an enchanted palace, so that the change when it comes is as complete as that in pantomime's fairy transformation scene.

Hardy's novels have also something of the charm, and charmedness, of the pantomime world. His country characters and settings, in the kind of dramatic and pictorial presentation he gives them, establish the link in the first place. Penelope Vigar notes of Keeper Day's house in *Under the Greenwood Tree* that it is 'described initially as a sort of fairy cottage'.[33] The cottage on the downs in which Anne Garland is besieged by Festus has, given Anne's situation, a strong element of fairy-tale about it: it evokes memories of the Three Little Pigs or the Fox and the Kid. Festus himself, his eyes 'glowing like carbuncles' on one occasion, has a touch of the pantomime giant and his 'fee-fi-fo-fum' about him. Rather surprisingly, however, it is the opening of *Jude the Obscure* which most vividly suggests the pantomime stage. Perhaps this is partly because the focus of the action is a child. The village-green, with its school-house, its 'draw-well at the edge of the greensward', and Aunt Drusilla's green-thatched cottage, is a typical pantomime setting – the curtain might just have risen on *Jack and the Beanstalk*, *Mother Goose* or even *Aladdin*. Jude as he loiters by the well seems cast for the role of Idle Jack, while Aunt Drusilla, formidable in name and nature, promises with her opening cry of 'Bring on that water, will ye, you idle young harlican!' to be a vociferous and vigorous Dame. This pantomimic sub-text continues with the young Jude's ensuing adventures: the assault from Farmer Troutham, an angry Giant as well as a Harlequin-figure; the meeting with Physician Vilbert, a startling figure 'wearing an extraordinarily tall hat, a swallow-tailed coat, and a watch-chain that danced madly', who would certainly be at home on the pantomime stage; and above all Jude's vision of the fairy city in the sky, Christminster, which for all its kinship with the New Jerusalem may have as its poor relation the fairy palaces to which the heroes and heroines of pantomime progress or are transported – the 'Enchanted Home of the Genii on the Golden Heights of Sunshine', for instance, featured in *Ali Baba*, the pantomime in which Hardy himself acted.

Enchantment, magic, so essential an ingredient of pantomime, permeates Hardy's vision too. This world where 'nothing is as it seems' is a mystery to him, and he sits before it 'like a bewildered child at a conjuring show'; or like Elizabeth-Jane when, watching by her mother's death-bed, she asks herself,

> why things around her had taken the shape they wore in preference to every other possible shape. Why they stared at her so helplessly, as if waiting for the touch of some wand that should release them from terrestrial constraint.

This is the entrancement of the gingerbread children in *Hansel and Gretel*. The 'helplessness' of the object world persistently impressed itself on Hardy. In *The Woodlanders* (77), the 'little things' in Grace Melbury's bedroom gaze at her 'in helpless stationariness'; a later passage (p. 189) speaks of the 'aspect of mesmeric passivity' things outside wear at daybreak. The poem 'Nature's Questioning' handles the same idea. The animism in these instances is not that of the harlequinade but that of the fairy part of the pantomime, expressing itself passively, in the stare, not the grin.

All things in Hardy's world, therefore, as in that of pantomime, are conscious and alive; but the nature of that life, again as in pantomime, is uncertain, fluid and changing. Much, perhaps all, is dream and illusion: 'You see the scene. And yet you see it not' (*Dyn.*, 3. II. ii). Impermanence and death suggest that experience is the work of 'some strange necromancy':

> But nought of that maid from Saint-Juliot I see;
> > Can she ever have been here,
> > And shed her life's sheen here,
> The woman I thought a long housemate with me?

> Does there even a place like Saint-Juliot exist?
> > > > > ('A Dream or No')

And love, of course, creates its own colourful dream, brilliantly illuminated not by gas or limelight but by the radiance of the lover's vision. Nature itself at times imitates the splendours of pantomime, themselves imitations of Nature. 'Who's for a transformation scene?' cries Christopher Julian. He touches a blind, up it flies, and 'a gorgeous scene' presents itself – sunrise over the sea (*HE*, 64). And the garden party in *A Laodicean*, with its 'lavender haze', its trees 'as still as those of a submarine forest', and later the description of the interior of the marquee viewed through rain, 'the brilliant forms of the dancers passing and repassing behind the watery screen, as if they were people in an enchanted submarine palace', is itself transformed by Hardy's imagination into what looks very like a pantomime spectacular.

Hardy's work shows awareness of and utilises the transformation scene in all its aspects – its splendour, its processes, and its subsequent harlequinade. There is a particularly elaborate example in *The Well-Beloved*. Here the sudden shock of hearing of Avice Caro's

death creates for Jocelyn a striking transformation, in which the
dinner party he is attending recedes into the background, to be
replaced by Avice as he remembers her in the Isle of Slingers.
A 'handsome marchioness in geranium-red and diamonds' becomes
a glowing sunset, the 'crannied features' of an 'evergreen society
lady' shape themselves to 'dusty quarries', while the ornaments
of the table are transmuted into the features of the island's coast-line.
The transformation is a gradual one, in slow motion as it were.
Closer to the transformation scene of pantomime in its suddenness
is the appearance of Troy as revealed by the rekindled lantern,
'brilliant in brass and scarlet', which has upon Bathsheba (it is
their first encounter) 'the effect of a fairy transformation'.

Life itself is full of transformations for Hardy, both sudden and
gradual. 'Time, the magician' (*MC*, 64) is responsible for many
of them. It is he who turns the green leaf to brown, 'muslined
pink young things' to 'market-dames, mid-aged, with lips thin-
drawn / And tissues sere', and replaces one scene with another. The
process of change, as experience and the theory of evolution both
show, is inbuilt into life. Death itself is a transformation: life is
thus a matter of waiting 'till my change come' ('Waiting Both').
And, as the poems 'Transformations' and 'Voices from Things
Growing in a Churchyard' indicate, the dead themselves may still
be 'maskers', turned 'to a dancer in green as leaves on a wall'
or clambering up anew as ivy-green, making actual in this way
Pierston's mental experience.

v

One further piece of evidence that Hardy's vision of life as a
drama was shaped by his experience in the theatre, not simply
by his reading of 'the dramatic masterpieces of the past', remains
to be considered. This is his fascination with stage gauzes. He
recommends them at the end of his Preface to *The Dynasts* as
suitable to be used to 'blur outlines' and thus 'shut off the actual'
in the 'plays of poesy and dream' he surmises may be produced
in the future, and mentions that they have already been employed
in this way 'in exceptional cases'. The use of gauzes to distance
a scene so that it seemed mysterious, dream-like and remote, however,
was not at all exceptional. Samuel Phelps had popularised the
device through his productions of *Macbeth* and *A Midsummer Night's*

Dream at Sadler's Wells in the 1840s and 1850s, in which the
effects of making the Witches appear to grow out of and then
merge again in mist, and of throwing a 'green fairy tinge' and
mistiness over the woodland scenes of the *Dream*, subduing 'the
flesh and blood of the actors into something more nearly resembling
dream-like figures',[34] were greatly admired. 'Transparency gauzes'
(that is, gauzes with scenery painted on them, lit from behind)
were used to create the vision scenes in Boucicault's *The Corsican
Brothers* and Leopold Lewis's *The Bells*. Stage directions in *The
Colleen Bawn* call for 'gauze waters all over the stage' to represent
Lake Killarney. Gauzes were also invaluable for the creation of
pantomime's fairy world. Their use therefore extended over almost
the whole of the late Victorian theatre, wherever illusion was called
for.

The gauzes that appear in Hardy's work reflect their stage-origins,
explicitly or implicitly. The earliest of them, which appears in
Desperate Remedies, is quite explicit. 'Days and months had dimmed
the form of Edward Springrove,' writes Hardy (p. 244), 'like the
gauzes of a vanishing stage-scene, but his dying voice could still
be heard faintly behind'. If he has a particular stage-scene in
mind, it could be that in *The Corsican Brothers*, in which one brother,
Fabien, from his home in Corsica sees through the gauze his twin,
Louis, killed in a duel near Paris. At other times the image seems
most probably to derive from pantomime. Thus Paula Power, recalling the scene in the marquee discussed earlier, comments 'How
the rain came down, and formed a gauze between us and the
dancers.' 'Remote Egdon' disappearing 'by degrees behind the liquid
gauze' (*TD*, 213), the 'irradiated gauzes' the sun stretches across
the 'damp atmosphere' (*W*, 323), the 'two shadowy figures seen
through the grey gauzes of the morning' (*WB*, 177) all seem reminiscent of pantomime. The form is explicitly recalled in the short
story 'For Conscience' Sake', in reference to the facial resemblance,
between the father and his unacknowledged illegitimate daughter,
revealed during sea-sickness. Hardy writes, 'It was as if . . . a mysterious veil had been lifted, temporarily revealing a strange pantomime
of the past' – a strangely elaborate image for the situation. With
the 'ghost-like gauze' of the poem 'In Front of the Landscape',
we seem closer again to *The Corsican Brothers* and the like: this
is a transparency gauze, the 'customed landscape' of coomb and
upland 'stroked by the light' appearing 'no substantial / Meadow
or mound'. The action takes place in front of this gauze, since

the revisiting dead of his visions seem more real to the poet than do the things around him.

Finally, in *The Dynasts* the natural gauzes of the world are given a full dramatic function. 'Through the gauze of descending waters' at Ulm, the French soldiery are seen climbing to the attack (1. IV. iv); as Marie Louise leaves Vienna for her union with Napoleon, 'heavy rains spread their gauzes over the scene' (2. v. v); and at Waterloo

> storm supervenes
> In heaviness unparalleled, that screens
> With water-woven gauzes, vapour-bred,
> The creeping clumps of half-obliterate red.
>
> (3. VI. viii)

At the end of Part First also 'a gauze of shadow overdraws', at once expressing and concealing both the darkness of the present and the uncertainty of the future. Other stage curtains are often essentially similar in character and (so to speak) texture: 'An evening mist cloaks the scene'; 'The night fog enwraps the isle'; 'The October night thickens and curtains the scene'; 'A curtain of smoke drops'. These recall, for instance, the 'gradually thickening folds' of gauze behind which the Weird Sisters in Phelps's *Macbeth* vanished at the appropriate time.[35]

Gauzes are for Hardy an intrinsic part of the human stage. Physically, in the form of mist or rain, they obscure or diminish vision. Mentally, through time, forgetfulness, or incomprehension, they may do the same. And ultimately we all disappear behind them:

> Folk all fade. And whither,
> As I wait alone where the fair was?
> Into the clammy and numbing night-fog
> Whence they entered hither.
> Soon one more goes thither!
>
> ('Exeunt Omnes')

4 Cinematic Arts

To render the visual experience that life is by visual means: this was always Hardy's aim. The examples of painting and the theatre provided valuable aid, supplying him not only with techniques but also with images expressive of his vision. Yet there came a point when he needed to go beyond them, to outstrip their limitations. Painting could suggest movement but could not create it: theatre could create movement but only within a relatively limited area. Both arts were limited by exigencies of time and space, which Hardy's art, while remaining pictorial and dramatic, sought to transcend. Exercising the freedom and flexibility which his chosen medium of words gave him, he blended picture and stage to create a dynamic, fluid, powerfully visual art, in which, as has long been recognised, the art of cinema is strikingly anticipated in verbal form.

Basically the anticipation arises out of the necessities of his art. He needed 'the camera eye' to express what he had to say, and found it. If literary precedents or models are required, he had them in Milton and Dickens, both of whom adopted a highly visual style of narrative which the Russian film-director Eisenstein has analysed in terms of 'film form'. And experience of various devices and forms of entertainment that have a place in the pre-history of the cinema may have been a stimulus. Hardy's appetite for 'shows' was all-embracing: it included not only pictures, plays, fairs, circuses, Punch and Judy, puppets, but also panoramas and dioramas, galanty-shows, and the magic lantern.

In Hardy's references to panoramas the idea of a show is almost always present. Today we normally use the word 'panorama' simply in the sense of an extensive view. In Hardy's day, however, the word still signified a type of entertainment in which such views were exhibited. Panoramas, which could take the form either of paintings arranged cylindrically around the spectator or of a painted canvas unrolled between two end-rollers so as to pass in front of him – in effect, a moving picture – were shown either alone or combined with other forms of theatrical entertainment throughout the nineteenth century. In pantomime and other spectacular productions the moving panorama was a useful device both for rapid scene-shifting and for creating the illusion of movement over great distances. Hardy's 'panoramas' reflect his experience of these various forms.

The train seen in *Desperate Remedies* (166) as 'a flashing panorama of illuminated oblong pictures' points to an experience of the panorama as a show on its own, the instructive kind of panorama which enlarged its viewers' knowledge of foreign places and events (for example, the Siege of Paris). So too does the 'little moral panorama' which on the eve of Waterloo the Spirit Ironic presents before Napoleon, consisting as it does of 'hundreds of thousands of skeletons and corpses' which rise from his various battlefields and gaze reproachfully at him, led by the Duke of Enghien 'as showman'. Shortly afterwards, however, in a scene 'on the road to Waterloo' (3. vi. viii), the panorama functions as a stage device: 'The focus of the scene follows the retreating English army, the highway and its margins panoramically gliding past the vision of the spectator.' In these and other instances, such as 'the panoramic glide of the stars past earthly objects' (*FFMC*, 47), it is movement that is stressed. They suggest that Hardy appreciated the panorama as a moving picture. In its theatrical application he probably appreciated the simultaneous enlargement of the fields of vision and of action that it made possible.

The magic-lantern show, with its painted and moving slides, also provided Hardy with expressive images. These may be of external Nature merely, as when 'the cold clouds hastened on in a body, as if painted on a moving slide' (*RN*, 224). Or they may help to define mental or emotional experience. Giles Winterborne, as the lease of his house runs out, is said to feel that

things are slipping away from him 'as if they were painted on
a magic-lantern slide'. Jude, at the moment the missile thrown
by Arabella strikes him, is preoccupied with dreams of Christminster
and 'looking at the ground as though the future were thrown
thereon by a magic lantern'. In both these instances the mind
operates as its own projector. Later, in *The Dynasts* (I. IV. v),
the lantern becomes emblematic of the predetermined nature of
existence. Napoleon is said to be

> Moved like a figure on a lantern-slide,
> Which, much amazing uninitiate eyes,
> The all-compelling crystal pane but drags
> Whither the showman wills.

In this scene from *The Dynasts* the Spirit Ironic, taking up the
image introduced by the Years, speaks of 'your phantasmagoric
show'. Again, the choice of phrase is precise: 'phantasmagoria'
was the name invented in 1802 by a certain Philipsthal for an
exhibition of optical illusions. Philipsthal 'exhibited on a transparent
screen at the Lyceum representations "in a dark scene" of apparitions
and spectres which appeared to advance or recede . . . by means
of lenses and concave reflectors'.[1] Hardy uses the word in this
precise sense elsewhere, when he writes of Eustacia crossing the
firebeams coming from Susan Nunsuch's open door: 'She appeared
for an instant as distinct as a figure in a phantasmagoria – a creature
of light surrounded by an area of darkness.' It seems likely, therefore,
that when later in *The Dynasts* the Years refers to the Victoria
festival at Vauxhall Gardens as 'this phantasmagoria', and even
when Hardy himself speaks, in his essay 'The Science of Fiction',
of 'the phantasmagoria of experience',[2] the original meaning of
the word rather than our more generalised sense simply of a collection
of images is again present. In any case, the Spirit Ironic's use
of the phrase itself invites us to see the spectacle of *The Dynasts*
as such a show.

The exchanges between the Spirit of the Years and the Spirit
Ironic concerning the phantasmagoric show culminate in the Pities'
cry,

> But, O, the intolerable antilogy
> Of making figments feel!

The full significance of the magic-lantern analogy is here established. In their unreality no less than in their predetermined actions, its 'painted shapes' mirror the condition of man. Man himself is, like his own dwindling idea of God,

> One thin as a phasm on a lantern-slide
> Shown forth in the dark upon some dim sheet,
> And by none but its showman vivified.

('A Plaint to Man')

If the magic-lantern show is an optical illusion, so too is life.

The affinity between Hardy's art and that of the film derives, therefore, in the first place from his vision of life. It is a matter of ontology, not simply of technique. For Hardy life is a *cinema mundi* even more than it is a *theatrum mundi*: neither the phrase nor the object of reference is available to him, but the idea is. When he describes Eustacia as 'a creature of light surrounded by an area of darkness', he is describing all living things: the image is repeated in a different form in the gnats which in *Tess of the d'Urbervilles* (229) have their brief moment of irradiation and are gone. But creatures of light surrounded by an area of darkness are exactly what the figures on the cinema screen are, as we watch them from a darkened auditorium. Stripped of metaphor Hardy's view of life is that of a 'brief transit through a sorry world', a phrase he liked well enough to use twice, at the end of *The Mayor of Casterbridge*, and in the Preface to *The Woodlanders*: again the idea of the 'brief transit' may suggest the motion-picture, especially if we associate it with other expressions, such as 'the transit of her form across the field of his vision' and 'that little space in which I flitted across the field of your vision', both from *The Woodlanders* (149, 214). Figments that feel are also more completely approximated by the figures of the cinema screen than by those of the stage. 'Life's but a walking shadow, a poor player', says Macbeth, but the player himself, insubstantial as he may be in essence, appears before us in all his substance. On the screen we see for ourselves the walking shadow – this is indeed a galanty-show or shadow drama.

The cinema screen is also suggested, although in miniature form, so miniature in fact that the television screen perhaps furnishes a more exact comparison, in Hardy's account of the dicing-match between Venn and Wildeve in the darkness of Egdon Heath. 'A complete diorama of the fluctuations of the game went on in their eyes', he writes, adding, 'A diminutive candle-flame was mirrored in each pupil, and it would have been possible to distinguish therein between the moods of hope and the moods of abandonment.' The diorama, like the panorama, existed in the nineteenth century both as a show in its own right and as a device employed in stage-plays to achieve quite complex effects of movement and lighting. Hardy's image clearly refers to the former – to the diorama considered as an exhibition of pictures, illuminated and viewed through an opening in a darkened chamber. By varying the amount of illumination and the angle from which it came, effects of changing light – moonlight, sunshine and shadow – and passing time were created. Hardy's application of the idea is again careful and exact, and again, as in his allusion to the phantasmagoria, the vision suggested is one of light and movement set against a surrounding darkness. So, in *The Dynasts* when the Pities speak of the Confederacy of Napoleon's enemies after Tilsit dissolving 'like the diorama of a dream' (2. I. vii), it is the fluctuating images of dream that are suggested. Gabriel Oak experienced a waking dream of the same order when 'beneath the screen of closed eyelids' he was 'busy with fancies, and full of movement, like a river flowing rapidly under its ice' (*FFMC*, 101). In both these instances Hardy is describing what is in effect a mental equivalent of the motion-picture show.

The individual's preoccupation with his own mental images, whether dreaming or awake, is a central theme of Hardy's. Repeatedly in his novels the outer world recedes while a character contemplates some inner scene: Dick Dewy driving homeward 'with the inner eye of reflection so anxiously set on his passage at arms with Fancy that the road and scenery were as a thin mist over the real pictures of his mind' (*UGWT*, 117); Christopher Julian, who, accompanied everywhere by a sublimated image of Ethelberta, 'would stand and look fixedly at a frog in a shady pool, and never once think of batrachians' (*HE*, 313); Melbury, seeing only 'a tragic vision that travelled with him like an envelope', through which 'the incidents of the moment but gleamed confusedly here and there' (*W*, 248). Absent-mindedness, it would seem, is almost an occupational disease of Hardy's characters, and one that they have caught from their creator: poems such as 'The Self-Unseeing', 'The Self-Unconscious', 'In a Seaside Town in 1869', 'In Front of the Landscape', 'The House of Silence' express the same experience, regretfully, defiantly, or even triumphantly. The mental images thus projected recall the cinema screen in a variety of ways. There is, first, the isolation of the image: like the spectator of a film, the Hardy character is alone with his vision, the world around him temporarily blotted out. His gaze, like that of the spectator, is sharply concentrated and focused. (Melbury's 'envelope' even brings us close to the portable television set.) Hardy's inclination to see such images as pictures or shows increases the resemblance. Jude, we remember, seemed to see his visions of Christminster thrown upon the ground as from a magic lantern. His are visions of the future: in *Under the Greenwood Tree* (48–9) Michael Mail, commenting on the changed times, is said to be 'regarding nobody can tell what interesting old panoramas with an inward eye, and letting his outward glance rest on the ground because it was as convenient a position as any'. The 'panoramas' here are once more not simply wide views; they are moving-picture shows, unrolling before the inward eye. In the poem 'The Flirt's Tragedy', the 'spent flames' project images onto the wainscot. The sense that an old film is being played over is here strong:

> Here alone by the logs in my chamber,
>   Deserted, decrepit –
> Spent flames limning ghosts on the wainscot
>   Of friends I once knew –
>
> My drama and hers begins weirdly
>   Its dumb re-enactment,
> Each scene, sigh, and circumstance passing
>   In spectral review.

Many such old films were stored in Hardy's own memory; or perhaps, rather, his memory itself was the film on which were preserved the images of the past, ready to appear again before 'the intenser / Stare of the mind' (*CP*, 304). And, when they do so, his present surroundings are dimmed: these images are 're-creations killing the daytime / As by the night' (*CP*, 303), and he is one

>   to whom these things
> That nobody else's mind calls back,
> Have a savour that scenes in being lack,
> And a presence more than the actual brings.
>
>   (*CP*, 353)

Most compellingly cinematic in character is the poem 'The Phantom
Horsewoman', in which the 'ghost-girl rider' of his vision endlessly
repeats the same actions, like the jockey repeatedly leaping the
same fence before the old Gaumont British News series or the
Metro-Goldwyn-Mayer lion forever turning its head majestically
as its roar dies away:

> But she still rides gaily
> In his rapt thought
> On that shagged and shaly
> Atlantic spot,
> And as when first eyed
Draws rein and sings to the swing of the tide.

The stress on action in most of these 'memoried scenes' – the 'girlish
form' and he climbing the road in 'At Castle Boterel'; hands 'in
play' on the knobs of 'Old Furniture'; fingers dancing on a viol;
a *procession* of dead days – increases the resemblance to the motion-
picture.

Like his horsewoman, most of Hardy's images are phantoms.
This does not mean that they are spirits: rather they are bodiless
imprints of once embodied forms, brought into existence by the
mind of the observer. But so too are the images of the cinema –
equally, or almost equally, thin and bodiless, yet bearing the same
relation to actual pre-existent or still existent bodies as Hardy's
phantoms bear. 'The photographic image is the object itself', says
André Bazin, 'the object freed from the conditions of time and
space that govern it.'[3] This is the condition of Hardy's horsewoman:
'Time touches her not!' We know 'things existent' – people and
objects – by seeing them, and it is by retaining what we have
seen that we are able to prolong that existence in the phantom
state. It is our gaze that takes the shot; in the familiar phrase,
'I am a camera.' By this means we ourselves are able to confer
or withhold immortality. Hardy makes this point in his two poems
'Her Immortality' and 'His Immortality'.

This recognition that the mental image shares a continuing identity
with its object, allowing it to be present for the observer in an
arrested 'moment of vision', changed in substance but not in being – a
true presence, that is, not a representation such as a painted portrait
is – again suggests the ontological nature of the affinity between
Hardy's art and that of cinema.[4] Hardy's sense of the life mysteriously

indwelling in the photographic image comes out in his poem 'The Son's Portrait', in which a mother buries the photograph of her dead son; and still more in the rather unpleasant poem 'The Photograph' – unpleasant because of the very vividness, amounting almost to relish, with which he expresses his feeling that in burning the photograph of a woman he is burning *her*. Averting his eyes as he sees the flames gnawing 'at the delicate bosom's defenceless round', he is compelled, presumably by fascination, to look again, and watches 'furtivewise / Till the flame had eaten her breasts, and mouth, and hair', when he exclaims, 'Thank God, she is out of it now!'

Other examples of this still-continuing identity between image and object are the shadow, and the reflection in a mirror. Hardy's poem 'The Whitewashed Wall' turns on this characteristic of the shadow. It is a touching account of how a mother habitually kisses her hand to a spot in the chimney-corner where under the whitewash lies the portrait of her son, traced in pencil around the shadow he once cast there:

But she knows he's there. And when she yearns
    For him, deep in the labouring night,
She sees him as close at hand, and turns
    To him under his sheet of white.

As for reflections, judging by the number of times images seen in mirrors or in window-panes functioning as mirrors occur in Hardy's lyrics and novels, they are a minor obsession of his. In the poem 'The Cheval-Glass' the glass is represented as perpetuating the images it has once held. It has been bought by and now stands by the bed of the disappointed lover of the parson's daughter to whom it once belonged:

There by my bed it stands,
    And as the dawn expands
Often I see her pale-faced form there
    Brushing her hair's bright bands.

There, too, at pallid midnight moments
    Quick she will come to my call,
    Smile from the frame withal
Ponderingly, as she used to regard me
    Passing her father's wall.

This irresistibly suggests the private picture-show: in the words of the popular song,

> I would give ten shows a day
> And a midnight matinée,
> If I had a talking picture of you.

We may also be reminded of the magic 'Mirror, mirror on the wall' of the Snow-white story, and there are indeed often hints of magic in Hardy's 'envisionings'. The conjecture in 'The Photograph' that, if the woman is still living, she may have felt a smart of anguish at the burning, introduces an idea of sympathetic magic similar to that involved in Susan Nunsuch's practices against Eustacia. More usually the magic is of the kind that raises phantoms, as in the poem 'Louie', for example. In the mysterious House of Silence 'figures dance to a mind with sight' – the poet is here a *magus*. The source of the magic is consciousness itself, the mind's own self-enclosed powers of perception and reflection:

> That mirror
> Which makes of men a transparency,
> Who hold that mirror
> And bids us such a breast-bare spectacle see
> Of you and me?

('Moments of Vision')

The 'all-compelling crystal pane' is, it seems, also a crystal ball. The lantern is truly a magic one.

For André Bazin the art of the cinema resembles that of the ancient Egyptians, which existed 'in a sphere of magical reality', and it does so because of the 'existential bond between fact and image, world and film'.[5] In Hardy's world of images it is the magic of consciousness that creates and maintains this bond. But there is also another kind of 'camera magic', the magic deliberately created by the magician or conjuror, or by a skilful cameraman or director. One of the pioneers in this kind of magic was Georges Méliès: in the early years of the cinema he and others amazed audiences with their visual fantasies – heads expanding and blowing up, buildings flying through the air, flowers growing and blossoming in a moment. These fantasies had had their forerunner in the strange permutations and combinations achieved by the magic lantern – different heads appearing on the same body; noses lengthening, faces changing, a fish or chicken reversing the order of nature by eating a man. The world of the pre-cinema had also had the ability, by means of the diorama and stereopticon (a double magic lantern), to show views dissolving, and thus to suggest the passage of time. Méliès himself was to develop the 'dissolve' and the 'fade-in' and to use them to assist his magical effects.

Hardy's inner vision similarly plays tricks with time and space. The poem 'The Head above the Fog' has a Méliès-like strangeness:

> Mere ghostly head it skims along,
> Just as it did when warm and strong,
>   Body seeming gone.

In other poems memory, longing, dreams, foreknowledge, Time itself superimpose one disparate image on another in a manner reminiscent equally of the magic lantern and of motion-picture devices. In poems such as 'St Launce's Revisited', 'The Man who Forgot', 'The Second Visit', past and present are in this way juxtaposed. In 'The Old Neighbour and the New' the speaker calls on the new rector but sees the old one still there:

> And on leaving I scarcely remember
>   Which neighbour to-day I have seen,
> The one carried out in September,
>   Or him who but entered yestreen.

The poem 'The Dream-Follower' employs dream to bring to the lover through the window-panes (which here operate like a 'transparency') a vision of the beloved as she really is – 'but a thing of flesh and bone / Speeding on to its cleft in the clay'. 'At the Dinner-Table' uses the distorting mirror, a device akin to the magic lantern in the bizarre effects it could produce, to make the same point: the speaker sees herself in the mirror as a 'haggard crone' and fifty years later sees the same image in the ordinary sideboard-glass which the other had temporarily covered.

In Hardy's poems the 'mind with sight' focuses, as both camera and observer, chiefly upon its inner visions. The figures that dance for it (as described in 'The House of Silence') have an animation and an emancipation from time and space which recall at times the world of Walt Disney. 'A Merrymaking in Question', with its 'headstones all ranged up as dancers', its 'cypresses droning a croon / And gurgoyles that mouthed to the tune', is literally a Silly Symphony. The delightful 'In the Small Hours' turns the poet himself into a Disney-type figure, a Gulliver or Snow-white, and creates a perfect piece of film magic, which, as the poet lies in his bed and fiddles 'with a dreamland viol and bow', brings 'figures of jigging fieldfolk' crossing 'the chamber in the gray':

Yea, up and down the middle
In windless whirls went they!

'Wagtail and Baby' too would translate easily and effectively into Disney-cartoon terms: it is a complete visual statement, clear and simple in outline. The strange poem 'The Pedigree', in which the branches of the family tree which the poet is studying seem to twist into 'a seared and cynic face', simultaneously recalls the dissolve of film fantasy, the distortions of some magic-lantern shows, and the transformations of the harlequinade.

Hardy's memory and vision in his poems fasten tenaciously upon the image, following it everywhere. His mode of expression consequently often acquires a cinematic character. 'Time, with its restless scene on scene' ('Every Artemisia') provides the scenario, but the shooting, cutting and editing are the work of vision and memory. It is they who choose, vary, or manipulate the viewpoint so as to embody the changing perspectives of time and space. In 'The Five Students' the actors move through both time and space straight into the eye of the camera, as it were. This poem begins with a close-up ('The sparrow dips in his wheel-rut bath') as typically cinematic as that opening of Dickens's *The Cricket on the Hearth* ('The kettle began it'), cited by Eisenstein to illustrate the direct links between Dickens and the 'American film esthetic' exemplified in the work of D. W. Griffith.[6] 'The Interloper' is another poem which seems distinctly filmic, both in its changing scenes and in its firm placing of the observer outside the scene ('I view them . . .', 'Next / A dwelling appears . . .'). Its opening lines set before us the chaise and its occupants and their surroundings –

There are three folk driving in a quaint old chaise,
And the cliff-side track looks green and fair;
I view them talking in quiet glee

As they drop down towards the puffins' lair
   By the roughest of ways;
But another with the three rides on, I see,
   Whom I like not to be there!

– in a manner familiar to film audiences. (One thinks of Ford's *Stagecoach* or Lang's *Moonfleet*.) Other poems – for example, 'During Wind and Rain' – employ montage-like juxtapositions. In 'Under the Waterfall' especially, in which the speaker describes how the act of plunging her arm in a bowl of water brings back to her the feel of a particular day of long ago, a striking piece of montage is created, dissolving the present into the past:

The basin seems the pool, and its edge
The hard smooth face of the brook-side ledge,
And the leafy pattern of china-ware
The hanging plants that were bathing there.

Finally, in 'A Man Was Drawing Near to Me' the presentation of the action from the speaker's viewpoint ('A man was riding up my way', 'The man had passed Tresparret Posts', 'The man was getting nigh and nigher') achieves an effect remarkably reminiscent of the cross-cutting by which the film hero in the old silent films was seen rushing to the rescue of the endangered heroine (as perhaps in a sense 'the man' was doing here, since this is Hardy riding towards his first meeting with Emma Gifford).

Such parallels with developed film techniques are common in the poems, whether the poems are lyrical and personal, or narrative and dramatic. But where narrative and drama are concerned, the main area of investigation must clearly be the novels and *The Dynasts*.

II

The cinematic nature of *The Dynasts* is self-evident and unmistakable. It is not merely a matter of its reminding us of the cinema: the cinema may also remind us of it. Robert Richardson in his *Literature and Film* asserts a direct indebtedness on the part of cinema to nineteenth-century closet drama, the cinematic character of which he sees as reaching its highest development in *The Dynasts*.[7] D. W. Griffith's influential *Birth of a Nation* (1915) shows, he suggests, a striking resemblance to Hardy's work. This could also be said of Olivier's *Henry V*: here the opening of the film, with its panoramic view of London and the Thames including the Globe Theatre and its flag, all seen from above, followed by the slow descent of the camera to the theatre itself, is strongly reminiscent of *The Dynasts*: we might be in the presence of the Phantoms themselves. Quite apart from the camerawork, there is a reminder of the Phantoms in the comments of the Chorus, which suggests in its turn that Hardy's creation of them may owe something to Shakespeare's play. The extent to which the combination of an 'Overworld' viewpoint with the use of a Chorus imparts a *Dynasts*-like character to Olivier's film is seen by comparing it with Sergei Bondarchuk's *Waterloo* (1970). This, employing the same material as Hardy's work and incidentally achieving some similar visual effects, seems nevertheless to belong to a different dimension, since it lacks the 'Overworld' framework.

Point of view is of paramount importance in *The Dynasts*.. Essentially the work is a dramatisation of a freely-ranging, mobile point of view, and in both senses of the phrase – with reference, that is, to physical sight and, within limits, to mental sight also. Whatever claims to greatness it has arise from this. Much of the dialogue and even some of the action may be unmemorable, but the vision – of this particular spectacle and of the human condition which it symbolises – is unforgettable. Seeing and feeling determine the character and shape of the work, to a large extent through the observations (again in both senses) of the Spirits. Indispensable as the Spirits are, however, the 'stage directions', which establish their, and our, point of view are still more important. Without them, and without the dialogue of the Spirits, the work would shrink to a fairly commonplace historical drama. Yet it is the stage directions above all that make it clear that this is a play that could be played on no ordinary stage. Theatre, in other words, here expands into cinema, and the directions are those not of a playwright or play-producer, but rather of a scriptwriter or film-director. Hardy here uses vision as if it were a camera, and in a strikingly flexible and sophisticated fashion.

Like the film-director, he has control of time and space. He acknowledges this freedom: the Spirits in the 'Fore Scene' announce

We'll close up Time, as a bird its van,
We'll traverse Space, as spirits can,
Link pulses severed by leagues and years,
Bring cradles into touch with biers;
So that the far-off Consequence appears
Prompt at the heel of foregone Cause.

Later they speak of 'our migratory Proskenion' (1. II. i), and again,
after Salamanca (3. I. iii):

What are Space and Time? A fancy! –
Lo, by Vision's necromancy
Muscovy will now unroll.

'Vision's necromancy' – the phrase provides a good alternative to
'camera magic'. 'Unroll', while looking back to the moving panorama, also looks forward to the film-reel. Movement is stressed
in all three passages: it is freedom of movement that shapes Hardy's
drama, as it does a film. As director, Hardy 'cuts' from scene
to scene, using techniques akin to those of the motion-picture camera.
   These techniques are immediately recognisable. Best remembered
probably are the wide, panoramic, aerial views, with their 'Dumb
Shows' of armies or other processions looking like cheese-mites,
a caterpillar, or 'a file of ants crawling along a strip of garden-mat-
ting', and other minutiae. With 'shots' like these the 'point of
sight' is, as Hardy says, 'withdrawn high into the air' (2. V. v).
Shots from above are Hardy's characteristic way of introducing
an action, but the length of the shot varies considerably. They
may be 'bird's-eye' without being quite so high as in the examples
given; or they may simply be from elevated ground, as when
for instance the Field of Austerlitz is viewed 'from the elevated
position of the Emperor's bivouac'. In his descriptions of the scenes
thus brought under observation Hardy often creates a sense of
deep perspective – for example, at the Field of Ligny (3. VI. v) or
on the Road to Waterloo (3. VI. viii). This, of course, is partly
because he is creating pictures. But they are pictures with movement
in them; hence truly 'motion-pictures'. People move up into the
middle distance or foreground, or alternatively recede and diminish.
The impression that they are moving straight into the camera
is very marked in Hardy's presentation of the retreat from Moscow
(3. I. ix). The point of observation is 'high amongst the clouds',

but, instead of the descriptive Dumb Show usually employed on such occasions, the episode is created for us by the comments of the Spirits. The scene is empty at first, a mere 'wild waste'. Then on the 'far land-verge there / Labouring from eastward toward our longitude' appears 'an object like a dun-piled caterpillar', which the Years identifies as the once Grand Army. It 'creeps laboriously nearer' until finally 'the whole miscellany arrives at the foreground'. 'Nearer' means nearer to the onlookers, high in the clouds though they are; nearer, that is, not to a specific place but to a point of observation – the equivalent of the camera. When the 'whole miscellany' reaches the foreground, they seem, although Hardy does not say so, to fill the picture, just as in the cinema they would fill the screen. The scene in the 'ballroom in the house of Cambacérès' (2. v. i) ends in rather similar fashion as 'The maskers surge into the foreground of the scene.' The action of the maskers itself anticipates a familiar effect in the Hollywood musical.

The episode, or sequence of shots, relating to the retreat from Moscow ends with the statement 'The point of vision descends to earth, close to the scene of action.' This happens many times in *The Dynasts*, and corresponds of course to the camera's moving in for a different type of shot. As in a film, it is not only the actors who move: the observer – the camera-eye itself – moves as well. Expressions such as 'the arid, unenclosed, and treeless plain swept by the eye' (2. ii. iv), or 'the vision swoops over the ocean and its coast-lines' (2. ii. v) create the actual sensation of this.

At Napoleon's escape from Leipzig (3. iii. v) his progress is tracked for us by a citizen 'at an upper window':

He is already at the garden-end;
Now he has passed out to the river-brim,
And plods along it towards the Ranstädt Gate. . . .

                                    He mounts,
And hurries through the arch. . . . Again I see him –
Now he's upon the causeway in the marsh;
Now rides across the bridge of Lindenau . . .
And now, among the troops that choke the road
I lose all sight of him.

This is a method Hardy often adopts. Like the good film-director, he frequently shows us the action through the eyes of a personage in the drama. Naturally, this often happens on the battlefield, where as in a film our double involvement, with observer and observed, intensifies the interest. Napoleon at Austerlitz, watching 'with a vulpine smile' as the ice on the Satschan lake breaks beneath the weight of the fleeing Russians, is one example that springs to mind. The citizen of Leipzig, being of no significance, is merely an embodied camera (as the Phantoms, in respect of their seeing merely, are a disembodied one), but Napoleon, Wellington and the other generals watching Waterloo both focus our attention and are themselves focuses of it.

The closures of Hardy's scenes are as cinematic as their openings. He repeatedly employs the elements (clouds, mist, rain, 'murk'), often combined with a receding 'shot', to create what are undoubtedly 'fades' or 'dissolves'. He often uses the words themselves, as in the statement, 'The silent insect-creep of the Austrian columns towards the banks of the Inn continues to be seen till the view fades to nebulousness and dissolves' (1. III. ii). Mist and haze frequently suggest the blur or soft-focus of the screen. Other elements are used with all the flare of an artistically-minded film-director to fade the scene dramatically and picturesquely: Rainbarrow seeming to become involved in the smoke from the beacon and slowly disappearing (1. II. v); the 'folds of smoke' wrapping the various scenes at Trafalgar as 'the point of view changes'; or, on a road in Spain, shortly before the battle of Corunna, the direction, 'The characters disperse, the fire sinks, and snowflakes and darkness blot out all' (2. III. ii). At times an effect akin to the 'dissolve', with one scene fading out as another fades in, seems aimed at, as in the statement, 'The point of view shifts across the Channel, the Boulogne cliffs sinking behind the water-line' (1. II. iii), or in 'The beholder finds himself, as it were, caught up on high, and while the Vauxhall scene still dimly twinkles below, he gazes southward towards Central Europe . . .' (3. II. iv).

The last quotation introduces an episode that is of interest on another account. Hardy here makes use of 'Vision's necromancy' to convey information in a stylised and symbolic fashion later to become a common device of the film-maker. 'Something broad-faced / Flat-folded, parchment-pale, and in its shape / Rectangular' is seen moving like a cloud from Vienna to Dresden. It is eventually seen to be a letter, 'magically' enlarged in size; it is Austria's declaration of war against Napoleon. Olivier uses a strikingly similar device in *Henry V*, when the pages of Shakespeare's play are seen floating over London. Other instances of Hardy's exploiting his medium in a suggestively cinematic way include the receding view of Milan Cathedral in which it 'smalls' and becomes 'like a rare, delicately carved alabaster ornament' (1.1.vi), and, at the end of the scene in which the palace of Godoy, the Queen of Spain's lover, is ransacked by the mob, the musical box which, swept off a table, starts playing a serenade as it falls to the floor and continues to play after the mob has left, while 'the taper burns to its socket, and the room becomes wrapt in the shades of night' (2.ii.ii). Visually this recalls such film-endings as that in *The Third Man*, with the fingers waving like the stunted trees of no-man's-land from the man-hole cover.

Nor should Hardy's effective use of sound be forgotten. This too is often in the manner of the film-maker. Natural sounds are used to enhance 'visuals' in many of the 'fades'. The musical-box just noticed is one example: another is the 'sputtering of the green wood fires' on the night before Borodino, which when the human tongues are still 'seem to hold a conversation of their own'. Hardy has also the good film-director's ear for the apparently irrelevant but significant sound – significant, often, for its power to establish the reality of a scene, or for its poignant commentary on it. Such sounds are the gusts 'calling' into the chimney and raindrops spitting on the floor as the Austrians debate their strategy before Ulm, or the 'soft hiss of the rain that falls impartially on both the sleeping armies' before Waterloo. Naturally too he uses the sounds of battle extensively, including 'the moans of men and the shriek of horses'. Many of the Dumb Shows become in this way not completely dumb. At the opening of Bondarchuk's *War and Peace* (1968) the shriek of horses similarly provided an unforgettably poignant accompaniment to the camera's movement over the vast, empty Russian landscape.

The Dynasts provides, therefore, a remarkable example of verbal cinema. It cannot, however, be characterised wholly in this way. Hypnotic as for long stretches may be our sense that we are watching a verbal-cinema show, our final impression, I would suggest, is rather more complex. The work is a hybrid, or perhaps a chrysalis: looked at in one way, it appears to be a stage-play in process of metamorphosis into a screen-play; looked at in another, as a screen-play still girded in to the limits of the stage. Paradoxically, this is in part due to those very panoramic views which do so much to establish its cinematic character. In any particular scene our downward gaze may seem to be directed by a camera, or its verbal equivalent, but taking the work as a whole the impression is, rather, of looking down upon a cockpit, hence a fixed stage. 'Can this cockpit hold / The vasty fields of France?', Shakespeare's Chorus doubtingly asks. But the insistent message of *The Dynasts* seems to be that the vasty fields of Europe are indeed no more than a cockpit. The introduction of the Spirits and their Overworld, together with their commentary, which persistently reduces the human actors to mere 'mannikins', sinks the message deep in our consciousness, so that although the human action often, so to speak, fills the screen, our experience of it can never be quite the same as, say, our experience of a Cecil B. De Mille spectacular: we have been too thoroughly conditioned to see the mannikin in the man, the cockpit in the vasty field, for that.

Although, moreover, the Spirits' role as watchers often corresponds to that of the camera lens, it does not invariably do so, and the prevailing impression they create is, rather, that of a theatre audience, discussing the play between, or sometimes during, the acts. The question of the Spirits' point of view, especially considered in relation to our own, is in fact a complex one. Do we watch the action *with* them? One assumes that Hardy intends this, yet, if so, they are for a theatre audience unusually peripatetic. When in the Fore Scene they move 'to the precinct', counting 'as framework to the stagery / Yon architraves of sunbeam-smitten cloud', they appear to be settling comfortably in the front row of the circle, but this is not so. Already by the end of the first scene they are on the move:

> To the drama, then.
> Emprizes over-Channel are the key
> To this land's stir and ferment. – Thither we.

The hybrid or evolving character of the work is thus epitomised in the double function of the Spirits, as theatre audience and moving camera. (They have, says the Years, the 'great gift' of 'the free trajection of our entities'.) Yet there are times when their position, whether fixed or unfixed, remains unclear. For instance, Part Second, Act III, scene one, opens with the statement 'The eye of the spectator rakes the road from the interior of a cellar which opens upon it.' This is imaginatively cinematic, as cinematic as Hardy's idea that, if he were a painter, he would paint a

picture of a room as viewed by a mouse from a chink under
the skirting. (*Life*, 235. Walt Disney, and Sir Frederick Ashton's
The Tales of Beatrix Potter, have accustomed cinema-audiences to
this view.) But are the Spirits really the mouse here? They speak
only once, and at the end of the scene. Are we to think of them
as within the cellar, or up in the air? Or as, on this occasion,
voices merely? Elsewhere they are silent for quite long periods.
For five scenes, for example, from the opening of the scene before
Corunna (2. III. iii) to the Field of Talavera (2. IV. iv), they are
apparently off duty. The sense of a camera-eye is still maintained,
however: on the Island of Lobau before Wagram our gaze is
directed by the author–observer himself; and at Wagram we view
the action through the field-glasses of the Emperor Francis and
his staff. But there are other scenes, in the dramatisation of Waterloo
especially, for which no 'point of view' at all is created, either
of the Spirits or of anyone else. The Brussels Ball is a striking
example. Another is the scene in Napoleon's quarters at Charleroi
immediately following that, which opens 'The same midnight.
NAPOLEON is lying on a bed in his clothes. In consultation with
SOULT, his Chief of Staff, who is sitting near, he dictates to his
Secretary orders for the morrow.' These are purely stage-directions.
The scene confronts the spectator–reader directly: there is no intermediary. It is theatre rather than cinema.

The drawing of stage-curtains from time to time also acts as
a brake upon the cinematic fluidity, imposing on it at such points
the circumscribed character of the theatre. 'The sun sets, and the
curtain falls'; 'The Dumb Show ends and the curtain draws':
such statements as these momentarily arrest the flow, bringing us
out of our waking dream, or at least changing its character, making
us feel ourselves to be not cinema-goers caught up by the power
of vision into a continuum, but rather members of a theatre audience,
watching a defined spectacle. Indoor scenes especially invite this
contraction. Thus, towards the end of the scene in the Tuileries
at the time of Napoleon's flight (3. IV. ii), we read, 'The curtain
falls for an interval. When it rises again the apartment is in darkness,
and its atmosphere chilly . . . .' The make-believe of theatrical performance is here very pronounced: the phrase 'for an interval' sets
the reader almost metaphysical problems of time to solve, since
it places him in three different time-streams: his own; that of
the imaginary theatre; and that within the drama itself.

At other times, Hardy's habit of using cloud, mist and suchlike to close a scene merges theatre with cinema. 'Draw down the curtain, then', orders the Spirit of the Years, whereupon 'Clouds close over the perspective' (2. 1. ii). The curtain has become a typical 'fade'. Conversely there are occasions when scenes 'open' or walls become transparent (at the Guildhall, Carlton House, the Brighton Assembly Rooms, for example) in ways which may suggest the cinema's 'necromancy', but which are probably to be related rather to theatrical devices, such as the transparency gauze.

The dramatic techniques Hardy adopts in this work are indeed many and various. In exploiting a freedom which the Victorian theatre aspired to without being able fully to attain, he transcended (within his verbal medium) the limits of the stage and anticipated cinema. Yet, if he went beyond it, it was the theatre which pointed the way. His Dumb Shows and panoramas, for instance, source of some of our strongest 'cinematic' impressions, are technically to be related to the moving panoramas and dioramas of the stage. If *The Dynasts* looks forward to *The Birth of a Nation*, it also looks back to the representations of Waterloo and other combats staged at Hardy's beloved Astley's.

The Spirits also by their commentary present a view of the 'play' which partly confirms our idea of it as cinema, but also partly reduces it. In their phrase 'Vision's necromancy' they assert (without knowing it) the cinematic approach. Their allusions to lantern-slides, phantasmagoria, diorama are consistent with this, although these are of course only rudimentary forms of cinema (or moving picture). But the central image they offer us is that of the clockwork toy. In their eyes this is a show performed by automata, 'earth's jackaclocks', 'homuncules', resembling those toys of the period ('Things mechanized / By coils and pivots set to fore-framed codes') in which the figures danced, fought, ran up and down stairs and did many other wonderful things, provided someone 'turned the handle of [the] idle show'. By means of transparencies they, and we with them, are allowed occasionally to see the inner workings, the mechanics of this particular show. Cinema too has its mechanics, of course, and we should experience the same shock of disillusion were we to visit a film set. But the image of life presented by the clockwork toy is very different from that presented on the screen. The Spirits' insistence on this image seems to me to have a reductive effect on our view of *The Dynasts* as cinema. It cannot erase our own impression of the work, but it modifies it (being itself part of that impression).

III

In Hardy's novels also, theatrical and cinematic modes are closely intermingled. Although, however, as we saw in the last chapter, Hardy creates a strong sense of theatre here through the use of theatrical forms and conventions, he does not, as in *The Dynasts*, deliberately simulate theatrical performance. There is therefore not the same tension between the two modes, nor the same sense of expansion (the 'free trajection') and recoil, and the novels consequently seem even more completely cinematic than the drama. Their cinematic qualities have of course been long acknowledged: David Cecil examined Hardy's visualising techniques from this point of view in his *Hardy the Novelist* (1942); more recently (1974) there has been an excellent article on the subject by David Lodge.[8]

Both writers very properly relate the resemblance first of all to the primacy of visual presentation in Hardy: like the film-maker, whose art is essentially a narrative one, he tells his story in a succession of scenes and pictures. But David Lodge also recognises in such visualisation a way of interpreting, not simply of presenting, experience. Quite correctly in my opinion, he questions J. Hillis Miller's argument that Hardy's use of 'specified and unspecified observers' arose out of his unconscious wish to escape involvement, and suggests instead that it demonstrates the importance he attaches to visual perspective. He quotes Alan Spiegel's statement that cinematic approaches to narrative material occur in the novel when the novelist is impelled 'not only to see his object, but at the same time to see the way that it is seen; to render the meaning of the seen object itself as inseparable from the seer's position in time and space'.[9] Since much of my first chapter was devoted to demonstrating the centrality to Hardy's art of precisely this endeavour, it will be clear that I endorse this view. To be seen is to be: Hardy's presentation of his creations as not simply objects of sight but objects *seen* ensures their existence: someone is around in the quad, and they therefore can continue to be. When the 'someone' is the unseen observer, he corresponds to the camera lens, mediating between us and the object of sight. When he is another person in the story (or a natural creature) he corresponds not to the lens itself but rather to the numerous watchers who direct our sight on film. Film is unimaginable without its internal watching – secret, suspicious, tense, enquiring, as the case may be. So too with Hardy. The existence of watchers, within and without the story, is a more important link between his novels and film than is the simple fact of visualisation as such.

Rather than informing us directly, Hardy prefers, says David Lodge, 'to enact the process by which we interpret visual information'. Thus, instead of telling us that Captain Vye, retired, walked on Egdon Heath, he states, 'Along the road walked an old man'; then, after giving details of his attire, 'One would have said that he had been, in his day, a naval officer of some sort or other.' The omniscient author, we might say, is masquerading as the innocent eye, thus ensuring the innocence of our own vision. The process is repeated in Hardy's treatment of the characters' visual experiences. Thus, in the passage under discussion from *The Return of the Native*, we next read that the old man 'at length discerned, a long distance in front of him, a moving spot, which appeared to be a vehicle', and it is only when he draws near to it that it is perceived to be a spring van, lurid red in colour. By such means we are made to share in the visual experience itself. Hardy repeatedly uses this method of presentation, even when no desire to arouse curiosity (as here) is apparent. 'She saw an oblong shape – it was a brougham' (*HE*, 380). Hardy could have said, as most writers would, 'She saw a brougham', but that, although it would have given us the same information, would not have communicated Ethelberta's visual experience. Similarly, Christopher Julian returns home to find not Faith, but 'the quaint figure of Faith' kneeling on the hearthrug (*HE*, 158), and Diggory Venn sees 'the form of Mrs Yeobright slowly walking towards the Quiet Woman' (*RN*, 117). Sometimes a character even speaks of his experience in this way. Thus in *Two on a Tower* (192) Lady Constantine's brother Louis reports his observation of Bishop Helmsdale's amorous antics:

The illuminated oblong of your window shone him full in the face between the trees, and presently your shadow crossed it. He waved his hand, and murmured some tender words, though what they were exactly I could not hear.

Most people would surely simply say 'The light from your window', with perhaps a reference to the shadow crossing *the blind*. But Louis is not simply telling what happened, nor even simply what he saw; he is also conveying something of what it felt like to see what he saw. The reader is made to share in the actual physical process of seeing, a process in which we see an illuminated

oblong before we see a window. Pictorially considered, this recalls
the Impressionists, but considered in relation to narrative it empha-
sises the priority being given, as in the cinema, to seeing as a
mode of experiencing.

As in film, therefore, we both see and see with Hardy's characters.
We both see their world and see their relationship to it. It is
also to a large extent the same world that we see in the novels
and on the screen, for although the cinema may use artificial
sets it need not do so: the real world lies all before it, and actuality
is its true *métier*. Its wide open spaces may be as truly wide and
open as the prairie, or as Egdon Heath. This sense of having
been brought into contact with a living natural world, and one,
moreover, which both authenticates and defines the personages we
meet there and their experiences, is one of the major factors in
our recognition of a resemblance between Hardy's art and that
of cinema. The similarity may be one of content and treatment
as well as technique. This is particularly so in the case of the
Western, as David Lodge also notices. The menacing black clouds
fringed with light that hang over Tombstone as Wyatt Earp and
his companions get their first glimpse of it at the beginning of
John Ford's *My Darling Clementine* (1946) recall those that lour
over Egdon, and the subsequent action, here and in innumerable
Westerns, great and not so great, acquires a heroic quality from
the landscape, as does that of *The Return of the Native*. Venn roams
the Heath like the Lone Ranger; Bathsheba's plough-horses flounce
into the pond, 'drinking, tossing up their heads, drinking again,
the water dribbling from their lips in silver threads' (*FFMC*, 312);
Laban Tall shrinks 'almost to a point' as he rides to get help
from Gabriel for the stricken sheep; Matilda turns out of a road-
waggon looking like a 'verdant caterpillar' (*TM*, 147): these and
many other such incidents have their parallel in the world of
film. Situations and community relations tend to correspond also.
Ford's Clementine is, like Fancy, 'the new school-marm'; and
in *The Man who Shot Liberty Valance* (1962) we find the same
central situation as that of *The Woodlanders*, with the educated
outsider stealing the strong silent man's girl. Hardy's chivalrous,
long-suffering heroes would fit easily into the world of the Western.

Like those of film, Hardy's characters have their being very
much through the element in which they live and move. This,
through (so to speak) skilled verbal camera work, may be made
to function as an additional dimension, turning a 'flat' character

into a 'round' one. In the case of Dick Dewy, it does so quite literally. When we first *see* him, Dick appears in profile only, 'like the portrait of a gentleman in black cardboard'. This profile is visible only to the shoulders. 'What he consisted of further down', we are told, 'was invisible from lack of sky low enough to picture him on.' Yet he is already known to us as much more than a cardboard figure, for, although we have not seen him, we have heard his footsteps and heard him singing. Above all, we have seen the wood through which he is walking, for Hardy's opening paragraph has particularised the sound and movement of the various trees, from the sobbing and rocking of the firs to the rustling, waving beech. He has also shown us the wood as it appeared to Dick when he glanced upward; his own glance has then moved down to show us the utter darkness surrounding him. He has thus done what the film-maker would do, and done it in the same way. He has established the reality of the world in which his characters are placed by a careful selection and direction of 'shots' – a close-up of the individual trees, a long shot of the horizon, a medium shot of the sides of the lane. Before we see him, Dick has been made known to us through his experience, which we have shared. Thus, as Lionel Johnson says (in a passage quoted above, in Chapter 1), 'the reader's mind falls into step with the writer's'. This falling into step is the equivalent of eyes following the changing images of the screen.

As the above example shows, Hardy has the compositional skills of the good film-director. He makes sequences as well as shots. As in *The Dynasts* and the poems, he employs in the novels various types of shot. One example of a tracking shot in which the activity of a camera seems almost openly acknowledged is the description of the rain spouting from the gurgoyle in Weatherbury churchyard. 'We follow its course to the ground at this point of time', says Hardy, and proceeds to track it 'over the plinth mouldings, over a heap of stones, over the marble border, into the midst of Fanny Robin's grave'. In *The Woodlanders* Percomb the barber is virtually converted to a camera, conducting us from one cottage interior to another, until we finally focus on Marty South at the fireside, followed by a close-up of her hair.

Hardy also uses cutting effectively, as anyone presenting a narrative primarily in visual terms must do. *Far from the Madding Crowd* again provides an illustration. Concerning Bathsheba's opening of Fanny's coffin we read, 'She went to the lumber-closet for a screw-driver. At the end of a short though undefined time she found herself in the small room . . . standing beside the uncovered coffin . . . .' The cut from the lumber-closet and screw-driver to the opened coffin would make effective cinema.

Even more noticeably cinematic is the cross-cutting or montage progression of parallel scenes which Hardy uses quite frequently, especially for his climaxes. To take *Far from the Madding Crowd* once more, chapter 52, entitled 'Converging Courses', aptly illustrates this. Beginning in Boldwood's house, where preparations for the Christmas party are afoot, the narrative moves to Bathsheba's, where she is 'at this time in her room, dressing for the event'. It then returns to Boldwood's to watch him 'dressing also'. Next it moves to Casterbridge to watch Troy and Pennyways planning Troy's return, then back to Bathsheba 'giving a final adjustment to her dress before leaving the glass'; back to Boldwood, now putting into his pocket the ring he has bought for Bathsheba; and so to Troy again, preparing to leave for the party he comes to spoil. The cross-cutting provides an ironical comment on Boldwood's hopes and Bathsheba's fears. As in innumerable films, from Griffith's *The Fatal Hour*[10] onwards, it heightens suspense in the reader, but it also suggests the inevitable collision-course on which the characters are set, not so poignantly as does David Miller's *Lonely are the Brave* (1962), where the idealistic modern cowboy and the huge van with its load of lavatory pans that is to strike him down are seen moving steadily towards each other, but with something of the same irony. (Hardy's poem 'The Convergence of the Twain' provides a more exact parallel with the film.) From the point of view of subject as well as method, we might also compare Renoir's *Le Crime de Monsieur Lange* (1935), in which the villain (a publisher) returns disguised as a priest while the co-operative created after his supposed death in a train accident is celebrating its success. We see the priest before we see the party, so that we are aware of impending disaster. The priest is later shot by M. Lange as he is assaulting Lange's girl-friend.

At the climax of *The Return of the Native* also, although there is less cross-cutting forward and backward, the montage progression through a series of scenes occurring simultaneously is equally clear. The parallelism by which, as Eustacia goes to her doom, her waxen image melts in the fire would, one imagines, have appealed greatly to Eisenstein, the acknowledged master of montage. For Eisenstein the art of the cinema was above all an art of juxtaposition. He particularly favoured a metaphorical type of montage, in which the meaning of an action or image is brought home to us through association with some other image. The outstanding example of Hardy's adoption of this device, in the sense that it is pure ready-made cinema, aural as well as visual, is his description of the birth of Avice the Third in *The Well-Beloved*:

> The sea moaned – more than moaned – among the boulders below the ruins, a throe of its tide being timed to regular intervals. These sounds were accompanied by an equally periodic moan from the interior of the cottage chamber; so that the articulate heave of water and the articulate heave of life seemed but differing utterances of the selfsame troubled terrestrial Being – which in one sense they were.

Another touching instance is the dawn wind's stirring of the 'dead leaves which had lain still since yesterday', followed by Fanny Robin's action in desperately turning round upon her knees, then rising to her feet (*FFMC*, 277). Fanny also provides the occasion for a typical piece of aural montage when, after her knocking-up of Troy at the barracks, Troy's expostulations at the ragging of his comrades 'became lost amid a low peal of laughter, which was hardly distinguishable from the gurgle of the tiny whirlpools outside'. This is essentially the same device that Hardy is to employ in *The Dynasts* to effect the transition from one scene to another, usually far distant, one. Eisenstein provides some close parallels. In the screen-play of his *Ivan the Terrible*, for instance, there is the statement 'The frantic clamor of the bells merges into a loud roaring of crowds', and again, 'It is far from the square to the apartments of the Tsar. The clangor reaches from far off to the nuptial hall. It merges with the shouts: *Bitter! Bitter!*'[11]

Allied to this, and equally cinematic, is the means Hardy uses in *The Woodlanders* to speed up the time to Grace's wedding. As the day drew near, he tells us, Grace's 'prophetic ear could in fancy catch the noise of it', hearing the murmur of the villagers as she came out of church and the jangling of the bells. Then, 'The dialogues seemed to grow louder, and the ding-ding-dong of those crazed bells more persistent. She awoke: the morning had come.' This seems curiously reminiscent of Dickens's *A Tale of Two Cities*, both of the famous 'Echoing Footsteps' chapter and of the actual moment of Sydney Carton's death. As literary precursors

of the cinema, Dickens and Hardy have much in common, including
a marked affinity with Eisenstein.

Hardy's sensitivity to light and shade too matches that of the
film-maker. His 'Rembrandt-lighting' has already been sufficiently
stressed. (See above, Chapter 2.) He shares the film-maker's knowledge of the aesthetic and poetic value of moving lights and shades,
as he shows when he describes those from 'the shining moon'
racing over Stephen Smith's head and back 'in an endless gambol'
(*PBE*, 108), and on numerous other occasions. Again, like the
film-maker he is well aware that coming events (and people) cast
their shadow before. He will write therefore of 'two friendly human
shadows' descending across the kitchen window, 'followed by Sol
and Dan' (*HE*, 194), or, when Boldwood arrives at the Malthouse,
he will tell us 'A shade darkened the door' (*FFMC*, 137). He
knows too the dramatic value of such shadows, their ability to
magnify and add significance to an action. The 'opalized haloes'
of the drunken Trantridge workfolk show this. So do the shadows
dancing 'merrily up and down, timed by the jigging of the flames'
at the rick-fire in *Far from the Madding Crowd*, and the 'two human
shapes, black as jet' that Gabriel sees on the slope of the rick
during the thunderstorm later in the same novel. These are as
dramatic and in the former instance as ballet-like as are the gigantic
shadows that accompany the celebrated sword-fight at the end
of Michael Curtiz's *The Sea-Hawk* (1940).

Hardy also re-creates motion for us. He does not merely tell
us that his characters moved; he re-creates the sensation. When
the movement is a rapid one, the resemblance to cinema can
be quite uncanny. This is because Hardy shows us what the camera
would show us: for example, 'the grass, loose stones, and other
objects' passing Anne Garland's eyes 'like strokes' as she is carried
away on the back of Champion; or the two banks of the road
'dividing like a splitting stick; one rushing past at each shoulder',
as Tess is borne down-hill in Alec d'Urberville's dog-cart.

'My art is to intensify the expression of things . . .': once again
it is this statement that provides the best commentary. If Hardy's
art is richly cinematic, it is because the art of cinema is rich
in means of making vividly visible the life of sensations and emotions
which his characters exemplify. Hardy's view of life itself as a
kind of book written in a universal sign-language of the visible
seems to join life, literature and cinema together in a circle of
identity. In the previous chapter I suggested that his presentation

of gesture and facial expression in this way – as something to be read, usually in close-up – is one of his links with Victorian melodrama. It is equally characteristic, however, of the language of the screen. At times, when we are invited not only to read but also to ponder, it has its counterpart only there. Only the cinema could give us that close view of Marty's face which would allow us to interpret 'every feeling and sentiment' as they unfold there 'in visible luxuriance'; similarly, the 'mere waste tablet' of Clym Yeobright's could be more fully perused on the screen than on the stage. The nuances of this visible language, which are able, for instance, to convey through the picture of his 'down-turned face, over which the twig shadows moved in endless procession' (*MC*, 318) all Henchard's misery and dogged determination as he walks from Casterbridge, are also shared only by the cinema.

But this, perhaps, is where we came in. There is essentially no discrepancy in associating Hardy's art with both melodrama and cinema, for the simple reason that the cinema itself has its roots in nineteenth-century melodrama, taking over its techniques as well as its materials, although greatly extending and developing them, as its medium enabled it to do. In its use of the panorama and diorama, its gauzes, even its picture-frame stage, nineteenth-century drama was moving towards cinema. Not only melodrama but pantomime too found an extended life on the screen, the harlequinade being reborn in the great comics of the silent era, the fairy part living again in the 'musical'. Thus Hardy's cinematic mode is at once prophetic and in step with the art of his own day.

5 Music and Dance

Hardy's devotion to 'Tune' was lifelong and, despite his self-reproaches in the Sala delle Muse, constant. It was part of his birthright: the *Life* prefaces its account of his birth with a description of the musical activities of his grandfather, prototype of old William Dewy of *Under the Greenwood Tree*, who played the bass-viol in the west gallery of Stinsford Church for thirty-five years; and of his father, who like Reuben, William's son, played the tenor-violin. He owed his very existence to music, for as the charming sonnet 'A Church Romance' tells, the love between his parents began over a violin string:

> She turned in the high pew, until her sight
> Swept the west gallery, and caught its row
> Of music-men with viol, book, and bow . . . .
>
> Thus their hearts' bond began, in due time signed. . . .

Hardy himself, the *Life* (15) informs us, was able 'to tune a violin when of quite tender years. He was of ecstatic temperament, extraordinarily sensitive to music', and some of the dance-tunes his father played at home in the evenings could move him to tears. At a later date he himself, both as a boy and a young man, played the fiddle at country dances and weddings, 'being wildly fond of dancing'. Throughout his life the appeal of music for him was always closely linked with that of dance: a good tune with a dancing rhythm was, one suspects, what always moved him most. Thus in old age he names 'the Blue Danube' and the 'Morgenblätter Waltz' as among his favourite music, and in the November before his death, having expressed the opinion that '*Il Trovatore* was good music', he was pleased to have his opinion confirmed next day in an article by Miss Ethel Smyth. Earlier in the *Life*, comparing himself with the later Verdi (see above, p. 1), he had quoted with approval an implicitly disparaging reference to *Il Trovatore*. The later statement, made in the privacy of his home, no doubt reflects his true taste: as he looks back nostalgically to his opera-going twenties, he cannot deny the appeal of Verdi's lilting melodies. He also affirms repeatedly his love of hymn tunes. The many folk-songs mentioned or quoted in his novels – 'Break O' Day', 'The Foggy Dew', 'I Sowed the Seeds of Love' – testify to his interest in that quarter, and it is worth noting that as far back as 1871, long before the folk-song revival had begun, he speaks of himself as filling up his leisure moments 'by writing down such snatches of the old country ballads as he could hear from aged people' (*Life*, 84). Nor did he despise the Victorian ballad: 'The Maid of Keinton Mandeville' is praised for her rendering of Bishop's 'Should He Upbraid!'; he builds another poem around 'The Mocking Bird'; and often looks back nostalgically to Emma's playing and singing. If the music that holds him comes generally in association with dance, it also comes very often in the guise of song.

His tastes in more serious music, orchestral and instrumental, are more difficult to gauge. He does not appear to have been very adventurously explorative: we are told in the *Life* (424) that, at the time when the composer Rutland Boughton consulted him about a proposed musical setting for *The Queen of Cornwall*, 'he had heard no modern compositions'. But the year was 1924; he was eighty-four years old, when a failure to be *avant-garde* is perhaps forgivable. The statement is in any case contradicted by Miss Imogen Holst's recollection that, when her father visited him in 1927 to discuss his composition, *Egdon Heath*, he was impressed with Hardy's comprehensive knowledge of music, including Holst's own recent suite, *The Planets*.[1] On the other hand, the *Life*'s reference to his 'doing his best to talk about music' when he met Grieg in 1906 suggest a certain embarrassed awareness of a lack of qualification for doing so. During his middle years, there are references to his attendance at concerts during his and Emma's periodic visits to London, but no record of the pieces performed. Such attendance would be socially *de rigueur*, whether accompanied by personal enjoyment or not. At this time his first love seems clearly to be the picture galleries and exhibitions. In the 1890s and early 1900s that situation is reversed: we hear little about visits to galleries, but much about his attendance at concerts, at the Imperial Institute and later at the Queen's Hall. Of the year 1901, for instance, we are told, 'May found them in London, and hearing music' (*Life*, 308), and in his account of 1905 (p. 324) a composer is actually named: he 'followed up Tchaikowsky at the Queen's Hall concerts'. This quickened interest in serious music, as it appears to be, is probably to be related to his turn to poetry-composition and the writing of *The Dynasts*, and perhaps to his reading of Schopenhauer, which would enhance his sense of the philosophical importance of music and lead to a desire to study it more closely. An expressed preference (p. 329) for 'late Wagner' over early (1906) may perhaps similarly be read in personal terms: 'a man not contented with the grounds of his success' who 'goes on and on, and tries to achieve the impossible' would naturally be 'profoundly interesting' to an erstwhile novelist who had just published Part Second of *The Dynasts*. In Wagner's case, we also know that Hardy had heard some of his music by 1886, at a time when, he recalls, proudly *avant-garde* in retrospect, the music 'was less familiar to the public than after' (*Life*, 181). The 'Lines to a Movement in Mozart's E Flat Symphony', begun in November 1898, should also be remembered. Altogether it seems probable that, where serious music was concerned, Hardy was, as in literature, something of an autodidact. With his innate feeling for and technical knowledge of music, it is inconceivable that there was not much in it that he enjoyed, although it evidently never held first place in his affections.

His experience at one concert at any rate has been recorded. A note for 25 June 1887 observes, 'At a concert at Prince's Hall I saw Souls outside Bodies' (*Life*, 201). The music that produced this effect was of no mean order, since it included, according to the advertisement in *The Times*, Beethoven's Sonata Apassionata, the andante and finale from Mendelssohn's Violin Concerto, Schumann's Quintet, a partita for violin and piano by Parry, and a string quartet of Dittersdorf.[2] Hardy was later to write of Botticelli's art in similar terms (see above, p. 47).

Hardy's love of music finds abundant expression in his work. Many of the characters in his novels take after their creator in being, as he describes Joan Durbeyfield, 'a passionate lover of tune', among them Tess, Henchard, Farfrae, the Dewys, Grandfer Cantle, and all the rustics. His poems return to music repeatedly in theme, image and allusion: the sense of 'haunting fingers' is seldom absent from them. Stripped of all their musical episodes and allusions, his works would appear as shrunken as Elfride Swancourt without her underwear.

The significance of music for Hardy's art, however, goes beyond its contribution to his description of manners. As he apprehends it, it is more than a social pastime, more even than an art: it is part of the very texture of life itself. 'Structures of sensation' that we are, there is music both outside us and within us. Thus hearing being, equally with seeing, a mode of perception, Hardy's rendering of the external world is made as much in terms of the auditory, of *natural* music, as it is in terms of the visual. But also, since experience involves feeling as well as perceiving, an affinity, even at times an identity, exists between human beings and music and, along with music, dance. This is due not solely to the emotional nature of music, its power to express and move the heart, but also to the fundamental characteristic it shares with the heart, its rhythm or beat. The life of music, and still more of dance, depends upon this beat, as much as does the life of man. Thus music is ideally suited to express the sense of life itself; not merely types of sentience, but the very state and experience of sentience. This is how it is used by Hardy: the 'feeling' of his 'figments' turns their bodies into musical instruments, their emotions into music.

II

Hardy described William Barnes as 'a man whose instinct it was to catch [so] readily the beat of hearts around him'.[3] This was Hardy's instinct too. Hearts beat loud and insistently all through his novels. He catches their beat quite literally, and is equally conscious of it as sound and as movement. At moments of intense

experience for his characters, sound and movement both seem
enlarged to an unusual degree. 'There, there, don't let that little
heart beat itself to death: throb, throb: it shakes the bed, you
silly thing', declares Miss Aldclyffe to Cytherea in that amazing
bedroom-scene in *Desperate Remedies*. At the death of little Sorrow,
in *Tess of the d'Urbervilles*, Tess is so horrified at the thought of
the damnation awaiting him because he has not been baptised
that, we are told, 'her nightgown became damp with perspiration,
and the bedstead shook with each throb of her heart'; while in
A Pair of Blue Eyes the strain of a game of chess with Henry
Knight on that 'palpitating mobile creature' Elfride is such that
'some flowers upon the table [are] set throbbing by its [her heart's]
pulsations'. By the end of the game her pulse is 'twanging like
a harp-string'. Elfride is one of Hardy's most impressionable and
nervous heroines, yet even the more self-contained Grace Melbury,
as she escapes from her father's house at her husband's return,
must surmount 'the sound of her strumming pulse' before she
can catch the sound of his carriage turning in at the gate. In
the last two examples, the words 'twanging' and 'strumming' (and,
of course, the comparison with a harp-string), make explicit, or
half-explicit, the parallel with music. Most of Hardy's heroines
(and some of his heroes) are 'highly strung': in his depiction
of them the dead metaphor takes on new life, as also does that
of 'heart-strings'. A nervous sensibility may turn a character's whole
being, not just his pulse, into a musical instrument. Of Sue Bridehead,
that 'ethereal, fine-nerved, sensitive girl', we are told (*JO*, 241)
that 'the fibres of her nature seemed strained like harp-strings'
during her life with Phillotson; and this describes a continuous
state, not simply a moment of high excitement. And when in
The Hand of Ethelberta Christopher Julian kisses Picotee in mistake
for Ethelberta, Hardy writes, 'Being in point of fact a complete
bundle of nerves and nothing else, his thin figure shook like a
harp-string in painful excitement at a contretemps which would
scarcely have quickened the pulse of an ordinary man.' The lives
of such sensitive beings are necessarily 'tremulous' (Angel Clare
speaks of 'our tremulous lives' – *TD*, 211), and may even produce
a *tremolo* in the voice, as in the case of Sue. 'Tremulous', a favourite
word of Hardy's to describe both life and character, almost always
carries a half-hidden musical reference, suggesting the vibrant, the
finely-tuned, the delicately poised, as is the 'blessed Hope' that
'trembled through / [The] happy good-night air' of the Darkling

Thrush. Part of the magic of the opening stanza of 'Afterwards' lies in this:

> When the Present has latched its postern behind my tremulous
>   stay,
> And the May month flaps its glad green leaves like wings,
> Delicate-filmed as new-spun silk, will the neighbours say,
> 'He was a man who used to notice such things'?

The poet's 'stay' has been as fine-spun, as delicately poised and sensitive as that of the new leaves, in whose movement some blessed hope again appears to tremble, or as the May month, which, flapping its glad green leaves like wings, may be seen not only as bird or butterfly but also as a ballet-dancer, a dainty Ariel, poised to take off, to begin its own delicate dance to life's 'shivering tune'.

Vitality and vibrancy: these are the qualities Hardy celebrates in his characters and in human life generally. Both are sustained by and expressed in the beating, throbbing, pulsing of the heart, which itself finds expression and correspondence in the beating, throbbing, pulsing of music and the dance. The parallel is pointed by Hardy's use of these and kindred verbs (such as 'palpitating') to express both activities. Thus, in 'Apostrophe to an Old Psalm Tune' he declares,

> So, your quired oracles beat till they make me tremble
> As I discern your mien in the old attire . . . .

The old house in the poem 'The Two Houses' affirms, 'Dancers and singers / Throb in me now as once.' At the Viennese court the dancers waltz 'to the throbbing strains of a string-band' (*Dyn.*, 2. III. v), while in 'The Romantic Adventures of a Milkmaid', as Margery and the Baron arrive at the ball at Lord Toneborough's and hear the sounds of music and dancing, we are told, 'At every fourth beat a deep and mighty note throbbed through the air, reaching Margery's soul with all the force of a blow' – the note of the Drum Polka. In 'The Dance at the Phoenix', not only do they dance, among other measures, 'the throbbing "Soldier's Joy"', but, as they do so,

>   over All-Saints', high and bright,
> Pulsed to the music Sirius white,
>   The Wain by Bullstake Square.

The story of this touching poem turns upon the very relationship – between music and dance on the one hand and the human heart on the other – the significance of which for Hardy we are discussing. In it the fifty-nine-year-old Jenny, who after a gay youth has led a sedate married life, is tempted out of bed by the notes of the dance the King's-Own Cavalry is holding at the Phoenix Inn. After a night of 'beating' out, toe and heel, the various dances –

> Each time and every time she danced –
>   Reels, jigs, poussettes, and flings

– she returns home, now '*bosom*-beating', lies down again by her husband's side, and dies of a heart attack. Heart-beat and dance-beat have here fatally coincided; but both have expressed the energy of life, and Jenny has gone out not with a whimper but with a bang.

Music and dance embody the beat of life: life itself is music and dance. Hardy's language often expresses this identity. In his sonnet 'Rome: On the Palatine', for instance, commemorating the same visit as the Sala delle Muse poem, he describes how he made the customary tour of ancient sites:

> When lo, swift hands, on strings nigh overhead,
> Began to melodize a waltz by Strauss:
> It stirred me as I stood, in Cæsar's house,
> Raised the old routs Imperial lyres had led,
>
> And blended pulsing life with lives long done,
> Till Time seemed fiction, Past and Present one.

Here the pulse of the waltz and the pulse of life in the present become one, and both together create the illusion of reviving the life of the past. In the much more impressive 'Wessex Heights' is the couplet

> I cannot go to the great grey Plain; there's a figure against
>   the moon,
> Nobody sees it but I, and it makes my heart beat out of tune

– an easy rhyme, if a false one, but a significant phrase. The feelings of the characters in the novels are often described in musical terms: Eustacia, who has longed for 'what is called life – music, poetry, passion, war, and all the beating and pulsing that is going on in the great arteries of the world' (*RN*, 290), drops into her 'old mournful key' (p. 291) when marriage to Clym fails to provide it; Marian's 'mood was tuned to its lowest bass' (*TD*, 173) at her realisation of the hopelessness of her passion for Angel Clare. In the violent scene between Bathsheba and Boldwood on the road to Yalbury, when he accuses her of betraying him for Troy, we read, 'The swift music of her heart became hubbub now, and she throbbed to extremity.' Later, in the description of the climactic scene by the coffin of Fanny Robin, as Troy bends to kiss Fanny, Hardy writes of Bathsheba, 'All the strong feelings which had been scattered over her existence since she knew what feeling was, seemed gathered together into one pulsation now.' Here the musical reference, though submerged and implicit, seems unmistakable: this is the top note, the big drum, the crash of brass. 'Palpitating drums, and breathing brass' (*Dyn.*, 2.1.v) are as appropriate to the expression of the swift music of the heart as are the trembling strings of harp and violin to that of the tremulous nerves. In music itself, there is a moving example of this identity of drum-beat and heart-beat in Stravinsky's ballet *Petrushka*, where during the final tableau the drums' rapid, insistent thud at one point clearly communicates the 'hubbub' within the puppet Petrushka; as Yeats wrote in a very different context, 'The heart of a phantom is beating!' – beating here too in a drama of passion not unakin to those of Hardy.

Hardy's acute, obsessional sense that man himself is but a phantom, a puppet, briefly galvanised into life by some showman's or magician's skill, gives his work a natural, underlying kinship with such ballets as *Petrushka*, *Coppélia* or *La Boutique Fantasque*. One remembers Napoleon's first appearance on the stage of *The Dynasts*:

> You'll mark the twitchings of this Bonaparte
> As he with other figures foots his reel,
> Until he twitch him into his lonely grave.

When the puppet comes alive, it begins to dance; and images of the dance of life are common in Hardy's work. Even in that

curiously dance-less novel *A Pair of Blue Eyes*, Knight finds in
the dance an image for the experience he now regrets having
missed: 'Of late years I have wished I had gone my ways and
trod out my measure like lighter-hearted men. I have thought
of how many happy experiences I may have lost through never
going to woo' (p. 292). Bathsheba Everdene, on the other hand,
having surrendered to the dance all too readily under the compulsion
of Troy's sword-arm, which makes a scarlet haze 'like a twanged
harp-string', finds herself, at the time of Fanny's death, obliged
to 'tread her giddy distracting measure to its last note, as she
had begun it'.

To live is to have motion and emotion, and the pride in the
possession of these faculties experienced by all living creatures is
the pride of life. (Hardy was fond of this phrase.) This pride
finds expression in the dance. It is present in many marvellous
dances recorded in the novels, in the wild jiggings at the tranter's;
the 'spinning and fluctuating' at East Egdon, where 'a whole
village-full of sensuous emotion . . . surged in the focus of an hour';
the rushing and racing of that 'multiplicity of Pans whirling a
multiplicity of Syrinxes' in the barn at Chaseborough (*TD*, 91).
This last dance, before it is described, has already had its counterpart
in 'the innumerable winged insects' dancing through the 'low-lit
mistiness' of the September evening, the mistiness itself corresponding
to the 'nebulosity' formed by the 'floating, fusty débris of peat
and hay' in the barn. It is typical of Hardy that this should
be so, for the dance of life as he sees it occurs throughout all
nature, 'from the leaf on the tree to the titled lady at the ball'
(*Life*, 213). Even the houseflies dance quadrilles (*Dyn.*, 3. VII. ii).
Those who portray Hardy in terms only of gloom and withdrawal
should remember that no one has re-created for us more often
or more vividly the joy and vigour, the fury and exaltation of
the dance. And the dance, as he describes it, it should be remembered
too, is a shared, a social thing, where, though as at East Egdon
'one happy man' may dance by himself 'with closed eyes, totally
oblivious of all the rest' 'the rest' may comprise 'forty hearts'
or more, which have come together and are beating as one.

The urgent sense of life that beats through the dance naturally
allies it to the sexual passions, to the urge to perpetuate life,
to create as it were a *perpetuum mobile*. In the couplings of the
dance marriages are both made and symbolised – sometimes disas-
trously made, as the Fiddler, in the poem of that name, intimates,

There's many a heart now mangled,
  And waiting its time to go,
Whose tendrils were first entangled
  By my sweet viol and bow!

The seductive power of music and dance is a recurrent theme
in Hardy's work, three outstanding examples being the description
of Eustacia's state of mind and behaviour at the dance at East
Egdon; the description of the effect of Angel's harp-playing on
Tess; and the short story 'The Fiddler of the Reels'. This last,
in its description of Car'line Aspent, compelled to dance on to
Mop Ollamoor's fiddling, has a touch of the folk tale about it,
as Hardy would very well realise: if Mop, looking at Car'line
out of one eye, is not the devil, he is first cousin to him. The
tale hovers on the brink of the supernatural; yet it is rather the
'natural supernatural' that is Hardy's concern here and in the
other two examples. The 'fascination' that all three women feel
is the fascination of excessive emotion, of feeling wrought to such
a pitch that it seems transmuted into something else. Hardy acknowledges its sexual origins in all three; even in the passage in *Tess
of the d'Urbervilles* the rankness of the grass and of the 'rank-smelling
weed-flowers' seems to symbolise that rankness of emotion of which
he speaks directly in *The Return of the Native*. Yet the rankness
of the animal passions is certainly not all, nor even the chief
part, of what Hardy is writing about. In Car'line's case her actual
seduction by Mop seems almost incidental, a matter of indifference
to him and of no lasting significance to her. ('I was so onlucky
to be catched the first time he took advantage o' me, though
some of the girls down there go on like anything!' is her matter-of-fact
view of its results.) Her story, with its laughter and tears, its
infatuation and 'nervous passion', is in the first place an accurate
image of the disturbed emotions of adolescence. Sexual awakening
is at the root of these, and Mop's power over her, the excruciating
sweetness of his bow which makes her the slave of his will, has
obvious sexual connotations. Yet the emotion which Mop's fiddle
both expresses and arouses, in children as well as in 'unsophisticated
maidenhood', is not exclusively sexual emotion. In its plaintive
passages, the fiddle makes the heart ache; would, in fact, 'wellnigh
have drawn an ache from the heart of a gate-post' or tears from
a statue. 'Sunt lacrimae rerum': these tears are the cry of man's
emotional nature, stirred to unconscious, inarticulate awareness of

itself and its predicament, and to indefinable longing for some
more satisfying state. The effect of Mop's fiddle on Car'line is
to urge her irresistibly towards an endless dance:

> Presently the aching of the heart seized her simultaneously with
> a wild desire to glide airily in the mazes of an infinite dance.
> The room swam; the tune was endless . . . .

What she is experiencing is not so much sexual emotion as such,
as rather the desire of senses and emotions for self-perpetuation,
or that *perpetuum mobile* I referred to earlier, which itself governs
and directs the sexual energies.

Eustacia's experience is rather different: there is no 'torture'
in the dance for her as there is for Car'line, since it brings her
not desire, by which she is already tortured enough, but fulfilment.
Of these 'Pagan' dancers on Egdon Hardy tells us, 'they adored
none other than themselves': this is an activity ideally suited to
the self-centred Eustacia. In the dance she achieves contentment
and even, paradoxically, a certain repose: her face becomes 'rapt
and statuesque', as it is not to be again until seized by the 'eternal
rigidity' of death 'in a momentary transition between fervour and
resignation'. Eustacia's desire for life had always seemed to be
complemented, as on the reverse side of a coin, by a desire for
death (one recalls her avowed 'agonizing pity for myself that ever
I was born'); the dance, in a sense, fulfils that desire by isolating
her temporarily from all that she finds unendurable in living. 'She
had entered the dance from the troubled hours of her late life,'
Hardy tells us, 'as one might enter a brilliant chamber after a
night walk in a wood'. There is a suggestion of salvation in this,
such as (despite the incongrousness of the comparison) is common
in hymns, with their emphasis on the 'encircling gloom', 'the
night of doubt and sorrow', and the contrasting Paradise of light
awaiting the pilgrim at the end of his journey.

No dancing is involved in Tess's case: when Angel had the
chance of dancing with her, he did not do so, otherwise Tess's
history might have been very different. As Angel's notes break
upon a soundlessness that is 'a positive entity rather than . . . the
mere negation of noise', Tess is drawn towards them 'like a fascinated
bird'. The 'outskirt of the garden' through which she moves is
'now damp and rank with juicy grass which sent up mists of
pollen at a touch; and with tall blooming weeds emitting offensive

smells'. The significance of this garden as a symbol of sexuality in its grosser aspect both without and within Tess seems unmistakable.[4] The effect on her of Angel's playing is described as follows:

> Tess was conscious of neither time nor space. The exaltation which she had described as being producible at will by gazing at a star, came now without any determination of hers; she undulated upon the thin notes of the second-hand harp, and their harmonies passed like breezes through her, bringing tears into her eyes. The floating pollen seemed to be his notes made visible, and the dampness of the garden the weeping of the garden's sensibility. Though near nightfall, the rank-smelling weed-flowers glowed as if they would not close for intentness, and the waves of colour mixed with the waves of sound.

By gazing at a star, Tess had said, 'our souls can be made to go outside our bodies when we are alive'; by fixing your mind upon some big bright star 'you will soon find that you are hundreds and hundreds o' miles away from your body, which you don't seem to want at all'. Mop Ollamoor's fiddle too, as Car'line had found, could 'draw your soul out of your body like a spider's thread, till you felt as limp as withywind and yearned for something to cling to'. Car'line's experience, in which a sexual element is clear, is a kind of exquisite torture of the body, not a repudiation of it. The parallel should nevertheless be remembered; Tess's experience in the garden has the same basis as Car'line's, even though it is more spiritualised. Her exaltation, in relation to the star and thus also to Angel's harp, is the exaltation of ecstasy, a state Hardy increasingly attributes to Tess as her love for Angel ripens. Tess and Angel – was he thinking of her great namesake, St Theresa? Her powers of levitation recall those of the saint; and the passage quoted above has a baroque quality reminiscent both of Crashaw (whose poetry Hardy certainly knew) and of Bernini's famous sculpture, which could have been among the 'statuary' Hardy saw during his visit to Rome in 1887. The question of influence is unimportant, however; what matters is that Hardy, though in such a very different context, is achieving an effect similar to that achieved by these two artists, and by similar means. Tess 'undulated upon the thin notes of the second-hand harp'. 'Undulation', waviness, is one of the outstanding features of Bernini's sculpture: the saint's entire body flows and ripples beneath the angel's dart. In the sculpture this waviness extends beyond the saint to the billowing clouds upon which she floats: so it does with Tess, with the 'waves of colour' from the weed-flowers mingling with the waves of sound. If Tess does not actually float here, in her unconsciousness of time and space she almost appears to do so, by the association of her undulations with the harmonies passing like breezes through her, and of both with the floating pollen. The mention of 'the weeping of the garden's sensibility' increases the baroque intensity of the writing: it has a peculiarly seventeenth-century air about it, recalling, to my mind, such things as George Herbert's 'The dew shall weep thy fall tonight'; Milton's daffadillies filling their cups with tears; even, since reminders of *Paradise Lost* are never far off in this novel, Nature sighing through all her works at the Fall. There is thus an ambiguity or tension in the weeping of the garden: it seems to weep both with and for Tess. This reflects an ambiguity or tension in the entire passage, in which flesh and spirit are held in an equilibrium corresponding perhaps to the 'delicate equilibrium' of the June evening, and summed up in the suggestive oxymoron (or near-oxymoron) 'weed-flower'. Despite her exaltation, this moment marks Tess's second fall, her fall into sexuality, to which she comes, as to the first, through a mist of pollen (itself a fertilising agent). But this fall, even as it happens, is redeemed by the 'purity' of Tess's response: she has left her body behind and is gazing at a star. Car'line's reactions have not this balance: her experience of 'the wild and agonizing sweetness' of Mop's music, 'projecting through her nerves excruciating spasms, a sort of blissful torture' seems, at this point of the narrative at any rate, unambiguously orgastic. In its mixture of pain and pleasure it too recalls the baroque – the 'sweet yet subtle pain' of Crashaw's St Theresa, for example. Hardy, however, knows what he is doing, as Crashaw perhaps does not.

'Lyric Ecstasy inspired by music to have precedence', Hardy wrote when planning his first volume of poems, at the very time of *Tess of the d'Urbervilles*'s publication (*Life*, 243). In relation to *Wessex Poems*, it is a puzzling statement, since apart possibly from 'The Dance at the Phoenix' none of the poems in that volume fits the prescription. In the novels it is certainly a theme that has, if not precedence, prominence. Such ecstasy belongs on the whole to youth, as do the pride of life, gaiety and vigour that find expression in dance and song – to youth, and to the young in heart, those who lack 'a perfect insight into the conditions of existence', such as Grandfer Cantle, whose approach is signalled by 'a light boyish step, and a gay tune in a high key' (*RN*, 383). Hardy in old age was no Grandfer Cantle, but rather, in his own view at any rate, a mere 'Dead Man Walking': 'I am but a shape that stands here, / A pulseless mould . . . .' It had not always been so, however:

> A Troubadour-youth I rambled
>   With Life for lyre,
> The beats of being raging
>   In me like fire.

Music and dance become in the poems virtually symbols for youth, in particular Hardy's own youth, and thus for the past. As such, they throb through the collection from beginning to end. At those private picture-shows that absorbed his attention when to those around him he seemed to be 'living within himself',[5] the showings often included a 'musical'. A solitary child dances 'in a dream'; 'figures of jigging fieldfolk' give way to 'wild whirling figures born / Of Jullien's grand quadrilles', and these again to the 'faery lamps of the Larmer Avenue', where 'to the booms / Of contrabassos, feet still pulsed from the distant rooms' (*CP*, 878). Very distant now are those rooms:

> Where once we danced, where once we sang,
>   Gentlemen,
> The floors are sunken, cobwebs hang,
> And cracks creep; worms have fed upon
>   The doors

(p. 95)

> for The years have gathered grayly
> Since I danced upon this leaze

(p. 70)

and our lutes are strewn 'With years-deep dust'. As Hardy harps (as we might appropriately say) upon this note, the illusory nature of the show is borne in upon us. Try to re-create it in the present, and it vanishes at once:

> From the night came the oddest of answers:
>   A hollow wind, like a bassoon,
> And headstones all ranged up as dancers,
>   And cypresses droning a croon,
>   And gurgoyles that mouthed to the tune

(p. 465)

The toys are back on their shelf again, the dolls frozen into immobility. The centre of the stage is empty. Unless, perhaps, there is
a dance of death to follow the dance of life, in which shrouded
figures pace with joy as they sing, 'We are out of it all! – yea,
in Little-Ease cramped no more!' to the accompaniment of fiddles
and tambourines (p. 511), or

> Whither have danced those damsels now?
> Is Death the partner who doth moue
>   Their wormy chaps and bare?
> Do their spectres spin like sparks within
> The smoky halls of the Prince of Sin
>   To a thunderous Jullien air?
>
> ('Reminiscences of a Dancing Man')

III

To express the emotion beating within those 'vessels of emotion',
human beings: this then is the first function of music in Hardy's
work. But human beings are not only moved: they move about.
They live and act within an environment, with which they exist
in a reciprocal relationship, seeing and being seen. For music to
express this situation also is not an alternative to its first function,
but simply an extension of it. Hardy uses music to express our
experience of the world as it impinges on us through our sense
of hearing, but that music outside ourselves often echoes and gives
back a music within. This function of music goes closely with
the dramatic vision discussed earlier: Hardy's novels, and many
of his poems, are quite literally *melo*dramas: that is, dramas accompanied by music. They are more than melodramas, however: they
are operas. The universe is his orchestra, accompanying the characters
and reflecting their emotion. Often when the speech of Hardy's
characters seems stilted and unnatural, as it does, for instance,
in some of the exchanges between Clym and Eustacia in *The Return
of the Native*, this matters as little as do the artificial phrases and
exaggerated gestures of the operatic hero and heroine, for as in
opera the emotion is being expressed by other and largely musical
means. This is why the sound of a character's voice is so important,
to Hardy and therefore to us. Eustacia's voice, he tells us, was
like a viola. Tess's, on the other hand, was 'fluty', (*TD*, 147)

and acquired a 'stopt-diapason note' when her heart was in her speech (p. 123). Sue's 'silvery' tones often have a *tremolo* in them, and at moments of intense emotion she 'drops' to a 'contralto note of tragedy' (*JO*, 168, 221) – as does Bizet's Carmen when she sees her own death in the cards. Donald Farfrae's voice 'musically undulated between two semi-tones, as it always did when he was in earnest' (*MC*, 118). A *basso profundo* was Boldwood's customary voice (*FFMC*, 179). Such statements and descriptions are a reminder to us that these characters as 'vessels of emotion' are vessels of music also, and communicate their emotions musically as well as verbally.

The use of music, or musical effects, in a purely melodramatic manner to emphasise or heighten the action 'on stage' is relatively rare in Hardy's work. When he tells us, as Mrs Yeobright and the reddleman gaze in on the sleeping Thomasin in Diggory's van, 'She seemed to belong rightly to a madrigal – to require viewing through rhyme and harmony', we perhaps hear the tender music ('a trill on the flute') played at the entrance of the juvenile female lead, as at the entrance of Mathias's daughter Annette in Leopold Lewis's *The Bells*. Description of the gloomy river-side where Henchard walked after his discovery of Elizabeth-Jane's true paternity introduces a complete 'inset' melodrama, music, audience, and all: 'In the meadow where Henchard now walked the mob were wont to gather whenever an execution took place, and there to the tune of the roaring weir they stood and watched the spectacle.' The corpse is at present missing, says Hardy; but the equally doomed Henchard supplies its place to *our* eyes, and walks to the same music. Apart from such isolated examples as these, the most extended instance of 'background' music used in a melodramatic manner is provided, appropriately enough, by *Desperate Remedies*, Hardy's most overtly melodramatic novel. Here Knapwater House, where the persecuted heroine Cytherea undergoes most of her trials, is provided with all the necessary 'noises off': a waterfall that is heard 'in every room of the house, night or day, ill or well', and along with that a 'whistling creak of cranks, repeated at intervals of half-a-minute, with a sousing noise between each', from the pumping-engine. These are the naturalistic means by which Hardy seeks to surround his heroine with an Udolpho-like atmosphere of mystery and terror. First heard as she approaches the house (with their sinister character pointed out by the coachman, lest it should be missed), they reappear like an obedient ghost at the

various crises of her story: on her first night at Knapwater House;
at her first meeting with the villain, Manston; and on the night
before her marriage to him, reinforced on the first occasion by
a death-rattle and a howling dog; on the second by a thunder-storm
and Manston's own organ-playing, which 'fascinates' her as Car'line
Aspent was fascinated by Mop Ollamoor; and on the third by
various inexplicable switching, creaking, and rattling noises, the latter
resembling 'a man playing castanets'. The same stagy devices accompany the scene in which Manston buries the body of his first
wife, watched from various points in the darkness by Anne Seaway,
Miss Aldclyffe, and a detective. When Miss Aldclyffe speaks to
Manston, her remarks are drowned for one eavesdropper by the
creak of the engine and for the other by the 'roar of the falling
water'. Here we have perhaps an equivalent of the music that
accompanied scenes of violence or horror in melodrama, the thunder
partnering the blood, as in the murder scene in *Maria Marten*
or the scenes in Sweeney Todd's cellar in *The String of Pearls*.

The background music in Hardy's novels normally exists in much
more organic and intimate relationship with the characters than
this, and becomes thereby something more than 'background' music,
requiring to be understood, as I have suggested, in operatic rather
than purely melodramatic terms. Hardy's experience of opera, particularly during the early, impressionable period of his life when
he attended performances at Covent Garden and His Majesty's
several times a week, had undoubtedly a marked formative influence
on his work. He refers in the *Life* to having seen operas by Rossini,
Bellini, Donizetti, Meyerbeer and others; and to having heard
Tietjens, Parepa and Patti, and, at the end of his career, William
Harrison, for many years the leading tenor with the Royal English
Opera. The repertoire of the theatres shows that over the years
1862–6 he would have the opportunity of seeing almost all the master-
pieces of nineteenth-century Italian opera, plus some French (works by
Gounod, Auber and Meyerbeer, for instance) and some German
(*Fidelio, Der Freischütz, Oberon*), together with a large number of
English works, many now forgotten, by such composers as Wallace,
Glover, Benedict and Balfe. Parepa sang with Harrison in *Maritana*
and *The Bohemian Girl* in October 1862; possibly these were the
performances Hardy attended. The Covent Garden season opened
that year on 8 April (Hardy arrived in London on the seventeenth)
with a production of *William Tell*, which was performed eight
times that season. There was a lot of Meyerbeer: *Les Huguenots*,

Le Prophète, Robert le Diable and *Dinorah* all figured prominently in the repertoire. But there were also eleven performances of *Don Giovanni*, ten of *The Barber of Seville*, and eight of *La Sonnambula*. *Il Trovatore* and *Un Ballo in Maschera* were given four times each, and *Rigoletto* twice. One wonders whether Hardy celebrated his birthday (2 June) that year with a visit to Covent Garden. If so, he would have seen Patti in *La Traviata*, her only appearance in the part that season. In succeeding seasons, this repertoire was largely maintained, augmented with such works as *Faust, Norma* and *L'Elisir d'Amore*.[6]

Frequent exposure to such works may help to account for some of the more obviously theatrical features of Hardy's novels. The sensation scene, for instance, was as characteristic of Meyerbeer as it was of Boucicault and his fellows. The spectacular fires in three of Hardy's novels – *Desperate Remedies, Far from the Madding Crowd* and *A Laodicean* – may in part owe their existence to the exciting climaxes of *Les Huguenots* and *Le Prophète*, in each of which a fire occurs. Indeed, the description of the fire in *Desperate Remedies*, with the bells being rung backwards and 'jangled indescribably', followed by the church clock striking midnight, its bewildered chimes wandering 'through the wayward air of the Old Hundred-and-Thirteenth Psalm', reads almost like a parody, conscious or unconscious, of that in *Les Huguenots*, which marks the start of the Massacre of St Bartholomew. Again, Hardy's frequent and sometimes mechanical reliance on the device of eavesdropping, with the true and false surmises it leads to, may have been encouraged by his familiarity with it in opera. Those scenes in which different characters, unknown to each other, stand at different points to observe the actions of some other character or group of characters seem particularly operatic, since in opera, of course, they provide the basis for an *ensemble*. The scene in *Desperate Remedies* referred to earlier is one such: here the sinister nature of the operation and the presence of the body in the sack recall the quartet at the end of *Rigoletto*, where Rigoletto and Gilda separately spy on the Duke and Maddelena. (This of course involves the conflation of two separate scenes in the opera, since it is Gilda who supplies the body there.) Another example occurs in *The Woodlanders*, where Giles and Creedle, Marty and Grammer Oliver, Fitzpiers and Mrs Melbury all stand to watch the Midsummer night's rituals of the village maidens, and an unspoken (or unsung) sextet may be imagined. In *The Hand of Ethelberta* there is a scene irresistibly suggestive of the second scene of *Il Trovatore*, in which Manrico and the Count di Luna watch Leonora's window from the darkness of the garden. In the novel Christopher Julien is in the grounds of Rookington Park, gazing at the lighted windows of the house, which contains Ethelberta. Suddenly he becomes aware of another man 'standing close to the shadowy trunk of another tree, in a similar attitude to his own, gazing, with arms folded, as blankly at the windows of the house as Christopher himself had been gazing'. The resemblance of the stranger to Manrico is increased when he begins to murmur one of Ethelberta's own poems 'in a slow soft voice'. Christopher, it should be added is no Count di Luna, being the most passive of all Hardy's heroes.

Finally, we may notice that opera offers as many examples as does the drama proper of those climactic ballroom or drawing-room scenes in which a shooting or other disaster occurs, at which the guests all crowd in from the adjoining rooms, cower against the walls, or throng the staircase – *Un Ballo in Maschera*, for instance, and *La Traviata*, but also *The Bohemian Girl*, which ends with a scene in which the jealous Gipsy Queen attempts to shoot the hero Thaddeus but is fatally wounded herself. Recollection of some or all of these, as well as of similar scenes in 'straight' drama such as were discussed in Chapter 3, may have contributed to Hardy's creation of the scene in which Troy is shot by Boldwood.

In addition to these mainly general resemblances, there is evidence at times to suggest a 'debt' on Hardy's part to a particular opera. Artistic sympathy is involved here: Hardy is seeking similar effects to those achieved in the opera, and, consciously or unconsciously, follows its example. The search for effect in itself establishes a link between him and the opera composer, particularly when the composer is Verdi: Verdi and Hardy share the same taste for heightened dramatic moments and striking and often ironic contrasts. *Jude the Obscure* may not immediately suggest itself as a notably 'operatic' novel, yet not only is its central action initiated by an act which, while paralleling that in Bizet's *Carmen*, makes Bizet's *verismo* pale by contrast – Arabella's throwing of the pig's pizzle and its effect on Jude are closely comparable with Carmen's throwing of the flower to Don José; but in addition it ends in a manner that directly recalls the last act of *La Traviata*. There Violetta, like Jude, lies dying of consumption; at the beginning of the act she is also, like Jude, separated from her lover, although, since Alfredo returns and is reconciled with her before the end, the parallel ends there. Before his return, however, as Violetta lies alone, the joyous noise of a carnival sweeps past the window, heightening by contrast the pathos of her situation. In Christminster too it is festival-time ('the Remembrance games'), and Hardy enforces the same contrast several times over, to ironic as well as pathetic effect. First the bells begin to ring, and their notes, coming in at the open window, 'travelled round Jude's head in a hum'. Then from the Theatre the notes of the organ being played at a concert roll over the housetops till they too, 'faint as a bee's hum', reach Jude's pillow. He dies alone and unattended, and, as Arabella, returned from her gadding, gazes at his dead body, 'the faint notes of a military or other brass band from the river reached her ears'. Finally, as Jude lies alone again and in his grave-clothes, 'the joyous throb of a waltz' enters from the ball-room at Cardinal. Thus Jude 'dies to music' as decidedly as Violetta, for life (and Christminster) in all its forms, spiritual, cultural, social, is rejecting him through the musical expression of those forms. The throbbing waltz, signifying the pride of life itself, and thus the love and life that were denied him, comes last; but in the bells, which sound first, is heard the mockery of his intellectual aspirations. Those bells had first sounded, actually or in imagination, for Jude when as a boy he saw from the Brown House the night lights of the city as a 'halo or glow-fog over-arching the place':

Suddenly there came along this wind something towards him – a message from the place – from some soul residing there, it seemed. Surely it was the sound of bells, the voice of the city, faint and musical, calling to him, 'We are happy here!'

Now they are heard again, just as the melody in which Alfredo had expressed his love and which she herself had echoed in the hopeful aria 'Ah, fors è lui' in Act 1, comes back to haunt Violetta's death-bed – a 'remembrance' motive, heard on Remembrance Day. The parallel *is* with the Verdian 'remembrance' motive rather than with the Wagnerian *leitmotiv*, for the chief function of the bells is not to characterise Christminster but to remind us of the changed situation. They are also heard – suddenly, by Jude – on another Remembrance Day, the day before the tragic death of his children. Here they strike an ominous, warning note, and, in their suddenness and the way in which they seem to sound for Jude's ears alone, invite comparison rather with the sleigh-bells in *The Bells*. They are heard yet once more, in the very last scene of the novel, where they have become a resounding *reprise*. As Arabella and Widow Edlin stand beside Jude's open coffin, 'The bells struck out joyously; and their reverberations travelled round the bedroom.'

Elsewhere in *Traviata*, the scene in which Germont, Alfredo's father, goes to Violetta to beg her to give up Alfredo for the sake of his daughter may foreshadow that in *The Woodlanders* in which Melbury pleads with Mrs Charmond to give up Grace. Their arias – for Melbury's long speech, beginning emphatically 'I am an old man', has something of the quality of an aria – are similar in tone if not entirely in content: there is the same full note of pathos as Melbury speaks of his child 'precious as the apple of my eye to me', Germont of his daughter 'pura siccome un angelo', before each makes his direct appeal for renunciation. Germont's aria is in fact closely modelled on the corresponding speech of Monsieur Duval in *La Dame Aux Camélias*, so that the recollection on Hardy's part, if recollection there be, may be of Dumas's play and not of Verdi. He is likely to have known the story first, however, in its operatic form.

Another work which Hardy would undoubtedly know both in its original and its operatic form is Goethe's *Faust*. J. O. Bailey, in his celebrated essay 'Hardy's "Mephistophelian Visitants"',[7] considers various possible sources for Hardy's knowledge of the legend, but omits Gounod. Yet that Hardy, an opera-goer, should not have known this, one of the most popular of the operas of his day, and known it well, is unthinkable. The first performance in London of Gounod's *Faust* was at Her Majesty's, on 11 June 1863. It was an instant success, and was given two or three times a week for the rest of the season. A rival production was also mounted at Covent Garden, the first performance being on 2 July. Thus Hardy would have ample opportunity to see the work, in this and of course subsequent seasons. Knowing his musical tastes, we may be sure he found the music captivating. Mephistophelian references in the novels, both explicit and implicit, are indeed numerous, as Professor Bailey has demonstrated. But for Hardy's visual *image* of Mephistopheles I think we need to combine his description of Lord Mountclere, in *The Hand of Ethelberta*, with that of Diggory Venn in *The Return of the Native* (of whom Hardy used the phrase 'Mephistophelian visitant'). Of Mountclere he tells us (*HE*, 241), 'Each eye-brow rose obliquely outwards and upwards, and was thus far above the little eye, shining with the clearness of a pond that has just been able to weather the heats of summer', and he stresses in his looks, a 'combination of slyness and jocundity' (p. 316), together with the 'dignified aspect' (p. 240) which he wore to a gazer at a distance. The Mephistophelian aspect of Diggory is, of course, his redness: he was 'red from head to heels'. Put these two descriptions together, and we have a close counterpart to the 'baritones with impossible eyebrows, who spend the evening in a red limelight and an ecstasy of sardonic smiling' of whom Shaw complained.[8] The scene in Melchester cathedral in *The Hand of Ethelberta*, in which Mountclere spies on Ethelberta from the shadows, to the accompaniment of 'diapason blasts' on the organ, seems designed to continue the parallel, recalling as it does (given the 'Mephistophelian' character of Mountclere) the scene in church in Act IV of *Faust*. Even closer to *Faust*, however, is the scene in *Tess of the d'Urbervilles* in which Alec d'Urberville startles Tess by appearing as an effigy on the altar-tomb of the d'Urbervilles in Kingsbere church. Professor Bailey, looking rather at the scene in the allotments, where the comparison is explicitly with Milton's Satan, denies any Mephistophelian character to d'Urberville, but in this incident it seems to me to be plain. Directions in the libretto of the opera at this point are for the tomb to open, revealing Mephistopheles, who bends to whisper in Marguerite's ear as she kneels in prayer. He tells her of the demons (who are heard as a Chorus) waiting to welcome her below. The counterpart of this in the novel is,

'I saw you come in,' he said smiling, 'and got up there not to interrupt your meditations. A family gathering, is it not, with these old fellows under us here? Listen.'

He stamped with his heel heavily on the floor; whereupon there arose a hollow echo from below.

D'Urberville certainly has something of the devil in him, as is indicated even by his name (D'urbErVILle), and as such is set in opposition to *Angel* Clare (albeit an inadequate angel) in a contest for Tess's soul, as in the last act of *Faust* good and evil forces do battle for the soul of Marguerite. 'But, might some say, where was Tess's guardian angel?', Hardy comments, on the occasion of her seduction. This recalls the striking reflection of Christopher Julien on Ethelberta's engagement to Mountclere: 'I should think her guardian angel must have quitted her when she agreed to a marriage which may tear her heart out like a claw' (*HE*, 318), where we suddenly find ourselves in the truly terrifying Faustian world, not of Gounod but of Marlowe. Gounod's *Faust*, it is worth recalling, is virtually the story of Marguerite only, a fact recognised in its German title, *Margarethe*.

Tess's situation, separated from and unjustly judged by the man she loves devotedly, gives her kinship with several operatic heroines, fallen and unfallen. Among the former is Leonora, heroine of Donizetti's *La Favorita*, performed at Covent Garden during the 1860s. Leonora has been the mistress of Alfonso, king of Castile, but now is claimed in marriage by Fernando, who is ignorant of her past. Leonora is torn by the same conflicting feelings, of love, doubt and fear, as Tess is, and expresses them in her principal aria, 'O mio Fernando'. Recognising like Tess that her future husband must be told the truth, she sends him a letter which, like its celebrated counterpart in *Tess of the d'Urbervilles*, fails to reach him. When she enters in bridal attire for the wedding, she finds him still willing to marry her despite, as she supposes, his knowledge of her past. This too finds its parallel in Hardy's novel. Leonora does in the end, like Tess, make her confession verbally, but the opera ends tragically. With Donizetti's famous heroine, Lucia di Lammermoor, the parallels are less close, although in the intensity of the passion, and the distraction it communicates, Tess's long soliloquy just before she stabs d'Urberville, which is, as Hardy says, 'a dirge rather than a soliloquy', is comparable with Lucia's Mad Scene. The occasion, after all, is not dissimilar: 'Too Late, Beloved' would be equally suitable to either work, as an alternative title. As it is, there is a suggestive similarity of structure in the existing titles.

A less passionate but very appealing heroine with whom it is tempting to associate Tess is Amina, the sleep-walker of Bellini's *La Sonnambula*. The resemblance lies in character rather than situation: Amina, pure and innocent, shows a touching, unshakable and selfless devotion to Elvino, though wounded by his unreasoning jealousy and rejection of her. She expresses her feelings as she sleep-walks: 'Elvino, abbracciami' and 'Quanto infelice io sono, felice ei sia'. And here a curious transposition has taken place: if there *is* a recollection of *La Sonnambula* in *Tess*, then Amina's role has been shared between Tess and Angel, for it is Angel who sleep-walks, and in the same direction as Amina – over the mill-stream. And, like Amina, he reveals his true feelings during his somnambulism ('My poor, poor Tess – my dearest, darling Tess! So sweet, so good, so true!'). It is curious too to note that *La Sonnambula* includes two characters named Theresa and Lisa.

One of the principal characteristics of opera is its delineation of character through emotion, and the musical expression of that emotion. This is the ultimate explanation of the resemblance between Hardy's personages and those of opera: it is a resemblance not simply as people, or in situation, but also in function and method of presentation. Hardy's characters do not habitually *sing*, though sometimes they do: Tess singing Angel Clare's favourite 'ditties' 'whenever she worked apart from the rest of the girls in this cold, hard time' is as much a figure of pathos as Marguerite singing at her spinning-wheel or in prison. He does, however, frequently achieve an effect equivalent to that of music by various means, chiefly through the isolation and emphasis of his characters' speeches, so that they become virtually *arias*, or through a lyrical heightening in their presentation or expression. Marty South's moving soliloquy at the end of *The Woodlanders*, for example, belongs undeniably to literature; yet in its note of triumphant love outsoaring death, combined with the 'sublime' image of Marty standing alone in the moonlight, it also suggests analogues in the world of music – for example, though the parallel is not an exact one, the union in death of Rhadames and Aïda to the pure strains of 'O terra addio; addio, valle di pianti'.

In *The Return of the Native* Eustacia on Rainbarrow, once the site of 'Druidical rites and Saxon ceremonies', brings to mind another 'sublime' operatic heroine, Bellini's Norma. The association here, however, is largely a visual one, rather than one of character. Eustacia, with her 'Pagan eyes, full of nocturnal mysteries' and her dark hair which, restrained in its luxuriance by a 'thin fillet of black velvet' still 'closed over her forehead like nightfall extinguishing the western glow', is an exotic and majestic figure such as Norma is as she sings the cavatina 'Casta diva'. The resemblance is closest on the occasion of Eustacia's return to Mistover after the mumming escapade, when as 'The form of Rainbarrow stood above the hills, and the moon stood above Rainbarrow,' we are told, 'Eustacia once more lifted her deep stormy eyes to the moonlight' and sighed 'that tragic sigh of hers'. In *Norma*, too, of

course, the exotic background and circumstances offset a familiar
tale of passion, and indeed the central situation, which is concerned
with Pollio's transference of his love from Norma to her priestess
Adalgisa, superficially resembles the initial one of Hardy's novel.
But essentially the resemblance is one of *image*: Eustacia wants
for herself, and Hardy wants to give her, a commanding presence
commensurate with her passion, such as we find in Norma.

Examination of the affinities between Hardy's work and opera has
not led me to find there much evidence of an operatic, contrapuntal
grouping of characters, such as Shaw, for instance, favoured in
his plays. The resemblance lies, rather, in his presentation of the
emotional state of the individual, as in most of the examples we
have considered. But, although little natural grouping, 'on stage'
so to speak, suggestive of the trio, quartet, and so on, occurs,
the underlying relationships between the characters constantly suggest
and indeed demand it. Thus Hardy's emphasis on emotion may
lead us to imagine a kind of shadow opera going on beneath
the surface action, with the relationships and the emotional reactions
of the characters finding expression in the vocal groupings that
would certainly have to be devised were the works presented as
operas. In *The Mayor of Casterbridge*, for example, where all the
characters live apart, each nursing his own secret, or secret life
(with the possible exception of Farfrae, who, being so well-adjus-
ted – 'like a well-braced musical instrument' – presumably has none),
there is one scene which already contains in outline an operatic
quartet. This is the scene in chapter 26, in which Farfrae and
Henchard take tea together with Lucetta, while Elizabeth-Jane looks
on and sizes up the situation. Hardy makes us aware, explicitly
or implicitly, of the feelings of all four characters; they are, as
it were, being contrapuntally presented in a quartet comparable
with, for example, that in the first act of *Fidelio*, in which Marzelline,
Leonore, Rocco and Jaquino all voice their separate hopes and
fears concerning the proposed marriage of Marzelline to the disguised
Leonore; or with that at the end of *Rigoletto*, as Gilda and Rigoletto
observe the Duke and Maddalena through the crack in the wall.
Again, a natural trio is suggested by the scene in which Henchard
reads aloud to Farfrae Lucetta's letters to himself, while Lucetta
listens, terrified, on the stairs. Normally, however, the counterpoint-

ing, blending or interweaving is more implicit than this, or takes place over a larger area. There is no bringing together of Henchard, Farfrae and Elizabeth-Jane to voice their feelings over Lucetta's death, for example, though we know what they are and can 'piece out' the trio for ourselves. Similarly, in *The Return of the Native*, Clym, Eustacia and Mrs Yeobright are never brought together; yet in a sense the whole central part of the novel is one sustained trio in which they voice their conflicting emotions, and is felt as such. In its confrontations between the characters this novel is indeed something of a Noah's Ark: the characters come in mostly two by two – Eustacia and Wildeve, Mrs Yeobright and Thomasin, Thomasin and Wildeve, Clym and Mrs Yeobright, Eustacia and Clym. Yet to think of it in operatic terms as a series of duets would be incorrect. What matters is the structure of emotions, which suggests a different grouping, setting Clym between Mrs Yeobright and Eustacia, Eustacia herself between Clym and Wildeve, and shaping the relationship between Clym, Eustacia, Wildeve and Thomasin to a quartet.

At the end of this novel (by which I mean the end of the main narrative), however, inner and outer form come together in what is in effect a fine example of the operatic ensemble finale. Like the ensemble finales of Mozart, it starts some time before the end, in Book v, chapter 7, 'The Night of the Sixth of November'. It starts, that is, with Eustacia's departure from Mistover, and builds up over the next two chapters to the culminating catastrophe. The titles of these chapters themselves indicate the *ensemble* nature of the action: 'Rain, Darkness, and Anxious Wanderers', followed by 'Sights and Sounds Draw the Wanderers Together'. 'The Wanderers' are, of course, the five central characters, Eustacia, Clym, Wildeve, Thomasin and Venn, who are all brought together to participate either as sufferers or as spectators in the final tragedy. The climax is musically built up: that is why 'Rain and Darkness', 'Sights and Sounds' appear in the chapter titles. Each of the characters is intensely involved emotionally in the situation, and, as they each struggle towards their destiny, vocalising their passion in unheard but still completely apprehended or imagined upsurges of song, Nature itself provides an orchestral accompaniment. This accompaniment spreads across all three chapters. It begins with night and increasing darkness, a darkness that itself seems to be apprehended musically, as it is in Holst's *Egdon Heath* Overture. Then a stormy wind arises, but as yet no rain. By the time Eustacia

leaves the house the rain has begun, and it increases even as
she stands there, and threatens to increase still further. From this
point it is in fact incessant, 'the whole expanse of heath . . . emitting
a subdued hiss under the downpour'. Meanwhile the wind continues:
we read of it rasping and scraping at the corners of Clym's house,
snapping at the window-panes and breathing into the chimney
'strange low utterances that seemed to be the prologue to some
tragedy'. From this 'drumming of the storm' at Blooms-End, we
accompany Thomasin across the heath, where the shrill wind 'whis-
tled for joy at finding a night so congenial as this'. Then, having
seen her on her way past Diggory's van, we join Wildeve, waiting
'slightly sheltered from the driving rain by a high bank', where
he listens to the wind, as it 'plunge[s] into the heath and boom[s]
across the bushes into darkness'. At this point the orchestral piece
reaches its climax: 'Only one sound rose above this din of weather,
and that was the roaring of a ten-hatch weir to the southward . . . .'
Again, the last act of *Rigoletto* comes to mind, with its storm
and darkness and sinister river in the background. But so does
Wagner: the effect Hardy creates, here and in similar passages,
seems to anticipate that 'weather and ghost music' which he was
later to recognise in Wagner's work.

Such 'weather music' is characteristic of Hardy. He likes it
for his climaxes, where 'the wild rhetoric of the night' underlines
and enhances the drama of the situation. Sue's final surrender
to Phillotson at the end of *Jude* takes place against a background
of storm: 'What a wind and rain it is tonight!' exclaims Mrs
Edlin. Similar weather, and weather music, had occurred earlier,
before a somewhat similar sacrifice: Ethelberta on the eve of her
marriage to Mountclere sings to Picotee in a kind of ironic 'Willow
willow' scene, and, as she sings, 'the music . . . mingled with the
stroke of the wind across the iron railings, and was swept on
in the general tide of the gale, and the noise of the rolling sea,
till not the echo of a tone remained' – a description which interestingly
foreshadows Hardy's remark to Grieg (*Life*, 329) that 'the wind
and rain through trees, iron railings, and keyholes fairly suggested
Wagner music'. Sue's last parting with Jude in the church at
Marygreen also has a storm setting: the scene, with Sue kneeling
by the altar and covering her ears with her hands as Jude, leaving
her, passes the end of the church and she hears his coughs 'mingling
with the rain on the windows', is a completely realised operatic
scene.

IV

Dramatic heightening is, however, only one of the uses Hardy has for 'weather music'. Such music, and the music of Nature in general, is central to his own experience of life and is used in a variety of ways to express that experience. His capacity to hear that music and to capture it in words reminds one of Elgar's remark that music is all about us: 'You just take as much as you want.' He is particularly sensitive to the music of trees – the 'musical breathing' of the young pines, the elm's 'Gregorian melodies' (*W*, 93, 119), the beeches on Norcombe Hill wailing or chaunting to each other 'in the regular antiphonies of a cathedral choir'. He strikes this note at the very start of his career, with the opening paragraph of *Under the Greenwood Tree*, which in its care to distinguish the individual voices of the trees is an overture, both to this novel in particular and to Hardy's work as a whole. In the novel, Dick Dewy now enters, singing: life is already being presented as a play, and a musical play, or opera. (The affinity with film technique noticed in the last chapter is consistent with this, 'background music' being one of film's most powerful aids to the articulation of emotion and meaning.) Even apart from the moments of high drama discussed above, Hardy's stress on life as something seen and heard, his habit of seeing it as a play and of hearing it as music, sustains the operatic character of his writing. Music of one kind or another often accompanies the activities of his characters: Stephen Smith on his evening walk at Endelstow is 'surrounded by the soft musical purl of the water through little weirs' (*PBE*, 113); the 'murmuring' of Tess and Angel during their idyllic autumn walks is accompanied by the 'buzz' of similar weirs; at Stonehenge the wind plays 'a booming tune, like the note of some gigantic one-stringed harp'. As Mrs Yeobright meditates alone on the morning of Clym's wedding, the heath before her is 'alive with butterflies, and with grasshoppers whose husky noises on every side formed a whispered chorus'. (Some of Verdi's husky choruses come to mind.) Sometimes it is a bird that comments in song on the situation of the characters in front of us 'on stage' – the 'weak bird singing a trite old evening song', for example, as Henchard and his wife and child walk the dusty road towards Weydon-Priors; 'the coarse whirr of the eternal night-hawk' bursting sarcastically from the top of a tree as Fitzpiers joins Suke Damson on the hay-cock; the 'solitary cracked-voiced reed-sparrow' with its 'sad, machine-made tone', greeting Tess on her solitary, sad walk, after the story of Jack Dollop had aroused bitter memories. The fine '1912–13' poem 'The Voice' ends with a similar dramatic presentation of the poet himself:

> Thus I; faltering forward,
> Leaves around me falling,
> Wind oozing thin through the thorn from norward,
> And the woman calling.

In all these instances the music of Nature harmonises with or is appropriate to the feelings of the characters: that is, it is a *fitting* accompaniment. The music within the character finds its echo in, or is articulated by, the music without. This is one of the principal means by which character and environment are brought into a living, dynamic relationship. One very explicit instance is Eustacia's departure from Mistover, in the storm we examined earlier. Hardy tells us, 'Never was harmony more perfect than that between the chaos of her mind and the chaos of the world without.' Another is that most memorable musical passage in the whole of Hardy's work, the description of the music of Egdon which accompanies Eustacia's walk between the two bonfires. Robert Liddell, in a generally imperceptive account of Hardy's use of background, tells us that this music is 'irrelevant' to Eustacia.[9] It is not: it is an exact evocation of her emotions and her predicament. The wild noise of the wind in the trees and hollows is in harmony with the passions within her, and with her spirit's longing for freedom; while the 'worn whisper, dry and papery' from the heath-bells at once echoes her *ennui* and dryness of soul, and mocks her aspirations with the withered voice of age – 'the ruins of human song'. Again, Hardy makes the point explicitly, by telling us that Eustacia's sigh 'modulated' so naturally into the rest that its beginning and ending were hardly to be distinguished:

> The bluffs, and the bushes, and the heather-bells had broken silence; at last, so did the woman; and her articulation was but as another phrase of the same discourse as theirs. Thrown out on the winds it became twined in with them, and with them it flew away.

To a student of opera at any rate, the music of this passage is perfectly comprehensible, very moving, and not at all irrelevant.

As a piece of musical description, the passage is intrinsically interesting. The music created by the wind on the heath is choral and apparently polyphonic:

> Treble, tenor, and bass notes were to be found therein. The general ricochet of the whole over pits and prominences had the gravest pitch of the chime. Next there could be heard the baritone buzz of a holly tree. Below these in force, above them in pitch, a dwindled voice strove hard at a husky tune . .

This 'dwindled voice' reaches Eustacia's ears 'but as a shrivelled and intermittent recitative'. Altogether this is really too complex for operatic choral singing, though it does suggest the quartet, such as I discussed earlier. Considered as a choral backing to Eustacia's music (her sigh), it suggests, rather, the oratorio. 'The infinity of those combined multitudes' (the heath-bells) reinforces the impression: massed choirs singing a Lilliputian 'Hallelujah Chorus' seem to be not very far away. Moreover, although the conception is clearly vocal, there is also a suggestion of instrumentation here: the 'combined multitudes' are in fact multitudes of 'tiny trumpets' – the massed bands of Lilliput added to its massed choirs!

Hardy's rendering of the music of Nature and of the environment takes both vocal and instrumental form. Even when his language is that of the voice, however, a symphonic effect is at times created, so that an instrumental reference seems implicit also. The opening paragraph of *Under the Greenwood Tree* once more provides an example. Here the 'sobs', 'whistles', 'hisses' and 'rustlings' of the various trees suggest an orchestral combination of instruments – cellos, flutes, violins – even more readily than they suggest a vocal combination. The passage from *The Return of the Native* quoted above is similarly, even readily, transposable into instrumental terms, even apart from the 'tiny trumpets': indeed, Hardy's reference a few pages later to 'the windy tune still played on the dead heath-bells' suggests that he himself was making no clear distinction between the two forms. In *The Mayor of Casterbridge* he has an elaborate and explicit orchestral passage. The occasion is that on which Henchard, meditating suicide after the skimmington and his lie to Newson, walks by the river and sees his own effigy floating in a pool. Hardy writes,

> To the east of Casterbridge lay moors and meadows through which much water flowed. The wanderer in this direction who should stand still for a few moments on a quiet night, might hear singular symphonies from these waters, as from a lampless orchestra, all playing in their sundry tones from near and far parts of the moor. At a hole in a rotten weir they executed a recitative; where a tributary brook fell over a stone breastwork they trilled cheerily; under an arch they performed a metallic cymballing; and at Durnover Hole they hissed. The spot at which their instrumentation rose loudest was a place called Ten Hatches, whence during high springs there proceeded a very fugue of sounds.

This is a little ingenious and self-conscious, but not precious. Hardy always liked to distinguish the individual qualities of sounds, noting, for instance, in *Desperate Remedies* (316), the variation in the noise of the rain according to the type of field it fell on: its 'soaking hiss' on a pasture, patter on 'some large-leafed root crop', 'paddling plash' on 'the naked arable'. His onomatopoeic words, as Eva Mary Grew noticed, are carefully chosen: the 'purr' of milk into the pails, its 'cluck' in the cans as it is carried to market, the 'smack' of the horse's hoofs on the moistening road (*TD*, 137, 213).[10] The point at which sound becomes music is a doubtful one, but for Hardy, with his sensitivity to varying tones and pitches, it clearly happened very readily. In a note of January 1881, on 'the Wordsworthian dictum (the more perfectly the natural object is reproduced, the more truly poetic the picture)' he observed that 'This reproduction is achieved by seeing into the *heart of a thing* (as rain, wind, for instance) and is realism, in fact . . .' (*Life*, 147). His own 'seeing into the heart' of rain, wind and other natural phenomena comes largely by way of sound, and consists in catching the music of the object, which is the expression of its inner being. In this way, an affinity becomes apparent not only with the operatic but also with the symphonic composers of his period. From *Fingal's Cave* to *La Mer*, the nineteenth century was the great age of descriptive music, with composers, having seen 'into the heart of a thing', endeavouring to communicate through their art what they have seen. The result may be naïvely if charmingly imitative – bird-calls on the flute or piccolo, rain drops on the violin – an imitativeness which on occasion finds its literary counterpart in Hardy; but it may also be profoundly realistic, with the imaginative realism Hardy mentions. This shared artistic concern, involving as it does the evocation of mood and sensation, gives Hardy an affinity with most of the Romantic composers not only in passages of explicit musical reference, but in his descriptive writing generally. The first chapter of *The Return of the Native* has been compared with the entrance of the Gods into Valhalla.[11] As a recognition of its stature and sublimity, this is fitting; but, looking at the *nature* of what is attempted (and achieved), a comparison with the beginning of *Rheingold* and its evocation in music of the waters of the Rhine seems even more appropriate. The existence of Gustav Holst's powerful symphonic poem *Egdon Heath*, confirms the impression that Hardy's chapter is in itself a poetic symphony. Holst's music marvellously captures the character of the heath in all its brooding sombreness, but it is the heath of the first chapter, not of the third or sixth. Humanity, that is, has not yet appeared on the scene. When it does so, as in chapter 6, where the brooding Eustacia mingles her sighs with its 'discourse', other parallels spring to mind, notably the music of Mahler. There is a moment in the last part of *The Song of the Earth* when the voice of the singer breaks upon the desolation of the instruments, which seems closer to this moment in Hardy than any other music I know. Eustacia herself hardly perhaps measures up to the comparison, but the Heath does. The deep feeling for Nature expressed throughout Mahler's work, and the stark questioning of Man's destiny, invite comparison with Hardy.

The basis for the musical and symphonic impression created by the opening description of Egdon is probably the fact that Hardy is not merely describing a place: he is also communicating a mood. Egdon could best be felt, he tells us, when it could not be clearly seen, and that is precisely the hour of which he is writing. The light is indistinct. The description opens,

A Saturday afternoon in November was approaching the time of twilight, and the vast tract of unenclosed wild known as Egdon Heath embrowned itself moment by moment. Overhead the hollow stretch of whitish cloud shutting out the sky was as a tent which had the whole heath for its floor.

The relationship between heath and sky established here is developed
in the next two paragraphs, and is presented as a contrast that
resolves itself into a similarity and even a fusion as the two draw
together. The movement of the thought, or the description, is,
it seems to me, to be understood and felt as we understand and
feel the movement of a symphony. Painting is involved too, of
course, but the description goes beyond painting because a *movement*
of light, or rather of darkness, is being presented. The opening
sentence states the theme: in its second half we can almost hear
the chords swelling out 'as Egdon Heath embrowned itself *moment
by moment*'. The next sentence states the second theme (sky, set
against heath). These two themes are then combined contrapuntally,
the heaven's 'pallid screen' being at first contrasted with earth's
'darkest vegetation', until with the coming-on of night the conflict
is resolved, as 'the obscurity in the air and the obscurity in the
land closed together in a black fraternization towards which each
advanced half-way'. This sense of symphonic structure diminishes
as Hardy's account of Egdon's qualities becomes more analytical.
It returns, however, midway through the description, with a direct
allusion to the heath's moods, reaching their greatest intensity 'during
winter darkness, tempests, and mists'. 'Then Egdon was aroused
to reciprocity; for the storm was its lover, and the wind its friend.'
Here once more we hear a chord struck, and have a sense of
musical climax. And at the end of the chapter, when we return
to our original standpoint ('To recline on a stump of thorn in
the central valley of Egdon, between afternoon and night, *as now* . . .'),
we recognise this as the recapitulation.

Elsewhere in Hardy's novels, a symphonic impression is created
by the orchestration of effects, sometimes quite extensive and sustained. One outstanding example is his description of the storm
in *Far from the Madding Crowd*. Particularly striking in this respect
is his description of the coming of the rain, where not only the
sound of the rain but also the actual movement of the wind may
be felt to have a musical value, or to exist in a musical relationship:

The air changed its temperature, and stirred itself more vigorously.
Cool breezes coursed in transparent eddies round Oak's face.
The wind shifted yet a point or two and blew stronger. In
ten minutes every wind of heaven seemed to be roaming at
large.

Here different musical phrases are, so to speak, introduced separately, from different points of the orchestra, till they finally combine in a crescendo of harmonies, or dissonances. A suggestive musical parallel occurs in Rossini's Overture to *William Tell* (incidentally, one of Hardy's favourite pieces).

For another, and somewhat different, example of the creation of an effect of dissonance we may turn to a passage in *Jude the Obscure* already discussed in relation to both painting and theatre: that in which the boy Jude lies looking at the sun through the plaiting of his straw hat and wishes he might never grow up. Here Jude's thoughts are first represented in terms of verse: 'Growing up brought responsibilities, he found. Events did not rhyme quite as he had thought.' But then, as his thought continues, the idea of harmony replaces that of rhyme: 'That mercy towards one set of creatures was cruelty towards another sickened his sense of harmony.' This thought leads on to a vision of life embodying dissonances of a kind characteristic of various twentieth-century composers:

> As you got older, and felt yourself to be at the centre of your time, and not at a point in its circumference, as you had felt when you were little, you were seized with a sort of shuddering, he perceived. All around you there seemed to be something glaring, garish, rattling, and the noises and glares hit upon the little cell called your life, and shook it, and warped it.

These three examples may serve to illustrate some of the various ways in which Hardy's writing acquires a musical character and texture, even without overt musical reference. His concern with mood and sensation and the expression of these, together with an acute sense of order and relationship, which also forms part of a musical sensibility, is chiefly responsible. Hardy responds to experience through its tones, rhythms, and harmonies, its changing tempos, chords and keys. Yet, as we saw in Chapter 2, his visual response is equally subtle and comprehensive. And the two responses, musical and visual, are only in part separate. They are separate in so far as they involve different senses, eye and ear; but in the expression of the total experience they are often fused. In this way Hardy creates 'acoustic pictures' (*RN*, 107). This has a twofold application: sounds may be apprehended pictorially, sights musically. Thus in *Far from the Madding Crowd* the notes of Boldwood's singing, accompanying Bathsheba at the sheep-shearing feast, 'formed a rich unexplored shadow, which threw her tones into relief'. This is predominantly the language of painting; in proximity to 'shadow' even the word 'tones' becomes ambiguous. Earlier in the same novel (p. 148) a predominantly musical language had produced a felicitous piece of synaesthesia: 'Beyond it [the gate of the meadow] the ground was melodious with ripples, and the sky with larks; the low bleating of the flock mingling with both.' And in the garden passage in *Tess* discussed earlier, a chromatic harmony of sight and sound is created as the 'waves of colour' from the glowing weed-flowers mix with the 'waves of sound' from Angel's harp.

One result of this approach is that Hardy in his 'musical pictorialism' comes at times to resemble the Impressionist composers as well as the Impressionist painters. Again the resemblance lies in the sensitivity to overtones, the rendering of shifting impressions and sensations, particularly the play of light and colour. 'The moving sun-shapes on the spray' (*CP*, 573) form a characteristic part of Hardy's vision, as they do of Debussy's or Ravel's. Comparison of Hardy's earth-based, even loamy, writing with the delicate art of Debussy may seem inapposite, until we remember that Hardy's art can be delicate too. Summer in the Froom Valley may be closer to that of Tennyson's Lotos-Eaters ('at mid-day the landscape seemed lying in a swoon') than to that of the *Prélude à l'Après-Midi d'un Faune* or Ravel's *Daphnis and Chloe*. But it is not utterly remote from them either: Hardy's evocation includes the 'still bright green herbage where the water-courses purled' and 'the languid perfume of the summer fruits, the mists, the hay, the flowers' which 'formed ... a vast pool of odour which at this hour [mid-day] seemed to make the animals, the very bees and butterflies, drowsy'. And if the Faun seems significantly absent from that description, he is present elsewhere, in the mysterious *winter* landscape of the poem, 'The Fallow Deer at the Lonely House'. What could be more delicate, more *Debussyish* even, than the second stanza:

> We do not discern those eyes
>   Watching in the snow;
> Lit by lamps of rosy dyes
> We do not discern those eyes
>   Wondering, aglow,
>   Fourfooted, tiptoe?

Here the 'rosy dyes' of the third line seem to spread out to include the deer, who is not simply 'wondering' but 'aglow', and the spreading out is like a musical progression, the melting of one chord into another. The 'radiant hum' with which 'Voices from Things Growing in a Churchyard' ends seems similarly comparable with the Impressionist composers' association of light and sound. And in poems such as the onomatopoeic 'On Sturminster Foot-Bridge' or 'Overlooking the River Stour' or 'The Sundial on a Wet Day' (except for its moralising conclusion), Hardy seems to be attempting to express in verse similar subjects to those Debussy chose for his *Images*, and by equivalent verbal means. The exquisite 'The High-School Lawn' also has in it something of the manner both of the Impressionist painters and of the Impressionist composers:

> Gray prinked with rose,
> White tipped with blue,
> Shoes with gay hose,
> Sleeves of chrome hue;
> Fluffed frills of white,
> Dark bordered light;
> Such shimmerings through
> Trees of emerald green are eyed
> This afternoon, from the road outside.

> They whirl around:
> Many laughters run
> With a cascade's sound;
> Then a mere one.

> A bell: they flee:
> Silence then: –
> So it will be
> Some day again
> With them, – with me.

The first stanza seems a perfect Impressionist painting, a verbal Monet or Renoir. Yet already in the very form of the lines there is the suggestion of a dance, of the 'whirling' of the next stanza; and the 'running' of the laughters in that stanza, together with the bell of the next and the contrasting silence, suggests rather a musical analogy. The terms used are near to those of

music – laughters 'running' together like notes or chords, or played
singly; and words themselves throughout the poem seem on the
point of turning into piano notes, partly perhaps because they
are so predominantly monosyllabic.

In addition, there are a number of poems written, like this
one, in his old age, in which Hardy is content simply serenely
to contemplate a scene or a mood, occasionally adding a moralising
reflection but without disturbing the impression created. In these
poems, though there is nothing in the language or structure themselves
to suggest music, the intention and effect still seem close to Debussy.
There is the same poise, the same sense of the sufficiency of the
moment. I am thinking of such poems as 'Last Week in October',
'The Later Autumn', 'Night-Time in Mid-Fall', 'Shortening Days
at the Homestead', which are all comparable with Debussy's *Brouil-
lards* and *Feuilles mortes*, in manner as well as in subject.

v

So constant and so deep-rooted is Hardy's musical response to
experience and so all-pervasive its presence in his work that it
scarcely seems an exaggeration to call music the 'informing soul'
of that work, the soul which

> With spirits feeds, with vigour fills the whole,
> Each motion guides, and ev'ry nerve sustains;
> Itself unseen, but in th'effects, remains.
>
> (Pope, *Essay on Criticism*)

As well as the elements of melody and harmony which I have
been considering, there are 'the measured movements and melodic
contours suggesting the underlying rhythm of the seasons, of mankind,
and of the universe' noted by Elna Sherman in her article 'Thomas
Hardy: Lyricist, Symphonist'.[12] Through these, his work acquires
a musical form in keeping with its musical texture and content.
'The underlying rhythm of the seasons' is a shaping force in nearly
all the major novels – *Far from the Madding Crowd*, *The Return of
the Native*, *The Woodlanders* and *Tess*. It determines the structure
of *Under the Greenwood Tree*, just as much as it does that of Vivaldi's
or Glazunov's *Seasons*. Hardy's sense of form is sometimes seen

as rather naïve and undeveloped, especially as compared with Henry James's: it is conceded that his novels have shape, but the shape is seen as the imposed shape of the architect, something transferred from the drawing-board, not growing naturally from within the material itself. Ian Gregor in his book *The Great Web* has offered a valuable corrective to this view by demonstrating that Hardy's novels are above all concerned with *process*, with the 'ongoing' involved in story and the 'web of human doings', and that this concern gives the novels their own special kind of unity and wholeness. I would not dispute this, but I should wish to add that the weaving of the web is in some respects a musical process. Music is the most 'ongoing' of the arts: it moves through time as well as in time. Hence its close association with dance. At the heart of Hardy's novels there is always a kind of dance. Hardy himself wrote of *Jude* (*Life*, 273), 'The rectangular lines of the story were not premeditated, but came by chance: except, of course, that the involutions of four lives must necessarily be a sort of quadrille.'

In earlier novels – *Far from the Madding Crowd*, for instance, or *The Mayor of Casterbridge* – the lines are less rectangular, the couples less evenly balanced, but in all of them the sense of a small group of people in their relationships with each other moving through the intricacies of a dance ('Cross hands, cast off, and wheel') is strong. J. Hillis Miller has described it as 'the dance of desire',[13] as indeed, in so far as it involves movements of attraction and repulsion, it undoubtedly is. Apart from *Jude*, its shape is most clearly seen in *The Woodlanders*. Professor Miller compares this novel to 'a slow minuet in which the characters one by one are shown making obeisance at a distance to other characters'.[14] Tempo and style are right there, but I think that in shape it is, rather, a five-handed reel, in which, as Hardy describes it in 'The Fiddler of the Reels', 'the five reelers stood in the form of a cross, the reel being performed by each line of three alternately, the persons who successively came to the middle place dancing in both directions'. Like Car'line, Grace Melbury soon finds herself in this place, 'the axis of the whole performance', and cannot get out of it, dancing towards the man in the two opposing partnerships, according as she is drawn by her 'primitive feelings' or 'modern nerves'. The existence of this dance at the centre of Hardy's novels creates in us a sense of pattern, linear and formal, if not stiff. Offsetting this sense of formality, however, there is the flexibility and fluidity of the narration itself, a fluidity so marked that it can lead the

inattentive reader such as Robert Liddell or (in this matter) Albert
Guerard to suppose that much of Hardy's natural description is
merely decorative. But both formality and fluidity are, I would
suggest, a necessary part of the 'great web': the formality, the
relatively rigid lines of the dance, supplies the spokes or warp;
the fluidity, or fluid parts of the narration, the woof that is woven
on them. And those fluid parts of the narration correspond to
the music that accompanies the dance. A web is a matter of
relationships, of the linking and interweaving, the holding in tension
together, of part with part. So is music: the idea of a web of
sounds is hackneyed and familiar. The web Hardy creates, which
has, as I hope I have demonstrated, its rhythms, melodies, and
harmonies, fully deserves to be called a musical one. My own
feeling is that Hardy's novels are in this respect a literary counterpart
to Wagner's music dramas, in which the voices and actions of
the personages are both set against and blended with a continuous
tissue of melody from the orchestra.

There is, however, a further implication in the phrase 'the great
web'. The phrase as Professor Gregor quotes it comes from *The
Woodlanders*, but, at the time when he was writing that novel,
Hardy entered in his notebook (4 March 1886) another version
of the idea. Thinking already of *The Dynasts*, he wrote (*Life*, 177),
'The human race to be shown as one great network or tissue
which quivers in every part when one point is shaken, like a
spider's web if touched.' F. B. Pinion seems to suggest that this
statement is an anticipation of Hardy's later hopes concerning the
development of altruism, rather than a vision of mankind as 'one
organism', such as he gives us many times in *The Dynasts*.[15] I
think it is both. But, in so far as it does relate to altruism, it
takes us back to certain topics discussed near the start of this
chapter: to the tremulousness of Sue (whom Jude often calls 'quiver-
ing') and others like her, including Hardy himself, a tremulousness
which makes of her 'a harp which the least wind of emotion
from another's heart could make to vibrate as readily as a radical
stir in her own' (*JO*, 292). The web and the harp are at one
in this; indeed, the web virtually *is* a harp. If, as Professor Gregor
rightly maintains, the 'great web' of Hardy's fiction makes us
aware of the presence of the author 'as a determining element
in the quality of the work',[16] then again we may see the web
as a musical web, the 'wind of emotion' from his fellow-creatures
reverberating on its creator's own heart-strings.

With *The Dynasts* there comes a change of perspective, as the 'Will-webs' are contemplated from a point of view above and outside them, rather than from within. The 'still, sad music of humanity' is still heard –

> These mortal minions' bootless cadences,
> Played on the stops of their anatomy
>
> (2. IV. viii)

– and the dance of life goes on, Napoleon footing his reel along with all

> the frail ones that his flings
> Have made gyrate like animalcula
> In tepid pools.
>
> (Fore Scene)

The 'eternal artistries' blindly woven by the Immanent Will are fashioned to a kind of dance, but it is a dance without pattern or purpose, a frenzied *perpetuum mobile* of 'coils', 'welterings', 'madding movements':

> Amid this scene of bodies substantive
> Strange waves I sight like winds grown visible,
> Which bear men's forms on their innumerous coils,
> Twining and serpentining round and through.
>
> (Fore Scene)

And the accompanying music is a mere *discordia concors*. One feeling poignantly embodied in the work is Hardy's longing to find music, music that will speak of order and purpose and compassion, within creation. The Pities voice that longing for 'a thorough-sphered melodic rule, / And governance of sweet consistency' after the death of Nelson, and again at the end of the drama, where in a spirit of wishful thinking they 'hymn' the Will for having achieved it, despite appearances, but are answered by the more sceptical and experienced Years:

> Something of difference animates your quiring,
> O half-convinced Compassionates and fond,
> From chords consistent with our spectacle!

And, in the Semichoruses that follow, the Years repeat the question, 'To what tune danceth this Immense?' And again,

> Last as first the question rings
> Of the Will's long travailings;
> > Why the All-mover,
> > Why the All-prover
> Ever urges on and measures out the chordless chime of Things.

A footnote to the last line refers to Horace's *Epistles*, 1. 12, where the phrase 'concordia discors' occurs. Hardy uses the phrase again in the poem 'Genitrix Laesa', where Nature is censured for supposing that she has created in life a 'rhythmic chime'. Relevant too is the poem 'The Lacking Sense', where it is asked of 'the Mother', 'Why weaves she not her world-webs to according lutes and tabors?' All these examples show Hardy regarding the universe as did Sue Bridehead when she imagined that it 'resembled a stanza or melody composed in a dream; it was wonderfully excellent to the half-aroused intelligence, but hopelessly absurd at the full waking'. He would like to believe in the excellence of that melody, but his wide-awake intelligence will not permit it.

What we see in *The Dynasts*, then, is man and the universe aspiring to the condition of music, but aspiring hopelessly. When Hardy speaks (3. 1. i) of 'the films or brain-tissues of the Immanent Will, that pervade all things' as being 'like breezes made visible' under the 'unnatural light' that reveals them briefly to the Spirits, he comes near to seeing music, itself so abstract and breeze-like, as the animating principle of the universe, or of Being. But to identify those breezes entirely with music would be to hear those harmonies his intelligence denied. In trying to hear them, in making his Years and Pities yearn for them, Hardy may, I think, have been partly influenced by Schopenhauer, from whom, it is generally agreed, he in part derived his notion of the Immanent Will. For in *The World as Will and Idea*, the work in which he expounds his doctrine of the will, Schopenhauer also gives an account of the arts as the primary means by which man gains intuitive insight into reality, and, arranging them hierarchically, sees music as the very summit and pinnacle, carrying us beyond the sensible and the conceptual to the Idea of the world. It represents 'the very ultimate essence of the life of will throughout the universe'.[17] Awareness of these ideas may, I think, have quickened Hardy's interest in music – that is, in serious music – in the 1890s and later, the period in which he was writing *The Dynasts*. He would have liked, I suggest, to have incorporated Schopenhauer's theories of music in his drama, along with his doctrine of the will. But he could not do so, because he could not hear that ultimate, metaphysical music. His experience answered rather to that described by Edwin Muir:

The desolations have no word nor music,
Only an endless inarticulate cry . . . .

And yet there *is* music in *The Dynasts*, the 'aerial music' which accompanies the Phantom Intelligences when they express themselves chorally or in antiphon. These Intelligences, according to notes made, like his note on the 'great network or tissue ... like a spider's web', on 4 March 1886 (a day fertile in ideas for his coming *magnum opus*), are 'Abstract realisms', 'the true realities of life, hitherto called abstractions'. Possibly only the Spirit of the Years conforms entirely to this description; the others, the Spirits Sinister and Ironic and the Spirit of the Pities, represent, rather, personified human attitudes, particularly attitudes within Hardy himself. Even so, their music may be a 'Schopenhauerism', the expression of an abstraction, of something that cannot be put into words. Whatever the nature of the Overworld they inhabit, these abstractions, after all, are abstractions from humanity. They are, in that sense, ethical forces. And Schopenhauer saw music as itself an ethical force, capable of embodying the ideal and of influencing conduct.

One must say of *The Dynasts*, as Goethe said of Marlowe's *Doctor Faustus*, 'How grandly it is all conceived!' And it is conceived, it seems clear, in part as a music-drama. Elna Sherman has a fine description of the work in these terms, likening the Fore Scene to 'a prelude of a vast music-drama or the introduction to a gigantic tone-poem', and continuing,

Although Hardy disclaims a perfect organic unity for his great epic drama, the musical undercurrent that flows through it from beginning to end supplies a unity of a more subtle kind. Whether or not Hardy was himself conscious of this is a matter of little consequence, but that a musical background was plainly in his mind cannot be denied.[18]

She also suggests that the 'interplay of Intelligences with the human action corresponds to the interweaving of motive and figure in the development of symphonic music'.[19] Various parallels suggest themselves: Wagner first of all, and his 'vast music-drama', *The Ring* – itself, we may remember, influenced by the theories of Schopenhauer, and, like Hardy's work, embodying the notion that virtue may be transmitted from man to the Gods. But, as well as opera, oratorio: the many recitatives (some by Recording Angels) and antiphons are a reminder of Hardy's fondness for this form and of his visits to Exeter Hall in the 1860s, and suggest a view of the work as an ironic *Messiah* or *Creation*.

In its complex ordering and blending of such a varied mass of material, allied to that 'aerial music', *The Dynasts* does suggest some musical work on the grand scale. This involves a paradox, however, for all this order and shapeliness and music is in the service of a vision of a world in which there is neither order nor shape nor music. Or, if there is music, it is perhaps the unearthly, inhuman, electronic music of our own day, sounding through the 'brain-tissues of the Immanent Will', the

> fibrils, veins,
> Will-tissues, nerves, and pulses of the Cause,
> That heave throughout the Earth's compositure.

Against this the plaintive voice of the Pities, answering the sardonic tones of the Spirits Ironic and Sinister and the disillusioned common sense of the Years, rises like the violin in one of Beethoven's last quartets. Otherwise there is little in this dry, rarefied atmosphere to remind us of the warmth and tenderness of the music heard in the novels and poems. The tune to which 'danceth this Immense' is not of that kind.

But, after all, it is the song of the earth, rather than the music of the spheres, that sounds most clearly in Hardy's work.

> Mock on, Shade, if thou wilt! But others find
> Poesy ever lurk where pit-pats poor mankind!

says the Spirit of the Pities to the Spirit Ironic (2. III. i). Not only poesy, we might add, but music too. 'Pit-pat' is a favourite and characteristic word of Hardy. Where 'poor mankind' pit-pats, hearts beat, music pulses, and feet tread a measure on the earth. That is why music and dance are inextricably interwoven in the fabric of his work.

6 The Composite Muse

The Muse who addresses Hardy in the Vatican embodies more arts than those we have been considering. 'But my love goes further', says the poet, mentioning by name 'Form', 'Story', and 'Hymn'. The place of Story in Hardy's work is self-evident. His affinity, even in his novels, with the ballad-writers has often been remarked: his tale-telling, however refined by art, follows the 'instinctive primitive narrative shape' of that of old wives and minstrels, and he accepts the role of entertainer as both a duty and a delight. 'Hymn' also, taken in the sense of lyric or poetry, is not so much a part of his work as its *sine qua non*. This is apparent, not from the poems alone, but also from what Jean Brooks has called 'the poetic structure' of the novels.[1] Hardy was first and last a poet, and if in his work the Muses are, as the goddess of the Vatican says, one, this is ultimately because the other arts have there been converted into poetry: hers is the final shape of which these are the 'phases'.

Without 'Story' and 'Hymn', then, Hardy's work would be as disembodied and unimaginable as the Cheshire Cat. But what of 'Form'? In the sonnet it represents sculpture, but in a broader sense it could be taken to include architecture too. Hardy's novels are notably well designed, a feature which has sometimes been attributed to his architectural training. Yet, although this element of design is certainly consistent with such training, it would be difficult to prove that it is specifically architectural in character (rather than, say, symphonic, choreographic, or simply literary). Rather, it reflects an innate planning ability common to both his architectural and literary activities, the same ability perhaps that enabled him despite his abhorrence of war to 'take a keen pleasure in war strategy and tactics, following it as if it were a game of chess'.[2] Hardy's own statements concerning Form in the novel relate mainly to plot, and are thoroughly orthodox, even neo-classical: he quotes Addison (on epic) and like Johnson on *Samson Agonistes* he looks for 'a beginning, middle, and end' (*Life*, 291), and insists on 'the well-knit interdependence of parts', or what Johnson would call their 'concatenation'. He relates the pleasure such 'constructive art' can give us to sculpture, not architecture, comparing it with 'the Apollo and the Aphrodite'.[3] This suggests that he thinks of the art of the novel less in terms of building around a space than of coaxing shape out of shapeless matter. He also thinks of 'artistic form' in terms of drama, particularly Greek drama – not surprisingly, since his critical theories go back ultimately to Aristotle's *Poetics*. He likes 'a well-rounded tale' and finds in the Bible 'the spherical completeness of perfect art' (*Life*, 171).

This is not to deny to Architecture a place among the sister arts which have helped to shape Hardy's work. Hardy himself draws attention to the parallel between poetry and architecture in general – that both arts have 'to carry a rational content inside their artistic form' – and between his own poetry and Gothic architecture in particular (*Life*, 301). He compares the 'cunning irregularity' of his verse to that of Gothic architecture and relates it to his adoption therein of 'the Gothic art-principle in which he had been trained – the principle of spontaneity, found in mouldings, tracery, and such like'. This produced, he claims, the 'unforeseen' character of his metres and stanzas, 'that of stress rather than of syllable, poetic texture rather than poetic veneer'. The irregularity and variety Hardy is stressing have already been too well discussed elsewhere, notably by Kenneth Marsden, to require fresh examination here. As Marsden says, the reader 'soon becomes acquainted with the most important consequence of their use, the cross-grained texture for which Hardy's poetry is well-known'.[4] This texture owes as much, however, to vocabulary as to verse structure. The oddity of Hardy's diction, its mixture of archaisms, dialect words, coinages, and so on, its stubborn individualism and defiant uncouthness, bring to mind the 'rough and harsh terms' of Spenser's *Shepherd's*

Calendar. And, just as Spenser's language helped to root both his poetic world and his poetry itself in the past, so too does Hardy's. Since, historically considered, the Gothic revival had its own roots in Spenser, the comparison may suggest that it is not merely fanciful to find something Gothic in the texture of Hardy's verse. Not merely a 'Gothic art-principle' but a love of Gothic itself may have led him to try to create in his poetry a verbal equivalent of those 'mouldings, tracery ... the carved leafage of some capital or spandrel' that he mentions.

Marsden also interestingly suggests that some of Hardy's poems reveal their architectural character by their very appearance on the page. He describes the effect upon the reader as being to force him 'to realize that there is a *complicated* pattern here, and yet encouraging him by assurance that there *is* a *pattern*'.[5] Our experience of the novels is perhaps a variant of this: we recognise the existence of a clear uncomplicated basic design, but are aware of a complicated pattern developing within it. Shapely and well-knit as Hardy's plots may be, the action itself proliferates incidents and develops through a series of 'unforeseen' twists and turns. Such intricacy, in union with an over-all structure that is both balanced and controlled, could perhaps plausibly be seen as an expression of the same 'Gothic' tendencies as are acknowledged in the verse.

One thing seems clear: the architectural features of Hardy's art derive more from his experience of actual buildings than from his experience at the drawing-board. He feels 'the poetry of architecture' (Ruskin's phrase), and he finds that poetry, it would appear, largely in its detail, in the products of the architect's – or stone-mason's – craft. His response is both visual and tactile; it is a response to surfaces, material, moulding, line and curve. In this respect it is at one with his response to sculpture: in each case it is the 'chiselled shapes' that hold him. Jude, feeling with his fingers the 'contours' of the mouldings and carving of the Christminster colleges (*JO*, 103) is aesthetically not so very far removed from Clym Yeobright with his exclamation, 'Let me ... dwell on every line and curve in it!' (*RN*, 212), as he gazes at the face of Eustacia, the 'exquisite finish' of whose beauty, I suggested earlier, approaches the sculptural. This feeling for mould and contour informs all Hardy's work, both verse and prose. It is present everywhere, from the shaping of plot and incident down to the structure of the sentence.

Above all, however, the importance of architecture for Hardy lies in the wealth of human associations that buildings gather round them. They embody 'memories, history, fellowship, fraternities', and it is, in his opinion, for these, even more than for any aesthetic qualities, that they should be preserved.[6] His many loving descriptions of such buildings, particularly dwelling-houses – Bathsheba's homestead, Melbury's house, Overcombe Mill, Oxwell Hall – reflect this view, with their eye for how Nature's 'filings and effacements' mingle with 'the marks of human wear and tear' (*TM*, 72). People and houses become through their shared experience part of each other. 'Part of her body and life it ever seemed to be', says Hardy of Tess's home; 'the slope of its dormers, the finish of its gables, the broken courses of brick which topped the chimney, all had something in common with her personal character' (*TD*, 369). Conversely, the old house of the poem 'The Two Houses' stands 'packed' with the presences of its past inmates.

Buildings are thus living records of the past and especially of the *social* past, which they preserve not only in its beginnings but also in its changes. Thus, as Hardy says of the Christminster colleges (*JO*, 108), they need do nothing but wait, and they become poetical. Clearly F. E. Halliday is right when he says of Hardy,

His historical sense, his feeling for continuity and the beauty of association were intensified by his architectural studies, and they lie at the root of his novels and poems, almost, it might be said, they are the roots.[7]

His works themselves resemble such buildings, coated like Hintock House 'with lichen of every shade', thronged and 'obsessed' as is the old house in the poem with remembered presences. Hardy in his works is a true preservationist.

Yet as with other buildings so in the house of life there are, he recognises, conflicting interests. Oxwell Hall 'had all the romantic excellencies and practical drawbacks which such mildewed places share in common with caves, mountains, wildernesses, glens, and other homes of poesy that people of taste wish to live and die in' (*TM*, 71). So with Stancy Castle: the conflict between ancient and modern expressed there in architectural terms gives *A Laodicean* a thematic centrality in Hardy's work, whatever its narrative deficiencies. For, as F. R. Southerington has said, there is in Hardy a conflict 'between the rationalism he wished to hold and the nostalgia for a lost past which he had wished to retain', and this conflict within the man finds expression in his art.[8] Not surprisingly, it often does so through architecture. The Crystal Palace *versus* St Pancras station: an art that could produce both within a few years of each other was well fitted to embody such oppositions. Nor is there an easy victory for either side. For all his nostalgia, Hardy is tolerant of new developments. The poem 'Architectural Masks', for instance, recognises that 'inner lives of dreams' may be lived in a villa of 'blazing brick and plated show' as easily as in an 'old mansion mossed and fair', which may harbour long-established but sordid materialists. Even Mr Woodwell's house with its depressing lack of mosses to disguise 'the stiff straight line where wall met earth' is acknowledged to be 'clean, and clear, and dry' (*L*, 259) – virtues of a kind. And in *Jude* the issues are joined. The 'lichened colleges' of Christminster may be poetical, but they are also rotten, like the traditions they represent. The 'precision, mathematical straightness, smoothness, exactitude' of the stone-mason's yard where restoration is undertaken are seen as praiseworthy. And yet of what use is restoration in a world being shaped by 'other developments', a world 'in which Gothic architecture and its associations had no place'? Jude fails to see, says Hardy (p. 108), 'the deadly animosity of contemporary logic and vision towards so much of what he held in reverence'. But Hardy sees it, and it is the source of much of his unhappiness. The tone of the remark recalls Keats's 'Do not all charms fly / At the mere touch of cold philosophy?' As an artist, this is where Hardy's sympathies lie. Significantly, it is after his artistic sense has left him and his appreciativeness become 'capable of exercising itself only on utilitarian matters' (*WB*, 186) that Jocelyn Pierston occupies himself in 'acquiring some old moss-grown, mullioned Elizabethan cottages, for the purpose of pulling them down because they were damp'.

II

'But probably few literary critics discern the solidarity of all the arts,' says Hardy (*Life*, 300). Perhaps not; yet, if so, one wonders how the idea could have escaped them, since it was decidedly in the air during the 1890s, the period to which this statement

relates. At the very least, a critic could have been expected to
know Pater's 'All art constantly aspires towards the condition of
music.' Unless he were culturally completely blinkered, he would
also be aware of the existence of Wagner's music-dramas and of
the composer's theoretical arguments in favour of a synthesis of
the arts. Wagner found an imitator within what could be regarded
as Hardy's own circle, in the experiments in the creation of a
'Pictorial–Musical play' of the artist Hubert Herkomer, which
attracted some publicity at this period.[9] A little earlier there had
been Whistler's *Nocturnes* and *Symphonies*. In France music, painting
and poetry showed a repeated tendency to converge, notably in
the work of Delacroix, Baudelaire and the Impressionists. Delacroix
had cultivated what he called 'the music of the picture', and
Baudelaire, noting in his study of the painter how he had achieved
his effects with 'the eloquence of a passionate musician', commented
on the aspiration of the arts of the nineteenth century to a condition
'in which they lend each other new powers'.[10] Baudelaire's own
verse owes much to synaesthetic experience, celebrated in his famous
sonnet 'Correspondances'. In music, one of the century's distinctive
creations was the tone-poem. From Berlioz to Tchaikovsky, composers
sought repeatedly to distil the essence of a literary work in sound,
or, as in Mussorgsky's *Pictures from an Exhibition*, reversed Whistler's
aims. Shaw commented,

> In the nineteenth century it was no longer necessary to be a
> born pattern designer in sound to be a composer. One had
> but to be a dramatist or a poet completely susceptible to the
> dramatic and descriptive powers of sound.[11]

And, even if some or all of the artists we have named were too
advanced for the kind of critic Hardy was thinking of, there was
still the example of the Victorian theatre itself, with its ceaseless
endeavour to turn the stage into a picture. In the theatre reviews
of the period the commonest adjective of praise is 'picturesque'.
Henry James could assume sufficient familiarity on the part of
his readers both with this picturesqueness and with the idea of
the oneness of the arts to make ironic play with both. 'If all
art is supposed to be one', he writes, then there is 'no great
violence of transition' in passing from a review of the London
art-exhibitions to a review of its theatres. 'The British stage has

indeed a considerable analogy to British painting', he observes. The reader awaits some interesting development of this idea from a critic who had said of Irving's Charles I that he 'might have stepped down from the canvas of Vandyke' and had found the scenery of the Lyceum's *William and Susan* 'as trim and tidy as a Dutch picture'. He learns that 'Both at the playhouses and at the exhibitions [the reader] encounters a good deal of Philistinism.'[12]

Philistine or not, the stage-pictures are there. In every kind of production, from Shakespeare to opera, melodrama to pantomime, the energies of actors, scene-painters, and stage-technicians were largely directed towards the achievement of striking pictorial effects. Wherever the action was set, in town or country, at home or abroad, strenuous efforts were made to re-create the scene. Total illusion, together with a dramatic heightening, was the aim. This is apparent in the anxious footnote of the playwright Watts Phillips to a stage direction in his Adelphi melodrama *Lost in London*:

The above explains my reason for requiring a great width of window at back. I wish the great city to appear *most distinctly*, as a background to the last act of the drama. The moonlight view will give a beautiful tone to the scene.[13]

Such 'beautiful tone', a stage-poetry arising out of the stage-pictures, was accepted as the theatre's crowning glory. Thus Clement Scott, writing of the Lyceum's 1890 production of Merivale's *Ravenswood*, recollects 'that lovely and poetic picture' at the end of the play, with 'the lonely Caleb, in the full glow of the evening sun, bending down in reverence over the eagle's plume of his lost and loved master' (who has just sunk in the quicksands).[14] And such enthusiasm was common. Hardy acknowledges this aspect of the theatre in his comment on the 'rosy cloud' following the sunset that closes the scene in the furmity-tent in *The Mayor of Casterbridge*: 'To watch it was like looking at some grand feat of stagery from a darkened auditorium.' His own 'grand feats' of description and his picture-making in general fill out his image of the *theatrum mundi*. And not Hardy alone but most nineteenth-century novelists were at one with the theatre-managers in this matter. United in their devotion to the picturesque, they share the assumption that this may best be achieved through the deliberate creation of pictures.

Creation might take the form of imitation: the stage-productions
of the period are as full of allusions to and reminiscences of actual
paintings as are Hardy's novels, from the tableau imitating Wilkie
in Douglas Jerrold's *Rent Day* in the early years of the century,
to 'one glowing pastiche of Turner after another'[15] in *Ravenswood*
at the end.

Literature and theatre were thus linked by their common devotion
to a third art, that of painting. Painters themselves often chose
their subjects from literature and the theatre. Music and theatre
were united in the very term 'melodrama'. Through melodrama
and pantomime the oneness of the arts could be experienced in
some degree even at the most popular level.

Much of what the nineteenth-century theatre was striving for,
in its melodrama and pantomime no less than in the operas of
Wagner, was to be realised in what was indeed the 'art work
of the future', namely cinema. As an art-form, cinema has its
roots in stage-melodrama, rather than in the embryonic cinematic
devices we noticed in Chapter 4, many of which had in any
case been utilised by the theatre. But its mobility and freedom
made possible the realisation of that ideal which James saw as
beyond the capacity of the London stage: 'To have the picture
complete at the same time the figures do their part in producing
the particular illusion required – what a perfection and what a
joy!'[16] It could go further than any of the other arts in the 'synchroni-
sation of the senses'. Eisenstein especially recognised this. 'The
problem of the synthesis of the arts is of vital concern to cinematogra-
phy', he wrote. 'Men, music, light, landscape, colour and motion
brought into one integrated whole by a single piercing emotion,
by a single theme and idea – this is the aim of modern cinematogra-
phy'.[17] This statement, which could serve as a description of the
kind of synthesis Hardy achieves within the verbal medium, helps
to explain why the anticipation of cinema is so marked in his
work.

Hardy was not himself to any significant degree a theorist about
art. If the various arts have a place in his work it is not primarily
in obedience to a theory; it is because, as the sonnet says, he loves
them all. They are a part of his experience, and his work reflects
his experience. He is also a little like Bottom, wanting to play
all the parts. Thus the other arts are 'influences' on his work,
supplementing and operating in the same way as the various literary
influences observable there. Hardy is, as he always insisted, highly

impressionable, and his cultural impressions have been readily assimilated to his own art. The composite Muse who appears to him in the Vatican is in this sense his own work personified. We may recognise his making common cause with the Victorian theatre in his combination of drama, picture, and music, but to go further and to associate his synthesis with the subtle and sophisticated ideas and experiments of such artists as Wagner, Delacroix and Eisenstein may seem mistaken. Yet I believe it is not.

I would point first of all to the remarkable resemblance between the Vatican sonnet and *The Well-Beloved*, both novel and poem. Just as Pierston is 'the Wandering Jew of the love-world' (*WB*, 77), so the poet is the Wandering Jew of the art-world. But the art-world here is itself a love-world: the poet is 'the wooer of all'. And Pierston's love-world is also the art-world: all his dreams of the Beloved he 'translated into plaster' (p. 64), and the statement describing him as the Wandering Jew goes on to reflect 'how restlessly ideal his fancies were, how the artist in him had consumed the wooer'. Hardy called *The Well-Beloved* 'A Sketch of a Temperament': the sonnet could be similarly described. And in both instances the temperament is essentially Hardy's own. He was as susceptible in his relations with women as he was towards the Muses, and the volatility of Pierston's affections parallels his own. As a sculptor, seeking to express in 'durable shape' the ideal beauty he has found in 'mutable flesh', Pierston fittingly represents his author: for Hardy too, art is a shaping, and in the sonnet under discussion his own art appears to him simultaneously as the manifestation of the Well-Beloved and as a piece of sculpture.

Also to be related to 'Rome: The Vatican' is the strange and disturbing poem 'The Chosen'. This tells how the poet's beloved (who may, as Robert Gittings suggests,[18] be Emma Gifford), becomes, on discovering that she has had five predecessors in his affections, a 'composite form', all five 'made one' with her and expressed in her face. This 'various womanhood in blend' he carries to 'an arbour small', where she lies curiously inert, almost as if she had become a piece of sculpture – one of (in Keats's phrase) 'the sculptured dead' perhaps – where he 'tends' her unceasingly, thus atoning 'in one . . . to all'. Whatever the poem's precise meaning, it clearly reinforces the sonnet's emphasis on the importance to him of the idea of the many in the one.

Both this lady and the composite Muse herself have something in common with yet another figure, that of the man in the poem

'So Various', who after presenting himself in a number of varied
and conflicting aspects is identified in the last stanza:

> Now. ... All these specimens of man,
> So various in their pith and plan,
>   Curious to say
>   Were *one* man. Yea,
>   I was all they.

This view of a human life or personality as a whole composed
of differing phases or aspects is characteristic of Hardy. We may
recall the phases of which both Tess's face and her story were
composed, or think of Eustacia, whose face in death 'eclipsed all
its living phases'. Pierston's sculptures portray Aphrodite 'in every
conceivable phase and mood' (*WB*, 75). 'Phase' and 'mood' come
close to being synonyms for Hardy – a reminder of the emotion-based
nature of his view of art and of life, as well as of his sense
of the fleetingness of impressions. And what eye and heart perceived,
science confirmed: Hardy's awareness of the phases of existence
had no doubt been rendered more acute by his study of Darwin.
Of the Well-Beloved herself it is remarked (*WB*, 64) 'Nothing
was permanent in her but change'.

The idea of the phases, used in such an aesthetic context and
explicitly associated at times with the moon, naturally suggests
Yeats, and in a sense 'Rome: The Vatican' is Hardy's 'Byzantium',
and the composite Muse his version of the starlit or the moonlit
dome. Hardy has little inclination to disdain 'the fury and the mire
of human veins'; rather, his art is truly, almost literally, the 'great-
rooted blossomer', rooted in the earth in a way, or to an extent,
that Yeats's never was. His love of perfection was nevertheless
probably as great as Yeats's. His aesthetic as well as his moral
sensibilities were offended by its lack. 'The cry of a child by
the roadway' wronged his heart, and not merely, as with Yeats,
the image of beauty within it, yet he too had his image of the
ideal. Mr Springrove's description of his son Edward and his 'seeing
too far into things – being discontented with make-shifts – thinking
o' perfection in things, and then sickened that there's no such
thing as perfection' (*DR*, 152) fits Hardy himself. Like Yeats too
he saw in perfection and imperfection a contrast between the states
of being and becoming. His admiration for 'the spherical wholeness

of perfect art' is comparable with Yeats's. His insistence that 'A novel is an impression, not an argument' is not so very far removed from Yeats's 'You can refute Hegel, but not the Song of Sixpence.'

It is closer still to the artistic creed and practice of Proust. Proust's admiration for Hardy is well known, and both writers acknowledged the resemblance between *The Well-Beloved* and *À la Recherche du Temps Perdu*, all that part of it, at any rate, that concerns Marcel's pursuit through various women of a phantom of his own creating. The basis for the resemblance is a remarkable similarity between the writers themselves in temperament and sensibility; even, discounting their very different social origins and upbringing, in experience. The little boy who 'danced in a dream' or who liked to recite 'And now another day is gone' while watching the 'chromatic effect' of the evening sun on the staircase's Venetian red (*Life*, 15), like that other little boy who was made to think melancholy thoughts by the sight of the images cast by his magic lantern on his bedroom walls at Combray, was at the start of a life that in its sensitivity and impressionability was afterwards to be fittingly characterised as a 'tremulous stay'. His art too, despite the more conventional and miscellaneous forms he worked in, was to be, like Marcel's, essentially a realisation of that life, a re-creation of the 'structure of sensations' (*TD*, 119), which defined its tremulousness. For Proust and Hardy are alike in their recognition of the subjective nature of experience, and of the paramount importance of the impression. Proust, much the more intellectual and analytical of the two, both expounds and acts upon his insights, thus filling out for us perceptions which in Hardy remain relatively mere *obiter dicta*, inklings followed intuitively rather than deliberately. The re-creation of past experience involves for him a strenuous effort to identify and express the exact sensations and feelings by which the experience impressed itself upon the mind. 'Every impression', he says, 'is double and the one half which is sheathed in the object is prolonged in ourselves by another half which we alone can know.'[19] By concentrating on this second half the artist is able to recover the impression itself in all its fullness. In this way art enlarges experience for us all, enabling us 'to know that essential quality of another person's sensations' in a way that love, as much of Marcel's history demonstrates, never can. 'Through art alone' he tells us, 'are we able to emerge from ourselves, to know what another person sees of a universe which is not the same as our own and of which, without art, the landscapes would remain as unknown to us as those that may exist in the moon'.[20]

Many of Hardy's statements about the nature and function of art, although made more tentatively and often only in the privacy of his notebooks, express an essentially similar view. His practice, moreover, like Proust's own, exemplifies it. Thus, much of Hardy's work is, like Proust's, a search for Lost Time, and one pursued in the same way, through the patient recovery of all the various sensations of which that time was composed. It is this that gives the sense of reality to his novels: their substance, the tissue of sensations of which they are so largely composed, was woven on the loom of memory. Despite obvious differences in subject-matter and technique, the two writers apprehend experience fundamentally in the same way. This is borne out in many parts of their work: in their recognition of the 'phases' of which a human face or personality is composed, and their extension of this perception to a human life as a whole and to the work of art in which such a life is realised; in their awareness of the transforming powers of 'Time the artist' (Proust's phrase; Hardy has 'Time the magician'); in their sense also of the significance of those moments when Time closes up like a fan (Hardy's phrase, occurring in one of Proust's favourite novels, *A Pair of Blue Eyes*). And in organising and expressing such perceptions both writers make use of the other arts. *À la Recherche* is, as well as a novel, both a piece of music and a painting, a fact reflected and symbolised in the great central images of Vinteuil and Elstir. But Vinteuil and Elstir (and Bergotte the prose-writer and Berma the actress) are, we might say, present in Hardy's work too, in the sense that it is shaped in the image of all these arts. Quite apart from these major presences, however, Proust's work resembles Hardy's in the way in which aesthetic analogies are woven into its very texture and fibre. They are, moreover, the same analogies: paintings of many schools, sculpture, theatre, the 'violin within us', the transparency, magic-lantern show, fairy play and transformation scene, and (explicitly in Proust, implicitly in Hardy) the cinematograph. Proust said that he needed 'to borrow comparisons from the loftiest and the most varied arts' in order to give some idea of the task he was undertaking, the realising of a life within the confines of a book.[21] Such allusions do more than this, however. They are one of the means by which the mind's distance from, yet possession of, the object is suggested. They help to create a world 'real without being actual, ideal without being abstract'[22] in which that possession is recovered and the 'doubleness' of the impression maintained. In all these respects Proust's employment of the composite Muse to intensify the expression of things both illuminates and confirms the seriousness of Hardy's.

There is a genuine simplicity in Hardy in relation to which such illumination may seem superfluous. But there is also a deceptive simplicity which has proved strangely tough and resistant to analysis. Here this approach may be more helpful. The 'solidarity' of the arts, as they combine in his work, helps to give the world he creates its remarkable solidity. They link internal and external in a form of stereoscopic vision and stereophonic sound that achieves an effect of high fidelity. They provide an outlet for the born aesthete that Hardy is, and at the same time enrich the expression of that 'power of observation informed by a living heart'[23] in the face of 'All the vast various moils that mean a world alive' (*CP*, 49) which makes Hardy's such a sympathetic and enduring art.

Notes

CHAPTER 1

1. *Thomas Hardy's Personal Writings*, ed. Harold Orel (Lawrence, Kan., 1966, and London, 1967) 120.
2. Ibid., 96.
3. Ibid., 105.
4. Lionel Johnson, *The Art of Thomas Hardy* (London, 1894) 72.
5. *T. S. Eliot, Selected Prose*, ed. John Hayward (London, 1953) 196.
6. *Hardy's Personal Writings*, 170.
7. Johnson, *Art of Hardy*, 70.
8. Albert J. Guerard, *Thomas Hardy, The Novels and Stories* (London, 1949) 7.

CHAPTER 2

1. Lloyd Fernando, 'Thomas Hardy's Rhetoric of Painting', *Review of English Literature*, VI (1965) 62–73.
2. Quoted by Carl J. Weber in *'Dearest Emmie': Thomas Hardy's Letters to his First Wife* (London, 1963) 100.
3. Some of the poems may refer to experiences of the 1860s or 1870s, and may have been written, or begun, at that period.
4. *Van Gogh, A Self-Portrait. Letters Revealing his Life as a Painter*, selected by W. H. Auden (London, 1961) 244.
5. Apart from a passing reference in the short story 'Alicia's Diary' to 'the beautiful altarpiece by Bellini' in the Church of the Frari in Venice (*SS*, 818).
6. The work in question is now attributed to Spinello Aretino. See *TD*, Notes, 436.

7. *Thomas Hardy, The Critical Heritage*, ed. R. G. Cox (London and New York, 1970) 4. See also Charles Morgan, *The House of Macmillan, 1843–1943* (London, 1944) 92.

8. *Hardy, The Critical Heritage*, 8.

9. Mario Praz, *The Hero in Eclipse in Victorian Fiction*, trans. from the Italian by Angus Davidson (Oxford, 1956) 11.

10. For example, Praz, *The Hero in Eclipse*; Raymond Lister, *Victorian Narrative Paintings* (London, 1966); Peter Conrad, *The Victorian Treasure-House* (London, 1973).

11. *Thomas Hardy, The Critical Heritage*, 21.

12. Reproduced in Christopher Wood, *Dictionary of Victorian Painters* (Woodbridge, Suffolk, 1971), 292.

13. This engraving appeared in the first number of *The Graphic*, 4 Dec 1869. A painting based on it, *Applicants for Admission to a Casual Ward*, was exhibited at the Royal Academy in 1874. (Present owner: Royal Holloway College.) In the painting the central figure is considerably changed; the marks of dignity have disappeared, and with them the suggestion of his higher social standing.

14. *English Influences on Vincent Van Gogh. An exhibition organised by the Fine Art Department, University of Nottingham and the Arts Council of Great Britain 1974–5*, Introduction and Catalogue by Ronald Pickvance, 43.

15. *Hardy's Personal Writings*, 176, 181.

16. Present owner: Royal Holloway College.

17. Graham Reynolds, *Victorian Painting* (London, 1966) 93 and 88 (plate).

18. Robert R. Wark, *Drawings by Thomas Rowlandson in the Huntington Collection* (San Marino, 1975) illus. 464.

19. Alastair Smart, 'Pictorial Imagery in the Novels of Thomas Hardy', *Review of English Studies*, n.s., XII (1961) 266.

20. Now attributed to one of Greuze's followers. See Smart, in *Review of English Studies*, n.s., XII; and *DR*, Notes, 393.

21. For example, in the Tate Gallery catalogue (to accompany an exhibition of the same name) *Landscape in Britain, c. 1750–1850* (London, 1973), compiled by Leslie Parris: No. 246, Linnell, *Harvest Home, Sunset (The Last Load)*; No. 247, G. R. Lewis, . . . *Harvest Scene, Afternoon*; No. 260, De Wint, *A Cornfield*; Nos 314 and 315, F. M. Brown, *Carrying Corn* and *The Hayfield*.

22. Wolfgang Stechow, *Dutch Landscape Painting of the Seventeenth Century* (London, 1966) 46.

23. Reproduced in the Tate Gallery catalogue *Landscape in Britain*, No. 272.

24. T. S. R. Boase, *English Art, 1800–1870* (Oxford, 1959) 109. Crome's *On the Skirts of the Forest* and De Wint's *Woody Landscape*, both in the Victoria and Albert, also have this character of 'immensity', and a certain mystery.

25. *English Influences on Vincent Van Gogh*, 18.

26. Reproduced in Edward Lucie-Smith, *A Concise History of French Painting* (London, 1971) illus. 211.

27. *Van Gogh, A Self-Portrait*, 106–7, 116.

28. Kenneth Clark, *Landscape into Art* (London, 1949) 94.
29. It is curious to note that Marlotte is the name of the village near the Forest of Fontainebleau where Monet, Sisley and Renoir painted during the 1860s. See William Gaunt, *The Impressionists* (London, 1970) 14.
30. Clark, *Landscape into Art*, 141.
31. A. Alvarez, '*Jude the Obscure*', in *Hardy, A Collection of Critical Essays*, ed. Albert J. Guerard, (Englewood Cliffs, NJ, 1963) 121.
32. Alison Fairlie, 'Aspects of Expression in Baudelaire's Art Criticism', in *French Nineteenth-century Painting and Literature*, ed. Ulrich Finke (Manchester, 1972) 44.
33. John Dewey, *Art as Experience* (New York, 1958) 18.

CHAPTER 3

1. *Hardy's Personal Writings*, 114.
2. Ibid., 142.
3. Ibid., 124.
4. Reprinted in *English Plays of the Nineteenth Century*, vol. III: *Comedies*, ed. Michael R. Booth (Oxford, 1973).
5. Sir Theodore Martin, *Helena Faucit (Lady Martin) 1817–1898* (Edinburgh and London, 1900) 270.
6. W. May Phelps and John Forbes-Robertson, *The Life and Life-Work of Samuel Phelps* (London, 1886) 323.
7. *Thomas Hardy, The Critical Heritage*, 311.
8. Martin Meisel, *Shaw and the Nineteenth-Century Theater* (Princeton, NJ, 1963) 18, 23.
9. Michael R. Booth, *English Melodrama* (London, 1965) 18.
10. Booth (ibid.) reproduces (following p. 144) a poster advertising *Human Nature* by Henry Pettitt and Augustus Harris at Drury Lane Theatre (1865). This shows a woman lolling at full length on a sofa in a loose gown. Another woman kneels, crying, 'Give me back my Husband'.
11. *The Actor's Art*, ed. J. A. Hammerton (London, 1897) 64.
12. *The Dolmen Boucicault*, ed. David Krause (Dublin, 1964) 166.
13. James L. Smith, *Melodrama* (London, 1973) 36.
14. Dutton Cook, *Nights at the Play* (London, 1883) 213.
15. He refers to 'the fictitious Elizabeth of *Kenilworth*' (*Hardy's Personal Writings*, 118). 'Amy Dudley' is mentioned in *The Woodlanders*, 242.
16. J. Coleman, *Memoirs of Samuel Phelps* (London, 1886) 251.
17. Booth, *English Melodrama*, 157–8.
18. *The Actor's Art*, 176.
19. *Hardy's Personal Writings*, 124–5. *Écorché*: an anatomical figure (ibid., 272).
20. Peter Brooks, 'The Melodramatic Imagination: the Example of Balzac and James', in *Romanticism, Vistas, Instances, Continuities*, ed. David Thorburn and Geoffrey Hartman (Ithaca, NY, and London, 1973)

214, 217. The first statement quoted relates immediately to pantomime, but is part of a larger argument concerning melodrama.
21. Ibid., 209.
22. *Hardy's Personal Writings*, 125.
23. Smith, *Melodrama*, 62.
24. Ibid., 10–11.
25. *The Times*, 27 Dec 1866.
26. A. E. Wilson, *Christmas Pantomime, The Story of an English Institution* (London, 1934) 126.
27. Covent Garden playbill in the Enthoven Collection, Victoria and Albert Museum.
28. Wilson, *Christmas Pantomime*, 169.
29. *The Times*, 27 Dec 1866. Hardy writes in *The Woodlanders*, 201, of Grace's 'sylvan home' – perhaps an unconscious recollection.
30. Cf. also the popular song 'Will-o-the-Wisp' by J. W. Cherry (1824–89), in which the phantom exults over the discomforts of the travellers he leads astray: 'Is merry sport for me', and 'I laugh Ha ha! I laugh Ho ho! / I laugh at their folly and pain'. Such gleeful practical joking seems to have appealed to the Victorians.
31. *Illustrated London News*, Jan 1863, 19. (From the Enthoven Collection.)
32. Wilson, *Christmas Pantomime*, ch. 8 ('Harlequinade'); William F. Axton, *Circle of Fire. Dickens' Vision and Style and the Popular Victorian Theater* (Lexington, Mass., 1966) 19–20; Douglas and Kari Hunt, *Pantomime, The Silent Theater* (New York, 1964) 51.
33. Penelope Vigar, *The Novels of Thomas Hardy: Illusion and Reality* (London, 1974) 93.
34. Henry Morley, in *The Examiner*, 15 Oct 1853. Quoted in George C. D. Odell, *Shakespeare from Betterton to Irving* (London, 1920) vol. II, 323.
35. A. C. Sprague, *Shakespeare and the Actors: The Stage Business in his Plays (1660–1905)* (Cambridge, Mass., 1945) 227.

CHAPTER 4

1. E. H. Gombrich, *Meditations on a Hobby Horse* (London, 1963) 121, quoting from Mary D. George's *Catalogue of Prints (1801–10) in the British Museum*.
2. *Hardy's Personal Writings*, 135.
3. In *What is Cinema? Essays selected and translated by Hugh Gray* (Berkeley, Calif., 1967) 14.
4. Cf. Bazin (ibid., pp. 96–7) on the cinema's ability to put us 'in the presence of' the actor, and his comment, 'It is . . . at the ontological level that the effectiveness of the cinema has its source.'
5. Peter Wollen, *Signs and Meaning in the Cinema* (London, 1969) 132.
6. Sergei Eisenstein, *Film Form. Essays in Film Theory*, ed. and trans. Jan Leyda (New York, 1949, and London, 1951) 195.
7. Robert Richardson, *Literature and Film* (Bloomington, Ind., and London, 1969) 22–4.

8. David Lodge, 'Thomas Hardy and Cinematographic Form', *Novel*, VII (1973–4) 246–54.
9. Quoted from *Novel*, VI (1973) 232 by Lodge, in *Novel*, VII, 247.
10. See Robert M. Henderson, *D. W. Griffith: The Years at Biograph* (London, 1971) 59.
11. *Ivan the Terrible, A Screenplay by Sergei Eisenstein*, trans. Ivor Montagu and Herbert Marshall (London, 1963) 60, 61.

CHAPTER 5

1. Elna Sherman, 'Thomas Hardy: Lyricist, Symphonist', *Music and Letters*, XXI (1940) 146.
2. This was the evening concert. There were other concerts at Princes Hall that day, at 11 a.m. and 3 p.m., but the music was much lighter in character.
3. *Hardy's Personal Writings*, 83.
4. See David Lodge, *Language of Fiction* (New York and London, 1966) 176–88.
5. *Concerning Thomas Hardy. A Composite Portrait from Memory*, ed. D. F. Barber, based on material researched and collected by J. Stevens Cox (London, 1968) 119.
6. Harold Rosenthal, *Two Centuries of Opera at Covent Garden* (London, 1958).
7. In *Publications of the Modern Language Association*, LXI (Dec 1946) 1146–84.
8. George Bernard Shaw, *Music in London, 1890–94*, vol. 1 (London, 1932, repr. 1956) 2.
9. Robert Liddell, *A Treatise on the Novel*, paperback edition (London, 1965) 119–21.
10. Eva Mary Grew, 'Thomas Hardy as Musician', *Music and Letters*, XXI (1940) 139.
11. William R. Rutland, *Thomas Hardy: A Study of his Writings and their Background* (Oxford, 1938) 179, quoting A. Stanton Whitfield.
12. In *Music and Letters*, XXI, 155.
13. J. Hillis Miller, *Thomas Hardy, Distance and Desire* (Cambridge, Mass., and London, 1970) ch. 5 ('The Dance of Desire').
14. Ibid., 163–4.
15. F. B. Pinion, *A Hardy Companion* (London, 1968) 102.
16. Ian Gregor, *The Great Web: The Form of Hardy's Major Fiction* (London, 1974) 32.
17. W. Wallace, *The Life of Arthur Schopenhauer* (London, 1890) 131.
18. In *Music and Letters*, XXI, 161.
19. Ibid., 163.

CHAPTER 6

1. Jean Brooks, *Thomas Hardy: The Poetic Structure* (London, 1971).
2. *One Rare Fair Woman, Thomas Hardy's Letters to Florence Henniker*,

1893–1922, ed. Evelyn Hardy and F. B. Pinion (London, 1972) 92.

3. *Hardy's Personal Writings*, 122.
4. Kenneth Marsden, *The Poems of Thomas Hardy, A Critical Introduction* (London, 1969) 117.
5. Ibid., 131.
6. *Hardy's Personal Writings*, 215.
7. F. E. Halliday, *Thomas Hardy, His Life and Work* (Bath, 1972) 16.
8. F. R. Southerington, *Hardy's Vision of Man* (London, 1971) 38.
9. See John Stokes, *Resistible Theatres: Enterprise and Experiment in the Late Nineteenth Century* (London, 1972) 69–110.
10. Edward Lockspeiser, *Music and Painting: A Study in Comparative Ideas from Turner to Schoenberg* (London, 1973) 47.
11. George Bernard Shaw, *Major Critical Essays* (London, 1932, repr. 1947) 265.
12. In *The Scenic Art, Notes on Acting and the Drama 1872–1901*, ed. Allan Wade (London, 1949) 141, 160, 162.
13. *Hiss the Villain, Six English and American Melodramas*, ed. Michael R. Booth (London, 1964) 269.
14. Clement Scott, *From "The Bells" to "King Arthur"* (London, 1896) 320.
15. Laurence Irving, *Henry Irving, The Actor and his World* (London, 1951) 529.
16. Henry James, *The Scenic Art*, 230.
17. Sergei Eisenstein, *Film Essays* (London, 1968) 85. Quoted in Stokes, *Resistible Theatres*, 104.
18. Robert Gittings, *Young Thomas Hardy* (London, 1975) 162–4.
19. Marcel Proust, *Time Regained*, trans. Andreas Mayor, paperback edition (London, 1970) 256–7.
20. Ibid., 262–3.
21. Ibid., 451.
22. Ibid., 231.
23. *Hardy's Personal Writings*, 138.

Index